Aging:

Spiritual Perspectives

Aging:

Spiritual Perspectives

Opera Pia International
Msgr. Ettore DiFilippo, Director
Francis V. Tiso, Editor

SUNDAY PUBLICATIONS, INC.
3003 So. Congress Avenue
Lake Worth, Florida 33461
1982

1982
Sunday Publications, Inc.
3003 So. Congress Avenue
Lake Worth, Florida 33461

Printed in the United States of America
Library of Congress Cataloging in Publication Data

ISBN 0-941850-03-X

248.85

Note to the Reader
All biblical references are to the Revised Standard Verion of the Bible. Old Testament Section, copyright © 1952; New Testament Section, First Edition, copyright © 1946; Second Edition © 1971 by Division of Christian Education of the National Council of Churches of Christ in the United States of America.

Contents

I. FOREWORD

Ettore DiFilippo

Opera Pia International and the United Nations World Assembly on Aging

The United Nations statistical studies indicate that throughout the world the number of older persons (over 60) is steadily increasing both absolutely and proportionately. At the same time, economic, social and cultural changes, associated with technological innovations often lead to the marginalization of the aging person, especially at the moment of the cessation of economically productive work. Moreover, in Third World countries, a high birth rate, coupled with a prolonged life expectancy, is presenting serious problems to policy makers and social planners. And rapid urbanization and industrialization are disrupting traditional social patterns and transforming the role of the aged both in rural and urban areas.

In this context, past traditions and approaches in responding to the needs and challenges of aging are breaking down. Clerly, there is a great need for governments, private institutions, religious and public organizations to join together in a well-coordinated effort to envision new approaches in this field, involving the planning of programs and activities in collaboration with the aged themselves.

Recognizing these needs, the General Assembly of the United Nations, in resolution 33/53 of 14 December, 1978, has decided to convene, in consultation with member states, specialized agencies, and concerned organizations, a World Assembly on Aging in July, 1982, as a "forum to launch an international action program aimed at guaranteeing economic and social security to older persons as well as opportunities to contribute to national development." Governments, international and non-governmental organizations. have been invited to participate in the preparatory work for the World Assembly on the Aging and in the Assembly itself.

It is expected that the Assembly will not be limited to economic, political, and social issues, but will offer an occasion to probe into the specific nature and deeper meaning and quality of life. The Assembly could help create the awareness that life is a dynamic process and aging is one of its most sacred revelations.

Bearing the above in mind and in response to the General Assembly's appeal to non-governmental organizations, Opera Pia International (OPI) is undertaking — in close consultation with the responsible UN agencies — with the collaboration of government and church groups, other non-governmental organizations, and recognized experts in sociology, medicine, gerontology and geriatrics from all over the world, and with the cooperation of the UN Fund for Population Activities and other private and public institutions, a three phase project for active aging.

The first phase of the project consisted of a prelminary meeting to formulate and develop the format and objectives of OPI's contribution and participation to the United Nations World Assembly on Aging and related activities, and to plan the organization and documentation of an international forum in preparation for the World Assembly.

An International Forum, which represented the second phase of the OPI program, was held in Castelgandolfo from August 31 to September 5, 1980, with the participation of all those who had attended the first meeting, plus additional representatives of the United Nations, international consultants, experts on aging, and religious representatives from Africa, Asia, the Middle East, Europe, Latin America, and North America. The Forum adopted the "Castelgandolfo Document on Active Aging" containing the basic principles and guidelines for all future activities of OPI in the field of aging and related issues.

The third phase, designed to follow-up on the conclusions and recommendations arrived at in Castelgandolfo, is now in full process. It consists of six regional conferences from September, 1981 through May, 1982. The reports of these meetings with their conclusions and recommendations are to be transmitted: A. Through OPI's headquarters to the UN's responsible organs, to interested non-governmental organizations, and to all OPI's regional groups; and B. Through OPI's regional groups to local government departments, to church national conferences, educational institutions, and to communications media on the local and regional level.

The immediate purposes of the entire project are to identify situations, needs, and ways and means, and to formulate objectives and guidelines in the selected areas of family life, education, ethics and spirituality that could be utilized as: A. input to the UN World Assembly on Aging, in particular the drafting of the World Plan of Action for the aging and its implementation; B. suggestions for innovative action-oriented pastoral programs for and with the aging; C. constructive orientation for a mutual collaboration with public authorities, policy-makers, secular and religious institutions. Opera Pia International itself is an educational, inter-religious, humanitarian, non-profit organization. It was established in 1978 with the goal of contributing, in the world context of economic, social and cultural changes, a totally human dimension (social, moral, and spiritual) to the items in the agenda of the international community as represented by the United Nations, in particular those issues concerning aging.

OPI's membership is convinced that there is an urgent need for science, religion, governments, and non-governmental organizations, to join together in a coordinated effort to develop new approaches and programs for and with aging persons.

OPI is equally convinced that the needs and the challenges of old age are met and answered primarily in the hearts and minds of the aging themselves. Therefore, if on the one hand it is important to reaffirm and promote the fundamental rights of older persons and care for their physical and mental necessities, on the other hand their psychological and spiritual needs must be emphasized and the often latent riches and resources of their age must be recognized and shared.

Although a very young organization, OPI intends to reach out and carry on the vision of the elderly as bearers of the fullness of life within human existence.

It is because of the recognized value of this vision in the temporal affairs of humanity that a suggestion has been made that OPI apply for consultative status in the United Nations Economic and Social Council, where the pertinent issues are discussed.

With the present volume, OPI hopes to make a concrete offering to an international and inter-religious network of persons who wish to collaborate in the realization of a new perspective on life which encompasses all that it is to be human, including an appreciation of the elderly as an active presence in our midst.

Thomas Berry

On Spaceship Earth, as has been noted by Buckminster Fuller, everyone is crew as well as passenger. To be an idle traveller is not acceptable. Everyone is needed. The captain without the cook cannot long guide the ship. So in the social order with professor and craftsman, farmer and city dweller, governor and sanitation worker. So too with the elderly and the youthful. Everyone is joined in the single human venture. What is done by each is different. That is why everyone is needed. Activities that differ most from each other are most needed by each other.

In this context, I present the following observations on the creative role of the elderly in the human community. Their contribution is of unique importance. What makes these reflections necessary is the extraordinary sequence of transformations in the entire earth process that has taken place in the recent past and which is presently entering into a new and dangerous, if also an entrancing, phase of its development.

The main difficulty in achieving a satisfying future is that we have not yet understood in any adequate way the order of magnitude of the changes that have already sent the human community into a series of convulsions and which are presently affecting all our securities, personal and social.

The real order of magnitude in the changes we face cannot, however, be understood simply by consideration of human security. Even beyond the human is the security of the planet itself and of all living beings on the planet. The changes wrought in the past century are not simply changes in cultural adaptation, in economic institutions, or in political regime. Nor are these changes equivalent simply to changes in religious or in moral orientation. The changes wrought in the past hundred years of science, technology, and industry are changes of geological and biological magnitude. The planet itself in its physical being as well as in its biological functioning has been extensively altered by human activities. While many benefits have been derived, these benefits themselves have become questionable when we consider what they have cost in terms of the deterioration of the planet and the uncertain future of all life upon the planet.

If the high benefits of this period have been experienced by relatively few persons, life has been profoundly affected for every living being on earth. A long listing would be required to identify those living forms that have benefitted most and those that have suffered most. What can be said is that the cost has been enormous. Many living species have disappeared forever. Tens of thousands of species could disappear before the end of the century. Since the lives of all the living from the one-celled bacterium to the human community are woven in a single fabric, we cannot but feel the loss and, ourselves, experience the deteriorating effects of an industrial establishment that is bringing about such consequences.

The ambivalence of the industrial age becomes increasingly manifest. A significant price must be paid for every advantage gained, a price that is seldom adverted to by the defenders of "progress" and mechanization as the ultimate norms of human value. The grime that has settled over our cities is invisible to those entranced with the power of the new technologies. The future itself is uncertain in the blessings it promises and the demands it makes.

But however this ambivalence of the industrial age might be viewed from any of the "three worlds" of differing economic and social status, the present elderly of the world carry within their being the blessings and the burdens of the twentieth century. Their lives coincide with the century. Their earliest memories go back to the beginning of the century when the automobile was just appearing on the dusty roads of the world, when the world was being electrified, when the first planes rose into the sky, when the entertainment industry took on its present forms in radio and later in television, when farms reached a new level of mechanization and the vast machines for planting and harvesting and processing began to move over the plains of Kansas and Nebraska. This was also the period when the great modern corporations were taking control of the economic life of the world and assuming charge of earth's resources. The scientific research centers were being set up in the universities and in industrial establishments, centers that eventually would make nuclear power available. Above all, perhaps, the present elderly of much of the world have lived in the petroleum age, the age not only of oil heating and gasoline motors, but the age of plastics and artificial fibres, of pharmaceuticals and fertilizers, all made of petroleum; an age, however, that already begins to see its own decline and even its termination.

Much else could be written describing their twentieth century which veers toward its conclusion as the elderly persons who lived through this period, themselves, pass on into the last two or three decades of their lives. Socially the most significant development for the elderly has been the urbanization of the human community. The great cities of the century in this period were attracting their huge populations in Shanghai and Mexico City as well as in Cairo, Calcutta, Tokyo and Rio de Janeiro, New York, London, and Leningrad. While tribal and village life have continued, the centers of vital transformation in all parts of the planet shifted toward the urban centers. Whereas in the early 19th century less than five percent of the world was living in these large urban centers, by the year 2000 over half the world's population will be in these large population centers, a change of enormous significance in determining the quality of life that the elderly will be living.

Without judging its human benefits or its human cost, its earth benefits or its earth cost, this has been an exciting century, a century that has given both the context and the content of life for many of the elderly of the world. They have participated in its achievements and in its tragedies, in its wars and in its efforts to achieve peace, in the rise and fall of its economic prosperity. Mainly the elderly as individuals have been caught in the swirl of forces beyond their control, forces that are only partially under any control. Once initiated, science and technology have produced a sequence of changes far different from those anticipated.

The New Vision

But whatever the present situation a new way of seeing the world, human life and the future is emerging, a vision shared on an extensive scale by peoples throughout the world, the vision of a post-industrial ecological age of intercommunion based on awareness of the inter-dependence of all the living and non-living forces of the planet. The machine metaphor that has for several centuries dominated our western sense of reality has definitely lost its validity as supplying the basic norm of the real. The vital, organic, person metaphor is finding expression throughout the human community. All professions, all human roles and institutions; education and values are being reconstituted in the context of this understanding of the world. The clock-world of Newton; the manipulative, exploitive world of high-energy technologies; the quantitative value system; none of these can any longer assume a controlling position in the human community.

If the period of primordial human spontaneity gave way for a time to a dominant rational manipulative period, this period is itself giving way to a third period, a period that can be identified as that of a critical naivete, a period of both scientific insight and intuitive understanding, a period when the emotional and aesthetic aspects of the universe find their proper recognition. This new attitude itself is coming about not by manipulative processes nor by compelling propaganda but by a pervasive interior attitude that is emerging from the unconscious depths of a long-suppressed human mode of being and of feeling.

Most significant is the fact that new developments are not emerging from the formal centers of professional training. The new sense of health, of nutrition, of exercise, of interior tranquillity, is not arising from medical schools. The new educational practices are originating outside the academic centers where the more integral development of the individual human person and the deeper spiritual disciplines needed by the child to deal with fundamental life issues is still not understood or appreciated. New legal attitudes needed to deal with man-nature relations are not developing first in the law schools but in the general public consciousness. New paradigms of commercial and economic life are being first enunciated outside the schools of business administration. So throughout the whole of contemporary life the organic-person understanding of the world is asserting itself with a transforming influence.

Most significant for the future, however, is the new sense of reality being manifested from within the scientific tradition. The sciences are discovering inner spontaneities, organic relations, intuitive processes, immediacies beyond mechanistic calculation, syncronistic happenings beyond explanation by simplistic causal processes. The involvement of the subject in all knowing, indeed the personal nature of human knowledge begins to be appreciated.

The total effect of all these changes cannot easily be indicated. We can, however, say that the great imperative of the present is that the human community respond creatively to the opportunities that are presenting themselves for shaping a more satisfying and sustainable world for the future. We can also say that no one is exempt from participation in this most signicant task. Both the infant and the elderly are integral to this activity along with all other components of the human community. Ultimately, this new orientation is something that must be brought about by the entire earthly community, by all the living and non-living beings of the planet.

The New Roles

By its own inner processes, the organic nature of reality is asserting itself in a spontaneous identification of the new roles that individuals and groups are called upon to fulfill at this time. Educators such as George Leonard, physicists such as Sir Bernard Lovell, biologists such as René Dubos and Lewis Thomas, naturalists such as Rachel Carson and Annie Dillard, energy specialists such as Amory Lovins, lawyers such as Ralph Nader, economists such as Willis Harman and Hazel Henderson, philosophers such as Alfred North Whitehead, theologians such as Teilhard de Chardin, member of the international political and economic organizations such as Robert Muller, ecologists such as John and Nancy Todd — all these and many more, from all parts of the world, have responded effectively in creating new roles in answer to the creative urgencies that are upon us if we are to shape a sustainable and satisfying world. That these individuals are profoundly affecting the institutional expression of these different areas of life is abundant evidence that an inner dynamism in the reality of things is asserting itself. The overall agreement of the hundreds and thousands of persons who are involved in such creative activities has been outlined extensively in the recent publication of Marilyn Ferguson, *The Aquarian Conspiracy.*

So too with the elderly, it is a question of the elderly themselves being sensitized to their own new situation and to their own role in creating the new order of earthly existence. The elderly alone can create their new roles, even though the assistance of the total society is needed. The elderly are natural leaders of the communities of which they are members. The elderly in the professions have wide control over the professions. The elderly in commerce have extensive control over commerce. So in education, in energy systems, in the arts, and in entertainment, the elderly have widespread influence and extensive control whether in Africa or Asia, Europe or the Americas. Especially in religious and moral affairs, the judgment and influence of the elderly is of supreme importance. Because they have significant influence, they have corresponding responsibilities. The elderly can ruin their own cause.

The image of the elderly as inactive, as non-participating observers of the world scene, or as having attained an age simply of enjoyment of life, of detachment from the turmoil of human affairs, is an image that is both illusory and damaging to the elderly. It is illusory because the elderly are absolutely involved in the total human and the total earth process. Elderly participation is not a matter of choice. They participate either as positive contributors or as negative burdens to the community and to the earth. While their mode of participation may be changed, their presence and their insight, their energy, their influence are demanded. For the elderly to remove themselves or to be removed from the earth-human process, is as unacceptable as is the removal of a functional organ from the human body, retiring it before the cessation of bodily life takes place.

Any effort of the elderly to escape their proper functioning, or any effort to isolate the active elderly, is destructive in a very direct way to the elderly themselves. They become victimized by the consumer economy. Withdrawal is an indication of the dying down of the will to live on the part of the individual or on the part of the community which finds itself unable to incorporate the elderly into the functional pattern of its life. Above all, the taste for life needs to be sustained on its proper scale and with its proper order of intensity. Generally, efforts at isolation are primarily due to the mechanistic model of the universe and of the human community. The organic model has a place for functional activities that are of value in themselves and not merely in terms of benefits to a consumer society.

The Historical Situation

A present reading of the historical situation indicates that a transformation of momentous significance is taking place on the planet earth; that this is due primarily to the scientific-technological developments that have taken place in the past hundred years; that amid its great benefits this period of exploitive technologies has brought about many disastrous consequences throughout the geological, biological and human realms of the planet earth; that a reaction is taking place to establish a new ecological equilibrium beneficial to the earth and to the human community in their integral dimensions; that all human roles, professions and institutions are being reevaluated and reshaped in accord with a new sense of the vital, organic, person nature of reality; that the elderly as a distinctive group within the familial and social context of the present are called upon to assume their share in bringing about this new ecological age in which they will achieve the fullness of their own lives along with the fulfillment that hopefully will be experienced by all living beings upon the planet.

The present elderly are unique in the range of their experience which reaches back, in many instances, to a pre-industrial experience and which extends into the beginnings of the post-industrial experience of the ecological or meta-industrial period of history. Hopefully in the future many peoples will be able to move more immediately from a prior stage of pre-industrial existence to a post-industrial ecological mode of existence that will incorporate the benefits of scientific achievements and non-destructive technologies into the advantages of intimate association with the environment with its air and water and vegetation and abundance of living beings.

For the elderly of the western industrial countries to make their full contribution to the future, there is need, first of all, that they reflect on the historical role that they have fulfilled throughout this century. The elderly of the present, whatever the benefits they have derived from the industrial developments of the century or whatever the difficulties they have sustained, are the ones who have carried through the great human vision that survives and makes possible the further adjustments that can lessen the damage and enhance the benefits for future generations. The elderly of this generation have carried out a unique role in earth history. Never again will a generation be assigned the historic task of sustaining the human vision at such a moment of transition; for this twentieth century transition of traditional civilizations through a scientific-technological age to an ecological age will never again take place. It will be extended and developed but the inauguration period that has taken place in this century will not be repeated. It is an irreversible process. While this has been a most conspicuous event in the larger industrial centers, equally conspicuous events have taken place in other countries where the shock of industrial expansion has been compounded by political and economic colonization. Here the difficulty of sustaining a world of human meaning has had its own special manifestations. As elsewhere the elderly in more pastoral or agrarian societies have sustained this difficult period in their own being even as they have been forced to make urgent decisions on behalf of their peoples and their traditions.

That so much of the human quality of life has been sustained and developed within this context must, then, be attributed mainly to the present generation of older persons. Amid all the new advantages of literacy and schooling and modern medicines along with city-building and all the institutions of a modern society, there has been an almost limitless amount of suffering, turmoil, and estrangement from a former way of life filled with human meaning and human values. But here too the need is to establish the new patterns of existence that can be described as a new way of life integral with the ever-renewing cycles of the natural world but intimately associated with a new and sensitive phase of scientific insight and with technologies coherent with the technologies of the earth itself. Hopefully in this way societies generally considered as less developed can begin to consider themselves as the *avant garde* of the new ecological age. They can see themselves as establishing functional patterns of earth-human existence that the industrial countries themselves will need as models and as inspiration for their own future adjustment if they are not to arrive at a total impasse in their exploitation of the planet.

In achieving this goal the elderly of the entire world have a most significant role to carry out. Their total experience, whatever its span over the past sequence of changes, enables them to envisage with special clarity this new period in their own societies and in the larger human community. More than others the elderly should have the capacity to identify the general direction of development. They have lived through the entire arc of changes that have taken place.

In this manner they should be able to fulfill their social role as the "wise old men" and the "old wise women" of the present generation. They will thus fulfill their life obligations to themselves, to the society, to their historical destiny, and to the future. Eventually all four of these identify.

The Life Stories of the Elderly

The wisdom of the elderly is carried not fundamentally in moralizations or in any philosophical or even religious principles but in the structure of their own being which finds its finest expression in their life stories. This is why the elderly reminisce so much and in their later years become story-tellers of the earlier years of their lives and all the particular experiences through which they have passed. While these experiences are individual they are also the archetypal experiences that reveal the depths of history of the human community and even of the earth process. They provide the perspective needed, the vital sequence whereby the human heritage has been saved from being overwhelmed by the harshness of this particular century.

The importance of such local personal history is being realized wherever efforts are being made to recover a vital contact with the pre-industrial past and with the sequence of changes that have led us through this century and now back to the dynamics of the living planet. These efforts can generally be summed up under the term of "bio-cultural regionalism," which is a "third way" now being fostered by such creative persons as John and Nancy Todd, Amory Lovins, Hazel Henderson and many others. This "third way", often referred to as an "alternative future", is a way that is not simple acceptance of the high-entropy urban industrial society. It is rather a reactivation of life within the ever renewing rhythms of the natural world but with a substantial if refined use of science and technology and with a high level of emotional-aesthetic-spiritual communion with the natural world. It is intended that well articulated human communities in intimate presence to the natural world can be a healing and activating presence that will give to the land as much as it takes from the land.

In carrying out this program a reflexive consciousness of what is being done requires that the land be understood in its prehuman, geological and biological formation, that its sequence of early and later occupations by human peoples be appreciated, that the later period of western-industrial commercial influence be understood along with the alterations that have occurred in the animal and plant life, in the quality of water and air and soil, and finally that the land be understood in its emotional-aesthetic impact upon human consciousness.

For an understanding of the present human renewal of life in any such bio-cultural region, the accounts of the ancients who still live in these regions and who remember the events of the past become extremely important. In many instances in North America, in the San Francisco Bay region, in the Passaic watershed of New Jersey, in some of the southern states, in New England, serious efforts are being made to record the stories of the elderly who have lived a substantial part of their lives in these regions; for renewal is a continuation of the past even when undesirable disturbances of land have taken place. Even in the region of the South Bronx in New York, a devastated slum area, it is of great value to know something of that area before the present devastation was brought about, what was its original condition, how the land there really is when in its fertile and fruitful condition and how perhaps once more a sustainable and vital form of life could be lived there in association with a blossoming landscape.

Here, then, is one of the unique creative roles for the elderly, a role so identified with their own being and the story of their own lives that it should find spontaneous and delightful fulfillment. While only a few of these life stories will be recorded in writing or find their way into print, there exists throughout the human community verbal traditions, group memories of past events. Only when such memories exist can a reliable sense of direction be identified by a community.

The Cultural Coding

These traditions of the human communities exist as cultural codings which function at the human level much as genetic codings function throughout the world of the living. In the human community we have a genetic coding for a further trans-genetic cultural coding to be invented, developed and carried on through the language, rituals, spiritual disciplines, social customs, the arts and entertainment, education and the various occupations of social groups. Whereas genetic coding at the prehuman level guides the various living organisms through their lives with relatively little additional education, the cultural coding of the human being is not communicated so completely at the time of birth. A long period of cultural development is required that takes place through imitation of elders, through family customs, through the language of the society, through participation in religious rituals, through instruction in behavior, through the teaching of values. These latter aspects of cultural development are generally communicated through the stories that are recounted in the society.

The elderly are considered endowed with special wisdom because their many years experience has given them a depth of insight into the structure and meaning of the cultural coding that guides the life of the society. They understand the language and rituals better than the others, they know the stories of the society, they have the depth of insight needed for making the major life decisions of the community, they understand the mysterious functioning of the natural world and how best to survive its destructive influence and how best to cooperate with its beneficent powers. In some parts of Africa, the death of an elderly person is considered like the loss of a library.

This cultural coding is of immense importance, for only through this coding do we know how to feed and clothe and shelter ourselves, how to think and speak and act, how to laugh and weep, how to play and sing and dance, how to communicate with the spirit powers of the universe, how to respond intelligently to the mysterious world in which we live.

While we have been mainly concerned thus far in this discussion with the nature and magnitude of change in human-earth relations and the role of the elderly in activating a new and more coherent world of the future, we must also be concerned for the role of the elderly in providing that continuity in the complex cultural codings whereby the human community sustains its sense of human meaning and human values throughout this sequence of cultural changes that we are experiencing. This eventually is the most difficult of our present human tasks. It is also the most important for unless this be achieved the various cultural heritages will continue to experience disintegration rather than creative transformation.

The transformation needed requires both continuity and creativity, both at a high level of expression. Nothing less than the personal and cultural resources of the entire human community, even of the entire earth community, are required. Our confidence in a successful outcome rests eventually in the larger dynamics of the planetary process which shaped the earth and brought forth all the living beings on the planet and finally gave to us our human form. This inner providence of the planet is a sustaining and guiding power. It moves by violent upheavals as well as by silent, soft and delicate processes; yet its final benevolent nature need not be doubted. Above all it moves by interior attractions, by the indestructible spontaneities hidden in the depths of the unconscious realms of the human mind.

The human community need only develop its proper sensitivity to this matrix out of which we emerged and in which we live and breathe and have our being in order to identify and make functional the cultural coding of the future that constitutes the supreme creative task of our generation.

The assistance and insight of the elderly is required in a special way for this achievement. Fulfillment of this role belongs not to the addenda of their lives, nor to further involvement in a consumer economy; nor does it further trivialize their enjoyment of life; rather it bestows upon the elderly a sense of profound personal significance, a sense of fulfilling a historical role in the human order; ultimately of being a participant in the larger dynamics of the planet earth and of the universe itself. While many of the present generation have forgotten what such an experience is, the elderly cannot but feel that life in this context has the expansive and meaningful quality that is expecially needed in their later years.

II. AGING IN THE WORLD'S RELIGIONS

Knowledge is Power, but Age is Wisdom: The Challenge of Active Aging from an African Perspective

Kofi Appiah-Kubi

Introduction

The geography, cultures, languages and customs of the continent of Africa are so diverse, wide and far between that it is almost impossible for any one writer to speak or write about any subject that will adequately represent the entire continent. Any such an attempt should accept its limitations from the very outset.

Notwithstanding the diversity, there is a common thread that runs through the continent especially in the areas of human values, religions, communitarian character and social responsibility of African societies. These aspects will permit some kind of generalization. But in dealing with a subject such as aging it may be expedient to concentrate specifically on one African society as a point of departure. In spite of limitations, this will give some clarity and in depth understanding of the issue at hand. I propose to use the term African in this context to refer to the Akan of Ghana, the African I know best. It is however, intended that these comments on aging will reflect most African societies, if not all.

Who Are The Akans?

The term Akan describes a culturally homogenous group of people who share the same culture, speak the same group of languages and form a matrilineal descent group. There are slight variations in the dialects, however, an Akan is generally understood by another Akan. The Akans can be found in Southern Ghana. They are made up of the Ashantis, the Akims, the Kwahus, Akwapims, Fantis, Nzimas, Brongs and Ahafos. They occupy the Ashanti, Western, Brong Ahafo regions and part of the Eastern region of Ghana.

Occupation

The Akans are mainly farmers and live in the fertile forest belt of Ghana. They produce both food crops and such cash crops as cocoa and coffee. The coastal dwellers are basically fishermen. A few of the people engage in trading, commerce and civil service. As a matrilineal descent group, inheritance passes from mother to daughter or from mother's brother to son. The Akans are the predominant ethnic group in Ghana. They form about 40% of Ghana's population. Despite the influence of Christianity, Islam, modern education and social change, the Akans have kept their social and cultural heritage intact. Thus, it is often said, Ghanaian cultural life goes as the Akan culture goes and Ghana has been identified as the home of African culture.

Concept of Human Personality
or the Individual

The individual is viewed by the Akan as a composite of "Mogya" (Blood) which he inherits from his mother "Sumsum" (Spirit) which he inherits from his father and "Okra" (Soul) which he receives from God his Creator. Without "Okra" (Soul) the life giving force the individual is merely "mogya" (Blood) and "Sumsum" (Spirit). It is in fact, the "Okra" (Soul) which gives meaning to life of the individual. Thus, the Akan proverb: "Nnipa nyinaa ye Onyame mma obi nnye Asaase ba." Meaning "All human beings are God's children, none is the child of the Earth." The individual gains his lineage ties through his mother's "Mogya" (Blood). The "Sumsum" (Spirit) from the father moulds him and gives him his personality. A person is believed to have the same temperament and spirit as his father. The spirit is the source of his distinctive personal gifts and virtues. Thus, the Akan proverb: "Oba se ose nanso owo nkyi" meaning, "The child is like the father but he has his kinship ties."

The Akans further sing: "Okoto nnwo Anoma. Onipa bone na owo oba bone. Onipa papa na owo oba pa. Adofo no mmo moden na mo nye papa na papa ye yi mu ara na Onyame behyiramo. Okoto wo ho yi obira nim se owo okoto okoto kowo anoma a wokyiri." Which is literally translated:

The eggs of the crab do not hatch into birds. It is an abomination should the eggs of a crab hatch into birds. For we all know that the crab always hatches crabs. But never birds."

The full or complete person therefore, among the Akans is made up of "Mogya" (Blood, physical being) "Sumsum" (Spirit, Individual personality) and "Okra" (Soul or life giving force). The "Okra" is believed to be the guiding spirit of the individual through his earthly life's journey. Through the union of "Mogya" (Blood) and "Sumsum" (Spirit), God gives the "Okra" (Soul) which determines the individual's destiny. The "Okra" is said to come from the day on which the individual is born. For example, if one is born on Friday, one refers to one's "Okra" as "Okra Kofi" when misfortune strikes, the individual is asked to cleanse his "Okra" (Soul) in case the "Okra" has been offended in one way or the other. The "Okra" (Soul) leaves the person at death to join the spirit world.

There is among the Akans a very marked belief in destiny. It is said that when God gives the "Okra" he also gives "Nkrabea" (destiny) but one's destiny is known only to God. No one can change one's destiny. Destiny, according to the Akans, is concerned with the general quality and ultimate end of one's life. Thus, the Akans say: "Obi rekra ne Nyame na obi nnyina ho." Meaning, "When one was taking leave of one's God no one was there." It was a matter between, oneself and one's God who gives one the "Okra" which shapes or determines one's destiny. God-given destiny is therefore, said to be unavoidable. Some people are destined to be healthy, strong, hard-working, honest and wealthy; others are destined to be sickly, weak, lazy, poor and dishonest. It is said that one's destiny can change only when one is born again after death. This is reflected in proverbs and songs in the daily life among the Akans. Thus, the Akan sing:—

"Wiase nkrabea mu nsem
Agya Onyame na onim
Obi wo ho a obaa wiase
Se obegye din ansa na wawu
Obi wo ho a obaa wiase
Se orebepe sika
Ansa na wafi wiase
Obi ara nni ho a
Wamma wiase ammeye hwee
Nanso wiase mmonsafo
Wompe adepa."

This is translated:—

"The destiny of a man in this world.
Is known only to God
Some came into this world
To achieve greatness
Others came to be rich and noble;
But the evil forces in the world
Often prevent them."

The Individual and Belief In Reincarnation

Since it is God who gives the destiny, He alone can direct one's path in life. Among the Akans, there is in fact a very strong belief in reincarnation. The Akans say that any ancestor who considered his work on this earth unfinished when he died may decide to return and finish it. Some people are believed to be reincarnations of the ancestors. It is believed that the same child keeps coming and going if a woman loses several babies at birth in succession, especially, if the baby dies at birth or is still born.

To stop this occurrence, the child is given several cuts on the cheek, and is also given strange or funny names. This is believed to render the child ashamed to return to the spirit world.

Barrenness and Impotence — The Greatest Curse

The average Akan looks for prosperity in marriage, work, child-birth and life in general. Failure in any of these is not envisioned. Among the Akan, the complete and perfect individual is the one who is successful in farming or business of any kind, the one who is not maimed in any way whatsoever, the one who has no incurable disease of any kind and who is potent and can produce a lot of children. Barrenness therefore, is the greatest curse that can befall an individual. Wealth is seen in terms of fulfilling one's social, moral and biological obligations. While a blind man may be seen to be handicapped and therefore command sympathy from society, a barren woman or impotent man is most pitied and even despised. Children are seen as economic and social security in the individual's life in times of old age, illness or any physical or social disabilities. Children are the insurance for the individual's unknown future. Thus, the Akans sing: "Obere a merebere beberebe yi ennye se

biribiara nti. Dabi mabrabo yi nti na ama merebere beberebe yi."
"I am struggling to-day for a better future." They further say that:
"Mfiase nnye anibere se awiei." "The beginning of life is not as
hard as the end." Thus, the Akans pray and say: "Mma menwu
awia; Mma menwu anadwo; Mma menwu koraa.: Which — literally means: "Do not let me die in the day (Do not make me blind);
Do not let me die at night (Do not make me impotent); Do not
make me die at all. (Make me fruitful and not barren or childless)."

The Problem of Suffering

Generally speaking, the Akan can be said to know no problem
of evil or problem of suffering as such; the vital question or most
important point is the source of the evil or the cause of the
suffering. There are evil forces sufficient to account for the
wickedness, tragedies and misfortunes of life. Their attack on the
individual takes various forms. It may result in sickness, calamity,
disaster, sorrow or premature death. Witchcraft attacks the
virtuous, ancestors attack the wicked.

The Individual and the Community

The family is the basic unit and this is a unit for the living,
(present) the dead, (past) and the yet-unborn (future). The present,
the past and the future life of the community are very important.
The individual is, because his family, kinship, the extended family
and clan are. From birth through puberty, adulthood and old age
the kin group is constantly involved with the individual. His world
is a cosmic reality. The Akan society is by definition communalistic.
The individual Akan is here contrasted with average western man;
"Whereas Descartes spoke for western man when he said: "Cogito
ergo sum" "I think therefore, I exist" Akan man's ontology is
"Conatus ergo sum" "I am related by blood, therefore, I exist or I
exist because I belong to a family."[1] The African or Akan personality is expressed in the communion with the dead, the living and
the yet-unborn. The individual is thus incomplete and at times
considered meaningless and empty except in the company of
others. He shares his life, achievements, failures, health and disease
with others in the community. The only real hell for the African is
the rejection of the community. The divine imperative therefore,
for every healthy individual is to care for each other, especially, the

old and the very young who are usually considered vulnerable and at the same time the fountain of life because of our strong belief in reincarnation. In every child there is an old man. "The child indeed is the father of man."

The mythical tradition demands of the Akan a sense of realism, commitment, creativity and responsibility for the aged, the young, the feeble in the society and the whole created order. This calls for a communal commitment which not only embraces the Akans' immediate neighbours but the whole family of humanity.

The following maxim sums up the Akan concept of the individual and the community. "I am because we are and because we are therefore, I am." The individual Akan lives in what might be termed a 'weistic' community with a 'weistic' philosophy and weism and not communism is the key to his philosophy of life together. It is 'weism' with God, nature and man at the centre which forms his cosmic reality.

The Aged, Time and Rhythm of Nature

The Akan philosophy holds that man is at the centre of the universe. God who is the creator of man and the universe is the author of time. Therefore God is the main explanation of man's contact with time.

Time is associated with growth, movement, life, death and destruction. The individual is bound with nature so much so that man's view of time is based on nature, for there is cyclism in the rhythm of nature of which man is not only a part but the center. The trees blossom and flower, the fruits appear, the fruits ripen, they dry and sometimes fall on the ground (or are plucked and planted again) and germinate again to produce trees which will in turn produce seeds. The life cycle of the individual is patterned to that of nature. The individual is born, he grows, he marries, bears children, becomes old and dies. He returns to the spirit world of the ancestors, he is re-born or reincarnated to begin another cycle again. The Akan life is thus characterized with movements from one stage to another as one season follows another in nature. Death is not seen as a terminus of life but as another stage for the preparation for re-entry into the world, just as the seed dies when sown before it germinates. There is a fundamental relationship between the individual and nature. Nature is therefore revered and respected. In Akan tradition, there exists a relationship between the individual and nature which is expressed in terms of kinship identity and mutual respect. Even though man uses nature he does not exploit it as a thing without life; for it is nature which gives the full meaning of the individual life.

The Akan sees life in terms of the three categories of time: — the past (the dead), the present (the living), the future (the yet-unborn).

Time in this respect, is a continuum and the categories overlap. The past inspires the present and the future gives meaning to the present. The presence of the dead is a reality in Akan society. In the children today (present) lie the seeds of the future generations, thus, the future is here in the present and there is no present or future which is not linked with the past.

It is generally believed that the rhythms of time are endless. There is no reason to suggest that these rhythms of time and the universe will suddenly grind to a halt. There is no end of time, no end of the world and therefore, no end of the individual. Man, time and the world have a created beginning but no ending.

In harvest festivals, farmers scatter the first fruits on the earth with the hope that these would germinate into seedlings or even plants in the future. The fishermen usually throw some of their catch back into the sea; this would grow to increase the future catch in the generations to come.

Most Akans live with the view that they will be survived by the future generations. The Akans believe that God is eternal, and sustains the universe and will not end it. The eternity of God, life, the universe and time gives meaning to the eternity of man. This idea of the eternal God is reflection of the unending time, universe and life.

This idea gives meaning to the Akan idea of aging.

The Akan Concept of Aging

Though the Akans believe that *Knowledge* is power they affirm that *Age* is wisdom. Hence they say: "Akyin Akyin sen anyin, anyin." — "The traveller is more knowledgeable than the aged" or "Travel makes man." But they at the same time say: "Wohu sumina so ntamago a susu piapia no, na wada adaka mu pen." —"Do not despise a piece of rag in the dunghill for its former home was the wardrobe." Furthermore, "Kyemferefa a eda akrofon so se wanyin na nea onwenee no a?" — "If it is said of a piece of broken pot in a deserted village that it is old, what of the potter?"

"Enne mma se worentie aden na wontu mmukyia mmiensa mu mmienu mgu na wonso baako so gya?" — "If the youth of to-day maintain that they know it all, why do they not break two of the three pieces of hearth and cook on only one?" All these sayings go to confirm the positive attitudes the Akans hold for the aged. They in fact consider aging or old age as a blessing and a sign of honest and sincere life; indeed a total fulfillment of life. Old people are adored, revered and respected. The Akan counts it his singular duty to care for the old people in the community. The cultural up-bringing and socialization demand of every younger person to serve the old person without hesitation for through such sincere and unflinching service comes the hidden treasure of blessings. This is not considered charity but a duty for everyone in the community for old age is a stage every sincere and honest person who conducts his life properly will pass through. Therefore, every young person is enjoined in the community to "Do unto others as they would have others to do unto them." Neglect of the service to the old folks carries with it all sorts of untold punishment from the ancestors for after all the old people in the Akan society are considered "living ancestors" — people who are on their last stage to becoming the ancestors.

The ancestors or the living dead are a reality in the Akan life. They are the custodians of the moral, ethical, social and legal life of the Akan. They can influence the living for good or bad. Good is rewarded and evil is punished. They are the real owners of the land, the chiefs and family heads therefore, hold the land in trust for the living. The land which is the backbone of the economic, social and spiritual life of the Akan is the pivot or the linking rod between the living and the dead. No one owns the land but everyone has the right to the use of the land. Sincere service and respect to the aged is considered "Entertaining the unknown angel." The Akan idea of respect, reverence and service to the elderly coincides with the biblical injunction to "honour your mother and father that your days will be long on this earth." The youth through socialization and all forms of cultural upbringing are asked (as in Proverbs 23 verse 22) "to harken unto your father who begat you and despise not your mother when she is old." Thus, the Akans maintain that: "Se obi hwe wo ma wose fifi a wo nso wo hwe no ma nese tutu." Meaning — "If someone nurses you to produce your teeth; you also nurse them when they begin to lose theirs." The Akans further say that: "Se obi turu wo kohwe nkwa a wonturu no nkohwe owuo." — "If someone carries you to see life you do not carry them to see death." The use of the term 'father' or 'mother' in these adages is for every elderly person, they do not necessarily have to be one's biological kinfolk.

The Attitudes of the Elderly
Towards Youth, Society
And Themselves

The old people consider it their duty to share their wisdom with the young generation. They help actively in the socialization processes of the children and the grandchildren in the society. They babysit for their daughters, sons and grandchildren. Growing up as a child, I remember that it was my grandmother who usually fed me. In fact, I refused to eat whenever she was absent from home. The old people who are the store of the society's history, wisdom and ethics are the natural teachers of the younger generation. My paternal grandfather, a great linguist and orator, always put me on his lap and taught me the wisdom of our people in idioms and proverbs and pith-sayings. I am told by my parents that I inherited my knowledge of our language, especially the ability to use proverbs, from him. They are a constant reminder to the young generation of what it means to be old and to accept old age as a natural process of life and also to accept old-age as a blessing and fullness of life. The old people accept their station in life and in the community as an answer to their prayer to God and the ancestors as the fulfillment of their life.

Aging as a Natural and
Biological Phenomenon

The Akans do not just idealize old age. They accept it as an inevitable natural process which everyone will eventually pass through if they live an honest and sincere life. There is nothing to prepare you for the experience of growing old. Living is an irreversible progression toward old age, eventual death and reincarnation. You see men of eighty still vital and tall and straight as oaks; you see men of fifty reduced to gray shadows in the human landscapes. The cellular clock differs for each one of us and is profoundly affected by our own life experiences, our heredity and, perhaps most importantly, by the concepts of aging encountered in society and in oneself. [2]

The Akans, both young and old, believe that from a biological point of view, aging is simply a process of change, a continuous development which takes place in a fairly regular manner throughout our lives. In each individual that pace may differ. Different parts of the body resist aging more than others and abilities fade at different rates. Everyone knows their physical appearance will change as they grow older. It can be emotionally unsettling, even depressing to look in the mirror and see the effects of normal aging process. It is not just vanity that makes people hate growing old, the sheer inevitability of the process is frightening, even terrifying. Every aspect of human life undergoes some change as the years march on: the structures and functions of the body gradually become impaired, motivation, perception, emotions alter, a person's position in society and adjustment to surroundings and other people are affected. We spend about one quarter of life growing up and three quarters growing old.[3]

As a people who live in inter and intra-generational society, we note that certain biological changes which occur as we grow older are apparent whenever you watch an old person. The hair becomes thin, brittle, dull and gray. The skin becomes paler and may become blotchy. These changes in the surface of the body are gradual, and vary according to diet, genetic factors and climate. The individual may appear to shrink with age. However the Akans do not consider old age to be a disease, but as a natural biological process.

For the Akan, as for all humans, the world becomes narrower as friends and family members die or move away. Needs may decrease, you may require less food, less sleep and at times fewer human contacts.

The Aged and Modernization in Africa

In Africa today the old people are as rich in resources both human and material as they are in years. Our grandparents and parents who were and in some respects still are farmers or small businessmen who tend to retire gradually if at all. They still manage to remain economically independent during their old age and they have large farms and large extended families which provide another kind of insurance against having to be dependent on public charity. The traders amongst them depend on accumulated savings. In fact in such jobs as farming and trading our grandparents rarely go into retirement. Even when physical frailty may permit early retirement old people can still remain overseers of the work.

With the introduction of formal education, modernization, Christianity and other factors of social change, economic security is no longer based on accumulated savings; and the resources of extended families, but on government and trade union pension plans. In modern Ghana for example, family sizes are shrinking due to the influence of the "Gospel of Family Planning." The shrinking and scattered families cannot be counted on for financial, social and emotional help. In fact, with the gradual breakdown of the extended families and concentration on nuclear families, the grandparents are gradually being squeezed out of the normal life of the normal family life.

But the irony of the situation is that in most African countries the number of dependent children and needy old people is growing out of balance. This complicates the economic aspects of aging, and thus, makes it impossible to separate them from the social and political aspects or problems of the community. The question that remains to be answered is: How can a community support the non-productive members — providing health services, housing, income to dependent children and old people — when the proportion of dependent to productive people continues to grow? How do we balance the need to protect and nurture the helpless especially the childless in the Akan community, against the limited resources of the community? This brings us to consider the future plans in Africa for active aging.

Active Aging and the Future —
Which Way Africa?

We in Africa have hitherto been living on borrowed language, borrowed ideology, borrowed culture, borrowed technology in the name of modernization and civilization. We have been gradually throwing away the essence of our being as Africans in the unholy name of development. We have been blindly importing coca cola, bottle-feeding, and the commandments of Family Planning based on the fear of a population explosion. We have tended to downgrade our social and cultural values, traditional healing practices and religions as primitive and pagan. But there still remain some aspects of our traditional treatment of the elderly, in spite of the impact of rapid social change and the influence of an educated elite — acting as the agents of change, some of whom despise the traditional cultural values.

I think the greatest contribution Africa can make to the world civilization is her treatment of the elderly in our midst.

1. We should see the elderly not as a liability but as an asset to the community.
2. We should plan our pensionable age differently and not blindly follow the Euro-American system.
3. This calls for new development strategy whereby the good elements in the traditional system are combined with the good elements in the modern system which may evolve a new approach which will be better than any of its forebears.
4. The old people should be encouraged to participate actively in the labour market and not waste away.
5. Young people should be helped by the government in some form of welfare services so that the elderly may be properly cared for. Jobs should not be created for the youth at the expense of the elderly.

Wherever financial needs arise the government should give these to the youth or young couples concerned. Whenever possible the society should encourage a healthy, useful, and helpful old age life within the family. The generations should be helped to live together in order to appreciate old age as a blessing, and not as a curse or disease. Death should be perceived as a stage in the life cycle and not as an end in itself. Therefore, death may be met with hope and thankfulness rather than with fear and despair.

To the agents of change and our social planners in Africa the caution is: "It is only a fool who says it is my neighbour and not me" (Yede meyonko na yenne me.") The elderly of our culture in Africa say: "If you are eating the fingers of a monkey watch yours for you may not be able to tell the difference." ("Woredi Efoo nsa a hwe wo dee.")

Since the western system of treating the old people has not been ideal, attempts must be made to avoid the route of public charity. Our elders in the Akan community say: "Dua a kwaku Ananse adi awuo no Ntekuma nkotra ase nto nko." "Na asem se be" — "A word to the wise is sufficient."

References

1. John S. Pobee, *Toward an African Theology* (Nashville: Abingdon Press, 1979), p. 49.
2. Sharon R. Gurtin, *Nobody Ever Died of Old Age* (Boston: G. K. Hall, 1972), p. 17.
3. Kofi Appiah-Kubi. "From the Womb to the Cradle." Unpublished Doctoral dissertation, Columbia University School of Public Health, 1981. (Chapter 2: The Profile of the Akans.)

Aging Among Native Americans
The Quest for Wisdom

John A. Grim

"Honor the aged, in honoring them you have life and wisdom." This traditional saying of the woodland Ojibway of North America can be paralleled by similar expressions from native peoples around the globe. Such widespread lore reflects the active role that the aged have in these societies not only in personal accomplishment but also in leading younger generations in their pursuit of life and wisdom. This chapter attempts to describe the significant role of active aging among native peoples by a consideration of the - *continuity* of the elderly with their tribal tradition, by an examination of their *celebration* of life in an ongoing experience of power, and by a discussion of their *creative* role in assisting native societies in their encounter with technology.

The Ojibway peoples of North America will be the primary source for documentation on aging among Native Americans although examples will also be presented from other tribal groups. A short article on this subject cannot fully describe the varied thought of the many ethnic groups in the Americas. It is hoped that by examining selected expressions the reader will come to appreciate the striking view of the world within which native peoples situate the cycles of life. While an article may claim to speak of "native peoples" it must be acknowledged that such a stance is not intended to overlook the particularity of each tribe's culture. In fact, there are only particular indigenous groups whose cultural views on aging are unique to themselves just as their language, rituals and customs are highly differentiated. Yet the traditional thought of the plains — Lakota, prairie — Gros Ventre and woodland Ojibway can each provide a context for entering into the special cross-cultural meaning that aging has for all native peoples.

It is helpful at this point to provide a brief statement on the use of the terms "tribal" and "elderly." Both terms have either been trivialized so that their reference is overly vague or they have been politicized so that their use is considered pejorative. Because of the cross-cultural nature of this chapter the term "tribal" is occasionally used but wholly in a positive manner. "Tribal" indicates a group of people who share language expressions, kinship terminologies, mythological stories, ritual actions and cultural values which enable them to respond to the exigencies of life. In referring to "Native Peoples" the same scope is intended with no consideration of higher or lower ranks as compared with multi-cultural civilizations or the contemporary technological system. "Elderly" is used as more of an indicator term than as an analytically precise cipher. It indicates that period of life in which the human individual and extended age-group leave off commitment to procreation of children and take on active nurturing roles with regard to self-fulfillment and social participation.

The essay opens, then, with reflections upon the continuity of aging as manifested in the natural world and in human longevity. We will present the Ojibway story of "four hills" in which aging is seen as continuing the heroic quest for vision power. This heroic endurance brings the essay to a consideration of the famous "age-group" systems of native peoples and their celebration of aging. Finally, the essay concludes with an analysis of the creative challenge confronting the aged in Native American societies as they respond to the current crises of self, society and environments

Continuity

All life rises up from the earth, prospers during its time of growth and then bends, finally collapsing back upon the bosom of the earth. Natural cycles of life are the intimate experience of native peoples in which each stage is seen as distinct and yet connected with those before and those that come after it. So also the human journey comes, as the Ojibway say, to the evening of life in which a new mode of living must be learned. The quality of human aging is distinct in many ways within the cycle of the natural world and it is perhaps this quality that native peoples especially honor. Human aging is sharply differentiated from our nearest primate cousins by our longevity after the period of reproductivity has passed.[1] This post-reproductive longevity, according to the individual ages of early human skeletal remains, appears to have developed with the increase in the skull capacity to house an enlarged brain. Moreover the earliest skeletal remains of an elderly person are also associated with the first cultural evidence of human ancestors, Homo sapiens.[2] This gradual development of an elderly group in the hominid species would seem to indicate some selective response or biological urge in the human family. Such genetic coding may very well have a parallel cultural coding. That is, tribal peoples may have gradually evolved their cultural attitude toward post-reproductive longevity as that culminative stage of an enlarged understanding of life.

For Native Americans, however, the uniqueness of the "evening age" is never seen as separate from the continuity of life. It is this view of continuity that helps to explain why some tribal people, such as the Iglulik Eskimo, may have abandoned their inactive aging during duress. The collapse of life back upon the earth has its own right and the inactive aging were exposed just as all natural life is exposed to the completion of its cycle. Thus the later years of native peoples are differentiated from the natural world and yet paralleled by the aging process in the plant, mineral and animal worlds. The active aging especially provide a unique insight into the thought of native peoples because of their distinctive witness to the total life process. The elderly complete the human mode of earth's life and, in bending with age, they manifest a new dance, a new song.

"Four Hills"

The need for a new understanding of life by the elderly is suggested in the Ojibway story of the four hills. It is a traditional dream-vision that is narrated in Ojibway lore as a means of reflecting upon the inner spirit and outer force that moves a person through their years. The story tells of the view from a high mountain across a wide valley to four great hills. The first was steep and difficult to climb. The second and third were higher but not as rugged. The fourth, was difficult to approach, entirely jagged, and mist enshrouded at its peak.

On the first hill infants crawled along its ragged heights. At its base the youngest babies appeared already in movement towards the older infants near the top. Along the ascent many fell, hesitated and soon stopped their upward climb. Those who scaled this height disappeared down its other side only to reappear slightly older as young boys and girls on the second hill.

The climbing adolescents also moved towards the hill's summit but they lingered more and played at children's games. Along the route, however, were those that fell and did not rise. Some stopped to comfort them a moment but then they too were urged along by some mysterious force. Near the top the maturer adolescents, guided by elder's voices, stopped to fast and pray, alone and exposed to life's harshest teachings. They stood in pity, humbled, praying for a vision. Many then continued toward the top, confident in their newly acquired songs of vision-power. Others went on in hope of later supernatural visitation and some fell aside unable to continue without spiritual power.

At the third hill young adults paired together and climbed towards the top, aging as they walked together. Here the greatest danger seemed to come from the humans themselves. Many dropped to the ground tended briefly by their mates. They were compassionated by others who could not stay behind but joined the throng moving relentlessly towards the difficult peak and beyond it to the descent fraught with dangers.

In comparison to the other hills there were few who began the ascent of the fourth hill. These were the elderly with whitened hair and wrinkled skin. It seemed that their limping walk would never take them up the nearly perpendicular fourth hill. But up they went, giving encouragement to one another and even calling back to those on the prior hills. Some of these aged walked in pairs, others alone. Some, who could not go on, urged their fellow climbers to go higher. Here on this hill was a special movement, slow and deliberate like a measured dance step that told of all the prior journeys. Those who could perform this dance advanced slowly up the mountain, aging as they went into the mist that shrouded the crest. [3]

This Ojibway story of life's movement from infancy to old age tells of our successive stages of life. It is the fourth stage which especially concerns us here. This is the period of active aging in which the continuity of life develops special capacities for self-reflection, for social commitment and for interaction with the earth.

Self-reflection on Spiritual Power

The path of life, as described in the popular Ojibway lore of the "four hills," is thronged with humanity. The power or force that drives the human onward is of special concern to native peoples. In many Native American societies adolescents are encouraged to undertake a ritual fast at puberty to establish a contact with this power. Most often the boy or girl is encouraged and assisted in this ritual by his or her grandparents. The relationship between the generations is most striking during this rite of passage. The youth who seeks a power identity is guided by the old ones who are themselves living examples of this quest for vision power. Moreover, a remarkable kinship is established between the youth and his elderly guide because of their special status in the tribe. The youth, by virtue of his ritual fast and humiliation, has become an outsider to his tribe, a liminal person. Yet the youth is guided by the elderly who, although well-established at the center of tribal life, are also liminal by virtue of their age. It is this liminal status that promotes the self-reflection of the elderly on the fourth hill. They are the tribal exemplars of the quest for power and wisdom.

While no general statement can be advanced for all tribal peoples, it can be said that traditional Native American peoples seek personal contact with a vital "power" that is believed to sustain all life on the earth. For the Ojibway this power is *manitou* which is often identified with extraordinary phenomena in the natural world such as mountains, high winds or exceptional trees. Manitou is also applied to select humans and their signal actions. This power is considered sacred or holy by virtue of the awe and exclusiveness it evokes. Yet manitou is personal, it is experienced by individual tribespeople as animate and alive. Manitou is also numinous in the sense that this term indicates an experience that is simultaneously terrifying and entrancing. This contact with sacred power is initially acquired for an infant by an elderly naming visionary and given to the child as their power-name. The numinous quality of one's name then becomes both an inner urge and the ceaseless unfolding of one's life story. Thus upon self-reflection the elderly may eventually become their own manitou presence.

Among the Ojibway the gradual identification of the aged with manitou arises from the length of time spent living the vision quest. Ojibway mythology speaks of a specific aged manitou placed in the west by the Great Spirit (*Gitchi Manitou*) with the following directions:

> "Now I place you here. Probably no one will be able to reach you. The Indian will fall short of his goal of old age. But when one does reach you, make white his head and show him the right way to the world of ever-beautiful sounds. Here is your obligation to the Indians."[4]

The manitou described here is not a distant spirit but a tribal mythic value physically embodied in the elderly. The active aging then become the ever-changing and yet continuous manitou they seek. The aged personify the personal power of manitou and, as such, become the ones most prone to metamorphosis, the ability to change. The elderly are often feared as well as respected for their ability to transform themselves. In their liminal state, then, the elderly are the ones most able to manage the great change at death.

Thus the vision experience of adolescence becomes the on-going quest of traditional Native Americans. For a vision is not a completed or accomplished experience but rather a direction that unfolds in meaning. Consequently it is with elderly self-reflection that the quest for the vision takes on those sacred qualities that are akin to power itself and that are often associated with the mystical path in religious literature.

Social Commitment

The active aged especially manifest their social concern in performing the community rituals. Among the plains tribes who still perform the Sun Dance an elderly holy man chooses the cottonwood tree which forms the center of the ceremonial lodge and which is the symbolic link with the Great Power *(Wakan Tanka)*. This role attests to that individual's endurance on the quest for vision power, his sanction by the elder religious leaders and the purity of spirit blessing manifest in his long life.

The Ojibway medicine society, Midewin, also underscores the Native American regard for age. In this secret and sacred society there may be four earth and four sky degrees of contact with healing power. To acquire these higher degrees takes years of personal training, active instruction and society approval. A person who achieves this status is afterwards addressed as an "old Mide Shaman" or "old man."

Likewise among the Pawnee tribe now located in Oklahoma and formerly of the Nebraska plains, the old men and women played central roles in the annual liturgical cycle based on the elaborate Pawnee cosmology. But even more telling is the silent presence of the aged along the edge of the ceremonial lodge during the Great Doctor Ceremony. The elderly attest, by their silent witness, to the spiritual sanction of this ancient hunting-culture. Unlike the Pawnee priests who precisely enacted the Cosmological rituals, the Pawnee doctors or shamans ritually reenacted the personal and spontaneous "calls" to their vocation by animal spirits. Their curing ceremonies consisted of dramatic performances of wild animal impersonations. The obvious ecstatic-hunting symbolism of the doctor's ceremony contrasts sharply with the dominant agricultural rituals of the Pawnee. Yet the presence of the most respected elderly leaders as silent witnesses emphasizes the traditional commitment of the aged to the power that once vitalized their society.

A final example of the role that the elderly have as active supporters of the tribal ethos or way of life is that of the Navajo chanter. There is no formal stipulation as to when a Navajo tribesmember can become an apprentice to learn a healing chantway. However, the elder chanters are the most authoritative ritualists. Currently, some Navajo chantways are in danger of being lost because of lack of ritual expertise and even interest by the younger generation. The role of social commitment by the aged is indicated in the following statements from the Navajo chanter, Claus Chee Sonny:

> We are losing the older people, every day. And when I die of old age, the ceremonies which I know will die with me. But if somebody learns them, they will continue. I am getting old and tired. I cannot be at all the places anymore where these ceremonies are needed.

> It is difficult to learn all these things correctly. But when you have learned, many people will know about it, and many will depend on you. Your parents, uncles, aunts, their children and your leaders, these will all be your relatives — in a good (not an exploitative) sense. And they will all recognize you because of your concern (for them), your learning and your respect for the ceremony. This is what is called 'one has come before them' (*bich'aah ajiiya*) — between your people and the bad influences. You have put your people behind you (*dine ane joo nil* — by acting as their shield) so that no harm will come to them. [5]

The social responsibility that the Navajo chanter has for his people is evident in this statement from Claus Chee Sonny. He becomes a guardian of his community's health. He anguishes over the prospects of ill-will that threaten his people if the medicine chants should fail to be passed on.

Thus the active aging among Native Americans manifest in many ways that unique social role which is suggested in the Ojibway story of the "four hills." They are the faithful executors of the tribal rituals and the living link with the tribe's ancient tradition. The grandparents among Native American peoples also bridge the generations and perform important kinship roles by giving encouragement and advice to their grandchildren. Finally, the most traditional social role of the elderly among Native Peoples is their stance as channels for the healing and sustaining power

conveyed by the great public rituals and the private observance of
vision prayers.

Interaction with the Earth

Perhaps no more significant personality among Native Americans summarizes the importance of the Earth to these peoples
than their shamans. While the formation and function of the
shaman is too complex a subject to develop here, it is helpful to
understand some aspects of this healing figure often referred to as
the medicine man. Generally the shaman-to-be is chosen by a
"call" from a numinous power. This call becomes the dramatic
base from which the male or female shaman develops an elaborate
ritual with which to contact his or her spirit-power. A misunder-
standing of spirit-power often blocks peoples with a Judaeo-
Christian background from a deeper appreciation of tribal religions.
Indeed, spirit-power is beyond academic formulation. But for
native peoples the power that sustains and nurtures life expresses
itself to them in natural forms, in voices from the Earth. It is the
shaman then who is best able to enter into these presences within
the earth. Basil Johnston, a traditional Ojibway teacher, maintains
that the healing wisdom of a shaman is acquired after years of
active quest:

> The inner being in which the gift to heal reposed, had
> to be enlarged.
>
> During the early years of his training, a young man
> or woman chosen for his special gifts, spent time in
> meditation and prayer. Alone in a secluded place, the
> young person sought a dream. At the same time he
> endeavored to impart his being to the plant and animal
> beings as he attempted to ingest substances and make
> them part of himself.
>
> In these retreats (the shaman), it was hoped, would
> increase his knowledge of himself and attain a high
> order of curative powers. Such retreats continued
> throughout the career of the medicine man. As the
> earth annually renews itself, so the shaman had, each
> year, to withdraw into himself in order to maintain his
> power.[6]

By solemn meditation and contemplative interaction with the
earth the shaman gradually develops the ability to heal his people
with herbs and ritual prayer. What is especially striking in
Johnston's statement is the implied continuity, the rediscovery of

that which is already known. For the shaman continues his introspective retreats into the earth just as the image of the "four hills" story would suggest growth in power and wisdom with growth in age. Power moreover, seems to import more of itself to the shaman as he progresses in his quest. Lame Deer, the elderly shaman of the Oglala Lakota, spoke of his experience of Earth's power in this way:

> The *wichasha wakan* (shaman or medicine healer) loves the silence, wrapping it around himself like a blanket — a loud silence with a voice like thunder which tells him of many things. Such a man likes to be in a place where there is no sound but the humming of insects. He sits facing the west, asking for help. He talks to the plants and they answer him! He listens to the voices of the *wama haskan* — all those who move upon the earth, the animals. He is at one with them. From all living beings something flows into him all the time, and something flows from him. I don't know where or what, but it's there. I know.[7]

This special way of knowing is reserved for those who can wait and listen. Not only do the accomplished medicine healers hear this power which the Lakota name *wakan,* and the Ojibway name *manitou,* but it is also heard by the aged who carry on the traditional ways of Native Americans. The aged Hopi hear it as they sing up their corn, the traditional elderly among the Iroquois hear it in the fire, some active aging of the Osage even hear it in their memories of Indian boarding schools. The elderly of native peoples come to that stage of life in which the presence of power and its manifestations are especially intuited, felt and apprehended as the continuous rhythms of earth's life.

Celebration

From the Ojibway story of the "four hills" it has been possible to situate particular roles of the Native American aged against the larger world view of a quest for personal contact with the power that pervades the cosmos. In this section the significance of aging as a celebration of this power is developed by considering the age-group system of the plains tribe called Gros Ventre.

A basic distinction in age-group systems has been articulated by Radcliffe-Brown between an age-set and an age-grade. Because both terms provide insight into the manner in which Native Peoples empirically organize their societies it is helpful to introduce this

complex subject, however brief and circumspect the discussion has
to be. An age-set is "a recognized and sometimes organized group
consisting of persons . . . who are of the same age . . . Once a
person enters a given age-set, whether at birth or by initiation, he
remains a member of the same set for the remainder of his life."[8]
Thus an age-set is an independent organization that a person is
born into or joins in order to acquire tribal identity and status.

Age-grades, on the other hand, are "recognized divisions of the
life of an individual as he passes from infancy to old age . . . infant,
boy, youth, young married man, elder or whatever it may be."[9]
The age-grade systems among native peoples are often the most
important ceremonial activity during the year. The ceremonies of
transition or rites of passage would take a person spiritually,
socially and often physically from out of their current tribal
position. In their "outsider status" or liminal position the tribes-
person would be in a fitting stance to be "pitied" by spirit-power.
Having experienced the sacred power this person would be ritually
placed in the next age-grade. The numinous energies that accompany these celebrations become more auspicious as one passes
through the acknowledged tribal age-grades. Thus it is possible by
means of the age-group systems of many tribal peoples to
understand why they celebrate aging as the accumulation of degrees
of contact with power.

A good example of a Native American society that combined
age-sets with age-grades forming a typical age-group system is that
of the Gros Ventre of northwest North Dakota, northeast Montana
and southern Saskatchewan. Like most of the plains tribes, the
Gros Ventre had an elaborate kinship organization that helped
determine, along with the age of an individual, what age-set they
joined. As the age-set matured they approached the second older
age-set for instructions in the performance of age-grade dances.
Thus the stages of life, through which each age-set group passed,
was marked by a religious dance of high ceremonial value.

The extreme religious status of the age-grade dances is peculiar
to the Gros Ventre. As with other plains tribes they valued
individual vision bundles, but the age-grade dances were even
more auspicious. Even more important than the age-grade dances
were the pipe bundles held by the most sacred elders with age-grade
status. Thus, parallel religious activity culminated with the active
aging who, as an age-set, had passed through the age-grade
ceremonials over a period of many years.

The names of the age-grade sequence also reflect the tribe's sense of reciprocity with the earth. For they amplify the vision quest experience as an encounter with power in both natural forms and celebratory activity. The age-grade dances were:

    I. The Fly Dance
    II. The Wonder Dance
    III. The Kit-Fox Dance
    IV. The Dog Dance
    V. The Drum Dance
    VI. The Law-Enforcers Dance[10]

The last two stages would take a warrior and his wife into the years of active aging. Moreover, their names, Drum and Law-Enforcers Dances, indicate the special celebratory and leadership roles that accrued to the aged among the Gros Ventre because of their progressive journey for power and wisdom.

Despite the encroachments of technology and the varieties of tribal cultures among most native peoples some form of age-group system still organizes these societies in a sacred celebration of aging. Thus those qualities of life experience and religious knowledge that come with aging determine and celebrate the elderly's auspicious place in the Native American age-group systems.

Creativity and Crisis

Just as the Ojibway story of the "four hills" situated the active aging within the continuous human journey, so also it indicated the personal resourcefulness and creativity required from the aged. This section focuses on the creative role of the elderly among Native Americans which they bring to the current crises of self, society and environment.

While the particular issues that face each tribal group are varied, there are larger problems which are pan-tribal. Such a dilemma is the quest for personal identity in a highly fragmented world. Native peoples face a severe crisis of living in-between the traditional and the modern. In living within traditional society and modern technological society they are faced with the enormous split between self, society, and environment, on the one hand, and science and technology on the other. The fragmentation of modern life is an enormous challenge to contemporary American society. Unfortunately the world views of Native American peoples are not finding extensive means of expression with either the tribal or larger American audiences. In this sense the challenge to the elderly among Native Americans is to creatively respond to this crisis of self-identity in a period of tremendous fragmentation. Their response must certainly come from their own experience of self, society and environment as mutual actors in the movement of life. The elderly among native peoples, while faced with the crisis of tribal identity, have a unique perspective from which to meet the challenge. For they are still in touch with a pre-industrial ethos in which the tribal world view can function as a source of meaning and orientation.

The crisis facing Native American societies is also of major importance. For the most part the attitude of the dominant American culture towards native peoples has been that of "assimilating" or "civilizing the savage." In overt and subtle ways this attitude has been predominant in American life. One of the most obvious methods of indoctrination was the Indian school which prohibited native languages and life-styles. The more subtle, often well-intentioned, approach was to foster native life in an American framework such as elected tribal councils and individual property allotments both of which were foreign to tribal life.

Again, however, the crisis of society requiring a creative response from the active aging of native peoples is a broader issue than was formerly recognized. For the technological mono-culture that is overwhelming Native American people is also intruding into the sphere of the dominant American ethos. The Native American aged therefore have a unique responsibility to actively foster their traditional tribal customs and values.

Only within recent years have we begun to realize the need for diversity and difference within life at its most basic cultural, ecological and genetic levels. Culturally then the aged among native societies hold the memory of a way of life that is beneficial to the dominant American ethos. Native life is also "organic" and must grow in continuity and change. Thus the active aging face the creative challenge of nurturing their native ethos and yet enabling it to develop and change.

Finally the most demonstrable crisis affecting the aged and the larger human age-group is the assault upon the earth by modern technological life. While technology is the result of the progressive dreams and creative hopes of humanity, it has become an end in itself. It is the most urgent challenge of the elderly among Native Americans to articulate their reverence for the earth as a sacred reality to be cared for and nourished. Moreover those Native

American aged who are capable must assist their tribe and the larger populace in understanding Earth's natural processes before we set them aside in favor of human technologies. The active aging among Native Americans can go beyond the charge of romantic environmentalism to respond to our ecological crisis from a perspective that intimately appreciates the complexity of the natural world.

Conclusion

While the Ojibway story of the "four hills" provides a traditional view of the trials and endurance of life, the secret and sacred lore of the Ojibway shamanistic society offers special insights that fittingly conclude this essay. The Ojibway shamanistic society is called *Midewin. Mide* means "mystic" or "sacred" and *win* is a participial form that means "doings." Therefore the Midewin teaches and practices the ancient wisdom lore of this Ojibway healing society.

The teachings of Midewin are secret not merely because of a prohibition against their recitation. Rather they are secret because an understanding of them requires a knowledge that comes from the experience of power. These teachings are also sacred by virtue of their origin in the world of the *manitou*. The teaching that is of significance here is that of the Mide path or pattern of life. It can be diagrammed as follows with eight separate stops or "lecture points" or "fires":[11]

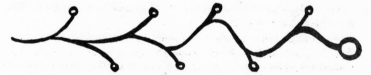

The Mide path bears immediate resemblance to the story of the "four hills" in its flow of continuity. Moreover, the Mide path also reflects the endurance needed to pass along life's path. For each circle is that point in life's passage where a person is tempted away from the right way. The circles begin with infancy and progress through adolescence, adulthood, middle age, married life, old age and beyond. Each challenge can be met by stopping at the temptation point, lighting the fire of reflection and calling together friends to "lecture" them back to the correct way.

The last two fires are of primary concern here. The second to last is the temptation of old age. Having successfully met the prior six trials of life, the temptation is to stop and give up. In this sense, the call for creative output from the elderly of native peoples is a call of encouragement to them. They must not give up their own traditional ways despite the desperation they feel at times. More than any other group in the Americas the elderly Native Americans can teach everyone endurance. Now they must creatively respond again from the depths of their endurance.

For the elderly Ojibway shaman the eighth circle is of cardinal importance. For Ojibway Mide lore says the eighth fire is that of peace or destruction and this fire, this temptation, can only be lighted by the dominant American culture. The white anglo-American peoples must meet this test say many Native Americans prophecies. But the active aging of native peoples also bear the challenge to help their younger generations to light the eighth fire of peace together. Thus the traditional role of active aging and the contemporary concern among the aged of Native American societies is still shaped by the enduring quest for wisdom.

References

1·E. E. Hunt, Sr., "Evolutionary Comparisons of the Demography, Life Cycles and Health Care of Chimpanzee and Human Populations," in *Health and the Human Condition,* eds. M. H. Logan and E. E. Hunt, Jr. (North Scituate, MA: Duxbury Press, 1978), pp. 52-58; Robert MacArthur and Joseph Connell, *The of Populations* (N.Y.: Wiley, 1966), p. 130.

2 Michael Day, *Guide to Fossil Man* (N.Y.: Meridan Books, 1968), pp. 162-167.

3 Basil Johnston, *Ojibway Heritage* (N.Y.: Columbia University Press, 1976), pp. 109-118.

4 Ruth Landes, *Ojibway Religion and the Midewiwin* (Madison, Wis.: Univ. of Wisconsin Press, 1968), p. 202.

5 Karl W. Luchert, *A Navajo Bringing-Home Ceremony* (Flagstaff, Ariz.: Museum of Northern Arizona Press, 1978), pp. 199 and 200, paragraphs 399 and 405.

6 Johnston, *Ojibway Heritage,* p. 82.

7 John (Fire) Lame Deer and Richard Erdoes, *Lame Deer, Seeker of Visions* (N.Y.: Simon and Schuster, 1972), pp. 145-146.

8 A. R. Radcliffe-Brown, "Age organization — terminology," *Man* 29 (1929):21.

9 Op. cit., p. 21, for an in-depth consideration of age-groups systems see Frank Henderson Stewart, *Fundamentals of Age-Group Systems* (N.Y.: Academic Press, 1977).

10. John M. Cooper, *The Gros Ventres of Montana Part II, religion and ritual,* Edited by Regina Flannery. Catholic University of America Anthropological Series 16. Washington, D. C.: Catholic University of America.

11 Francis Densmore, Chippewa Customs (Minneapolis, Minn. Ross and Haines reprint, 1968), p. 89; also cf. Johnston, *Ojibway Heritage,* p. 86.

Bibliography

Benedict, Ruth. *The Concept of the Guardian Spirit in North America.* American Anthropological Association Memoir 29. Menasha, Wisconsin, 1923.

Boas, Franz. *Race, Language and Culture.* New York: Macmillan, 1940.

Civilization of the American Indian Series. Norman, Oklahoma: University of Oklahoma Press.

Cooper, John M. *The Gros Ventres of Montana Part II, religion and ritual.* Edited by Regina Flannery. Catholic University of America Anthropological Series, 16. Washington, D.C.: Catholic University of America, 1957.

Densmore, Francis. *Chippewa Customs.* Minneapolis, Minn.: Ross and Haines reprint, 1968.

Eliade, Mircea. *Shamanism: Archaic Techniques of Ecstasy.* Princeton: Princeton University Press, Bollingen Series 76, 1964.

Halloway, Irving. *Culture and Experience.* Philadelphia: Univ. of Penn., 1955.

Johnston, Basil. *Ojibway Heritage.* New York: Columbia University Press, 1976.

Kluckhohn, Clyde and Dorothea Leighton. *The Navajo.* Garden City: Doubleday, 1962. First published 1946.

Kroeber, Alfred. *Handbook of the Indians of California.* Bureau of Ethnology Report 78, 1925.

Lame Deer, John (Fire) and Richard Erdoes. *Lame Deer: Seeker of Visions.* New York: Simon and Schuster, 1972.

Landes, Ruth. *Ojibwa Religion and the Midewiwin.* Madison, Wisconsin: Univ. of Wisconsin Press, 1968.

Lowie, Robert. *Primitive Religion.* New York: Liveright, 1948.

Maximilian, Prince of Wied-Neuwied. *Travels in the interior of North America.* Early Western Travels, 1748-1846, Vols. 22-24.

Edited by Reuben G. Thwaites. Cleveland: Arthur H. Clark, 1906.

Morgan, Lewis H. *League of the Ho-De-No Sau-Nee or Iroquois.* Edited by Herbert M. Lloyd. New York: Dodd, Mead and Co., 1901; reprinted by Human Relations Area Files Press, 1954.

Neihardt, John. *Black Elk Speaks.* New York: William Morrow, 1932; reprinted by Univ. of Nebraska Press, 1961.

Parsons, Elsie Clews, ed. *American Indian Life.* Lincoln: University of Nebraska Press, 1967.

Powell, Pewter. *Sweet Medicine.* Norman, Oklahoma: University of Oklahoma Press, 2 vols., 1969.

Radin, Paul. *Primitive Religion: Its Nature and Origin.* New York: Dover reprint, 1957.

_____. *The Road of Life and Death: a Ritual Drama of the American Indians.* Bollingen Series 5. Princeton University Press, 1945.

Rasmussen, Knud. *The Netsilik Eskimos. Social Life and Spiritual Culture.* Report of the 5th Thule Expedition 8, nos. 1 and 2. Copenhagen, 1931.

Schoolcraft, Henry. *Information Respecting the History, Condition and Prospects of the Indian tribes of the United States.* Philadelphia: Lippincott, Giambo and Co., 1853.

Sturtevant, Wm. C., Ed. *Handbook of North American Indians.* Washington, D.C.: Smithsonian Institute, 1978.

Tedlock, Dennis and Tedlock, Barbara. *Teachings from the American Earth.* New York: Liveright, 1975.

Vizenor, Gerald. *Tribal Scenes and Ceremonies.* Minneapolis, Minn.: Nodin Press, 1976.

Wissler, Clark. "The social life of the Blackfoot Indians." *Anthropological Papers of the American Museum of Natural History 7 (1911):1-64.*

Underhill, Ruth M. *Red Man's Religion.* Chicago: University of Chicago Press, 1965.

The Elderly and Moral Percepts
In Chinese Tradition

Albert Chi-Lu Chung

1. Individual, Family, and World Order

In Chinese history, the elderly have never been a social problem, even up to the present day. This fact is rooted in the guiding philosophy of Chinese life.

In the Chinese mind, there are unbreakable linkages among persons, families, the nation, and the world in general. One starts with oneself, and subsequently takes one's place in family life, in society, in the nation, and eventually in the world. This relates to the Confucian idea that all things have their roots and branches; and activities always have their ends and beginnings. To know what is the first and what is the last will lead one close to the primordial principle of the universe. The basic task for anybody, from the Confucian point of view, is to cultivate one's self. If one does not attend to that fundamental duty then no good can come in the end. The Confucian philosophers asserted, therefore, that the ancients who had intended to promote the prevalence of virtue all over the world, first had to administer their own countries properly. However, in order to administer their own nations well, they first had to regulate their own families properly. In order to regulate their own families properly, they had to properly cultivate their own selves. In order to cultivate properly their own selves, they had to set their own minds properly. For the purpose of setting their own minds properly, they first sought to be sincere in their own thoughts. For one to be sincere in thoughts, he or she must first seek and extend his or her own knowledge. To seek and extend knowledge one must focus upon the investigation of things.

The Confucian approach is philosophical. It is in fact an epistemology with ethical implications. The key point raised here is that the future hope of our world is inseparably linked to the soundness of both the individual and his or her family. The family receives its happiness from the individual who heads it. In Chinese tradition, this is the basis for the importance of the elderly, since the time the family itself was first established.

The Great Learning, a Confucian classic from which the above assertions are quoted, was believed by Chen Yi-Chuan, a Confucian philosopher of the Sung dynasty in the 11th Century, to be the work of Confucius himself. However, this was disputed by another well-known Confucian commentator, Chu Hsi (1130-1200, A.D.). Nevertheless, *The Great Learning* was a typical work of a Confucian writer or writers, as judged by the ideas indicated in both the texts and their commentaries.

The inseparable linkages among an individual, his or her family, community, country, and the world has long been a distinctly Chinese way of thinking. The tradition has its primary source in one of the oldest of Chinese ancient classics, the *Yi Ching,* or the *Book of Change.* It was the only known ancient Chinese classic that escaped the fires of the Chin dynasty in the third century B.C.

In the thirty-seventh of the sixty-four hexagrams of the *Yi Ching,* it is said that for the wholesomeness of a family, it is most advantageous for the female to be proper and persistent. This statement is from a particular hexagram called Chia-jen, or Members of a Family. The commentary that follows the text of the hexagram reads: "Members of a family: The female takes up her place properly and persistently within; the male takes up his place properly and persistently without. Both the male and the female are properly and persistently in their places. This is the great righteousness of both the Heaven and the earth. Among the members of a family, there are the revered, strict elders, namely, the father and the mother. If the father acts as a father; a son acts as a son; an older brother as an older brother; a younger brother as a younger brother; a husband as a husband; and a wife as a wife; then the rule of conduct for a family is rectified. If each and every family were to rectify its rule of conduct, there would not be any disorderly families; and the whole world would achieve stability and security."

This principle of rectification directs each individual to live according to his or her designated role. This enables the social duties, and in some cases legal obligations, to be properly and correctly fulfilled, so that a family may live in harmony and real happiness. In the same manner, this principle will lead our world in general to realize its potential for peace and security. The ontological foundations of the principle of rectification are epistemological, ethical, and aesthetic, in the sense that no one can act correctly, either morally or legally, without knowing about what is involved, especially in regard to one's role and the relationships to others in family and social life. Once the necessary knowledge is acquired, then the moral considerations become

possible and attainable. Successful perseverence in carrying out
the principle of rectification requires an aesthetic appreciation and
enjoyment in a deeply persuasive sense. This is the difference
between the Confucian and the Kantian point of view concerning
the moral imperative.

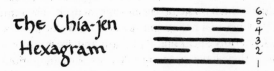

The principle of rectification in the *Yi Ching* as indicated clearly
in its 37th hexagram, Chia-jen, or the Members of a Family, was
accepted whole-heartedly by Confucius himself and his followers
throughout Chinese history. It was also the most cherished
preeminent principle of both Plato and Aristotle in the ancient
Greek world. The Socratic and Platonian notion of justice and a
just society stressed that each and every sector of the society do the
occupation for which they were best equipped to do. The
Aristotelian concept of the proper function of man, which is
inseparably linked to one's goodness, also does not differ greatly
from the rectification of name or title, in the social or legal sense,
of the *Yi Chang,* and later on, of the Confucians. They all agreed
that everyone could attain goodness, if he or she did what ought to
be done, according to the social, moral, and political-economic
implications that underlie or define one's role or title within the
family, society, or any sort of group. The principle of rectification
would thus be applicable equally and validly to the elderly.

The Chia-jen hexagram of the *Yi Ching* has more to say about
how the orderliness of family life can be attained, and about the
moral roles the elderly have to perform for the purpose of achieving
that orderliness implied by the Chinese word, cheng. The classic
text of any one of the 64 hexagrams of the *Yi Ching* consists of
lineal symbols, namely a composition of two radically different
lines, the yang(—) and the yin (- -), in varying formations, according
to the law of probability in logical sequence. Following the lineal
symbol formation, there is a short formal text concerning the
entire hexagram; then comes the main commentary (called chuan)
and finally the hsiang, which analyzes the naturalistic phenomena
implied in the formation of the hexagram itself with covert or
conjectural moralistic explanations. This is followed by a short

assertion for each of the six posited lines, each with its own explanation (also called hsiang and known as the "little hsiang") distinct from the "major hsiang," or "big hsiang."

In the case of Chia-jen hexagram, the mention of male and female, parents, sons, older and younger brothers, husband and wife is derived from the intended meanings of the six differently posited lines which make up the hexagram itself. The sequence of reading the lines in a hexagram starts from the bottom line up to the top. Generally speaking, if the top and the bottom lines are yang lines, they have been regarded as the completion of the images of father and son in a hexagram. The top yang symbolizes the father, and the bottom the son. This is exactly the case in the hexagram Chia-jen. The fifth yang in a hexagram has always been deemed as either the king, the father, the husband, or the older brother; and the second yin, the virtuous minister, the sage, the mother, or the wife. In Chia-jen, they denote the father and the mother, and also the husband and the wife in their hexagramatic implications. The chuan of hexagram Chia-jen states: "In a family, there are the strict authoritative rulers who are the father and the mother." In terms of brotherhood the fifth and the third yangs represent the elder and the younger brothers respectively. This is also the case in the Chia-jen hexagram. The fourth yin line in Chia-jen refers specifically to the woman of the house who enriches and renders great luck to the entire family.

A hexagram in the *Yi Ching* is composed of two trigrams with three lines in each of them as sub-units. The bottom is known as the inner trigram, and the top, the outer. The bottom trigram of Chia-jen is called the Li denoted the second daughter; and the top, the Shun signified the elder daughter. They are actually represented by the second yin and the fourth yin in their respective units, Li and Shun. In the hexagramatic structures of the *Yi Ching,* both the second and fourth lineal positions have been so considered as the weak places occupied properly only by the yin, which are regarded to be weak as opposed to the yang, the strong lines.

The inner trigram of Chia-jen is to be regarded as the inner world of a family within which the mother or the wife is the authoritative ruler. It is represented by the second line, yin. Since it is in the middle between the first and the third lines, it signifies the concept of moderation between two extremes. The second is arithmetically even in number, and can be properly taken only by the yin line. The second yin of Chia-jen possesses all these characteristics and attributes; and so is its fourth yin line. The hexagram statement of Chia-jen says, therefore: "For members of a family, what is most advantageous is that the women be firm and rectified." The women referred to here mean, first of all, the mother, or the wife; and secondly, the two daughters, designated by the Li and Shun.

As we pointed out earlier each of the 64 hexagrams of the *Yi Ching* has six lines which make up the hexagram itself. However, the essential lines are merely two radically different lines, namely, the yang and the yin, the strong and the weak. The strong yang line is designated numerically by "9"; and the weak yin line, by "6," in the *Yi Ching*. Since there are only six lines in each hexagram, thus one, three, and five are the only odd numbers; two, four, and six, the even numbers. The lineal positions of the former are supposedly to be occupied properly only by the yang; and the latter, by the yin. If a yang line is on the top, it is called the "upmost nine," the bottom, the "primary nine," etc. The yang may actually occupy, by chance, any lineal position in a hexagram; and so is the case with the yin. But the proper places for the yin to take are only the second, the fourth, and the sixth on the top. A top yin is called the "upmost six"; the fourth yin, the "six-fourth," etc. The varieties of lineal formations in the 64 hexagrams of the *Yi Ching* are derived from the law of permutations and combinations.

The first line, yang, of the Chia-jen asserts that the household must establish strict preventive measures, in the form of rules of conduct for the family, in order to avoid later on any occasion for repentance. A warning of this kind is also sounded in the explanation of line three, also a yang, by declaring that when members of the family are grumbling due to the stern strictness of disciplinary measures taken, there might be an occasion for regret. Nevertheless, if the firmness of disciplines remains unchanged, good fortune might still result. It might lead to regret and disorderliness in family life, if women and children were chattering and smirking. This is because such conduct will weaken or rip apart the rules of conduct in family life. It is to prevent this sort of worrisome situation that a red flag is raised in the explanation of the first line of Chia-jen. A more or less identical idea is stated in the interpretation of the top yang line of this hexagram. It says: "The upmost nine (yang line equals 9; yin line equals 6): If there are sincerity and respectability, there will always be good fortune in the end." We have pointed out earlier that the top line of Chia-jen, a yang, represents symbolically the father, the elder in the family. We also mentioned that the principle of rectification of names is involved in the achievement of orderliness in family life. As a matter of fact, it is thought to be absolutely necessary for a wholesome family life to have strict rules of conduct communicated straightforwardly. Analogously, a set of principles is indispensable for any well governed nation, and for the whole world as well, if peace and security are to be achieved. In this sense, we can see clearly that what an elder did with his or her family in the past was not merely to provide good example, but also persuasive guidelines for the community, nation, and the world in general, in their respective ways of managing the public affairs for the purpose of attaining the common good.

The cement that holds the members of a family harmoniously together is mutual love, also suggested by the hexagram of Chia-jen. Without it, orderliness can merely be accounted a shallow existence. Good fortune, *gi,* in Chinese, could not possibly be attained or sustained.

The fifth line, a yang of Chia-jen, is explained: Nine-five, under the kingly influence, a family comes into being; no worry; good fortune. The commentary following reads: Under the kingly influence, a family comes into being, because the mutual love is there. The fifth line in any hexagram is always the position for the king, the son of Heaven, according to the ontological implications of hexagramatical structure in the *Yi Ching.* This starts with the first hexagram, Chien. Its fifth line, nine-five, says: The flying dragon is in the sky. It will be advantageous to meet with the great man. Its commentary asserts that the flying dragon in the sky is just like the rising of the great man. The great man here means a sage who possesses the great virtues, the heavenly virtues, or the dragonfly virtues, *lun di.*

Therefore, the kingly influence mentioned above signifies the virtuous influence of the great man. The word, kingly, used here has another hexagramatic implication. In the original trigram designed by Fu Hsi in earliest antiquity, there were only three lines. Its top line denotes symbolically the Heaven, the bottom the earth, and the middle the human. This triplicity is called the three genuises, *san tsai,* in Chinese. It applies to the hexagram which has six lines divided equally into two sub-units. The six-lined hexagram was believed to be the creation of King Wen of the ancient Chou dynasty, 12th century, B.C. The upper two lines, the fifth and the sixth, in any of the 64 hexagrams of the *Yi Ching,* still represent the sphere of the Heaven; the lower two lines, the first and the second, the earth; and the third and fourth lines in the middle, the human. It is for this ontological distributive reason that the fourth yin line in the Chia-jen hexagram has been regarded as the woman of the house who acts authoritatively as a ruler in the family. This is due to the fact that the fourth line is very close to the sphere of Heaven, and yet remains on top in the human "province."

The fifth line, a yang, in the hexagram Chia-jen carries the inherent implication of kingliness because the fifth line is in the sphere of Heaven, yet remains close to the "province" of man. The lineal statement says: Nine-five, as a king he extends his influence to his family. There need be no anxiety. Good fortune. The lineal commentary asserts: "As a king he extends his influence to his family. They are in mutual love." The suggestion here is clear that an elder in a family must have the characteristics of being moderate and correct, as shown by the attributes of the fifth yang line in the hexagram Chia-jen, being in the middle between the fourth and the sixth, and being a yang with firmness in its proper place.

From these examples we can see that the *Book of Change, Yi Ching,* is very rich in philosophical implications. The hexagram Chia-jen defines the role each and every member of a family must play under the moral principle of mutual love, and with a self-imposed discipline of firmness, as determined by the principle of rectification. It also points out that the stability of the world rests indispensably on the stability of a sound family life.

2. Filial Piety and the Elderly

On the day this writer started to work on this section of chapter, the news-break over television reported that His Holiness, Pope John Paul II, was shot repeatedly and seriously wounded. In the view of Chinese tradition, the person who committed such a serious crime against a world religious leader, devoted to world peace, universal love, humanity and brotherhood, must be a man without any sense of filial piety. Had he been a pious son to his parents, or held pious feelings toward any other elder, there would not have been such a crime in the first place.

It has been widely asserted that the chaotic social situation everywhere and the international turmoils since World War II, are primarily due to the breakdown of morality in general, and the rules of conduct in family life in particular. The collapse of morality has subverted the law. Laws can maintain order effectively, only when the unwritten power of morality is in full force.

Filial piety, as a paramount moral drive in a man's social life, is undoubtedly a yardstick by which the close relationships between elders and the younger generation can be correctly measured. It is also a powerful binding force producing a stable, orderly, and meaningful society. In the perspective of Chinese tradition, filial piety can be counted on as a source of world peace and order. For these reasons, it is thought to be the supreme principle of man's morality. That is why the Chinese people often say that filial piety comes ahead of every good result. Chinese philosophers, specifically the Confucians, esteem filial piety as the essential moral principle that can define the very meaning of a man's being in this world.

The Confucians hold that a man would not be a man unless he observes filial piety toward his parents and other elders in the family. To be filially pious toward one's parents and other elders in the family is a moral duty for a son or daughter. If he or she could not be so, then the authenticity of his or her own existence would be in serious doubt. For this reason, in the *Analects,* one of the disciples of Confucius was condemned by the Master for not being virtuous when he denounced the conventional rule of conduct to mourn the death of one's parents for a period of three years. This disciple named Tsai Oh contended that the mourning period of three years was too long and wasteful. Confucius maintained that the first three years of a child's life were under the complete care of the parents; and that the mourning for the death of parents for a period of three years was, therefore, universally adopted and practiced. The complaint of Tsai Oh indicated, from the viewpoint of Confucius, that he did not have filial love and due respect for his parents. The Chinese word which Confucius employed here to criticize his disciple is *"jen,"* which we interpret here as love and respect. It was defined by Confucius, and also by Mencius, a loyal Confucian in the third century B.C., as "to love others." When the question, "What is jen?" was raised by Fan Chih, also a disciple of Confucius, the Master answered: "To love people." Confucius also asserted that a young man should be filially pious when he is at home; respectful toward elders when he goes out; and he should also remain earnest and truthful at all times. He should love all and cherish jen (the human love).

In the case of Mencius, he simply defined "jen" as "being a human being." He declared that the combination of being a human being and jen was to be regarded as the Tao, the primordial principle of universe. Mencius also contended that a man of jen loves all; and in the opposite a man without jen shows only an insincere love. Mencius also argued that everyone has something which he cannot bear; and that by extending that feeling to what he can bear the result will be jen.

Mencius made a distinction between a highly virtuous gentleman and an ordinary soul. He maintained that the difference between them is what they keep in their minds. The former, *chun-tse* in Chinese, constantly keeps both the *jen* and the *li*, propriety, in his mind. Mencius asserted furthermore that the man of jen loves people; and the man of propriety respects people. The one who loves others is always loved by others; and the one who respects others is always respected by others. Mencius also pointed out that the essence of jen is to serve one's parents piously; the essence of yi, righteousness, is to obey one's elder brother; and the essence of wisdom is to understand these two things.

From the assertions of both Confucius and Mencius on jen, we can see that filial piety is the manifestation of jen in its most spontaneous form. It never could be an artificial action of any sort. But to put filial piety into practice and action does require, Confucius contended, observation of the rules of conduct in propriety, which is called *li* in Chinese. Li is based upon sincere respect for others. When the sense of sincerity and respect are absent; then li would become artificially ritualistic and therefore meaningless. We found that there were numerous occasions in which the disciples of Confucius enquired about the meaning of filial piety. The Master always gave them different answers to as to reveal the true essence of the moral principle in question. When Tse Yu, a disciple from the home state of Confucius, Lu, asked about filial piety, Confucius said to him: "Nowadays filial piety has been thought to be the same as being able to support (his parents); but dogs and horses can also be supported. If there is no reverence, it makes no difference at all." Another disciple named Tse Hsia also asked about the meaning of filial piety. Confucius told him that the difficulty is with the countenance. The latter is perhaps due to the fact that the facial expressions usually indicate the presence or absence of sincerity and respect for others in one's doing or serving.

Therefore Confucius pointed out: "No adversity," to Meng Yi-tse, a noble official in the state of Lu, who asked about filial piety. The possible meanings of "No adversity" could be at least twofold: it might first denote to do nothing that could cause mental distress to the parents or other related elders; secondly, it could mean not to depart from moral principles, namely, the jen and the yi specifically. Confucius once asserted that one should not take a trip to faraway places while the parents are alive; and that if he does go far away, the destinations must be known to them beforehand. Confucius also stressed the point that in serving the parents one should give less advice; and that upon noticing that the parents would not accept his advice, he must show even greater respect for them. In rendering service to parents, Confucius advocated steadfastly that there should not be any complaints or adversity. Here again the idea of no adversity was asserted, as was the idea of respect.

In the *Classic of Filial Piety,* Confucius pointed out that there were five different ways for a son or daughter to serve his or her parents or the other elders of the family, namely, (1) to show reverence in residence; (2) to render joy in supporting; (3) to manifest deep concern in sickness; (4) to illustrate grief and sadness in death; and (5) to show seriousness and sincerity in memorial offerings. We quoted earlier the answer given by Confucius to Meng Shun, Meng Yi-tse, who asked about the meaning of filial piety. Confucius said to him: "No adversity." Fan Chih, a disciple, asked the Master what this meant. Confucius replied: "To serve with propriety, while the parents are alive; to bury them with propriety when they are dead; to perform memorial offerings with propriety." The word 'propriety' translates the Chinese word, *li,* which could be various sets of rules of conduct. But the real substance of *li* was sincere respect. The latter is grounded in *jen,* according to the Confucian point of view.

For a son or daughter to show filial piety requires more than just carrying out these five steps. Confucius declared, according to Hsian Ching, that anyone who wants to serve his or her parents well must not be arrogant when he or she is in a higher rank over others; must not be disorderly or unruly when he is in a lower position; and must not be quarrelsome when he is with his peers. If one could not get rid of arrogance, disorderliness and belligerence, then one would not be filially pious, even if the parents were being served daily with beef, lamb, and pork. Ridding oneself of these three things is intended to free one's parents from unnecessary shame, worry and anxiety. In the *Analects,* Confucius pointed out that while a man's father is alive, observe what he resolves to do; when his father passes away, look at his conduct. If for three years he does not change from the exemplified way of his father, then he may be called pious. Here again the mourning period of three years is suggested.

Thus filial piety is not only the most significant moral idea of man; but also a universal value constituting, with the respect for elder brother, a single principle that is in union with the gods and spirits.

3. The Significance of Death in Connection with Virtue and Fame

Death, like birth, is merely another basic occurrence in the whole process of being in this world. But there may be different sorts of death: Death with weight of the Chinese Mountain Tai; and others are just like light feathers floating away without any trace, as the Chinese people are used to say. The question here, as far as the issue of death is concerned, is whether a person, particularly the aged, has been dwelling in the principle of jen and acting according to the principle of yi, as pointed out by Mencius, the second sage of the Chinese people. To him the principle of jen is the tranquil habitation of man, and the principle of yi, righteousness or justice, his straight path. A man who holds fast to these two moral principles, from the viewpoint of Mencius is the man whose death carries a heavy weight like the Mount Tai. The death of the wicked, on the other hand, is not worthy to be noticed. A person of *jen* and *yi* is a great man, a "*ta chang fu*" in Chinese. He is a man with great virtues. He possesses the great spirit, the so-called "*hao jan chih ch'i.*" He is a person who dwells in the widest dwelling under heaven, stands in the most straightforward place under heaven, and walks the greatest path under heaven. He will join with others in practicing the great principles, according to his desires. If others go astray, he would follow principles alone. He can be debauched neither by wealth nor honor. Neither poverty nor mean conditions can swerve him from the great principles he cherishes. He would not be submissive to either menace or force. The death of such a person, with such rich virtue and great courage, would naturally be mourned by people everywhere with a deep sense of loss and grief.

When Confucius asserted that a virtuous gentleman, *chun tse,* would be sick if he were to be unknown after death, he probably intended to mean that a virtuous gentleman would become ill if he could not be virtuous in all his deeds. He was not actually concerned about being unknown by others. A virtuous gentleman always regards righteousness or justice as essential for everything. He always acts in accordance with the rules of propriety. In talking to others he is always humble and courteous. In completing all undertakings, he always is sincere and earnest.

Confucius declared that the way of being a virtuous gentleman is threefold, but he was not capable of any one of them: being virtous, a man of jen is free from anxieties; being wise, a man of wisdom is free from perplexities; being brave, a man of courage is free from fear. But Tse Kung, a disciple, said that the Master was describing himself. A *chun tse,* virtuous man, also has three awes in mind, according to Confucius, namely, an awe for the ordinance of Heaven; an awe for great men; and an awe for the words of sages. There are also three things about which a virtuous man must constantly take precautions: watching against lust in youth when his physical growth is not yet settled; watching against fighting with others in the years when his physical strength gets stronger; and watching against greedy desires in his older years when he is feeble. Besides the precautions to be taken, the nine thoughts, Confucius added, should be kept in mind by a virtuous man, namely, (1) thought for clarity in seeing; (2) thought for distinctiveness in hearing; (3) thought for gentleness in expression; (4) thought for respectfulness in manner; (5) thought for faithfulness in speech; (6) thought for considerations for others in conducting business; (7) thought for inquiry in doubting; (8) thought for difficulties in anger; (9) thought for righteousness in gaining things. The last, thought for righteousness in gaining, is a warning given specifically to the aged. it can and should be, of course, applicable to men and women of all ages.

The term Heaven, used by Confucius, like others in antiquity was to mean seemingly a mystic Being that possesses supreme power and moral governance over all other beings in the world. Confucius employed the term, *tien min,* Heaven's ordinance, three times in the *Analects* when he once said that he himself knew Heaven's ordinance at the age of fifty; in another occasion, to point out the three awes; and when he said that a mean man, having no knowledge of the ordinances, does not, therefore, have any fear of them, and that a mean man despises great men, and condemns the words of sages. What could the term, great man, mean here? The Chinese words, *ta jen,* great man, first appeared in the Yi Ching in its first hexagram, chien. The phrase was cited in explaining the second and the fifth lines in the hexagram. In the attached commentaries, the so-called "great man" was defined as one whose virtue is in union with that of Heaven and earth; whose brilliance is equal to that of sun and moon; whose orderliness is identical with that of four seasons; and whose good and bad fortunes are like that of the spirits and gods. Some commentators contended that the great man meant the sovereign or duke who might or might not govern his nation with virtues in accordance with the decrees of Heaven. Others maintained that only the ruler who was a sage within and a king without could be regarded as the great man, i.e., a man whose virtues make him the equal of a sage, who is also able to govern his country in accordance with the decrees of Heaven. In this sense, he would be the man of Heaven, *tien jen,* of Chuang Tse, a leading Taoist philosopher in about third century B.C.

That which makes the sages what they are, and which enables a king to achieve what he accomplishes originate from one source, according to Chuang Tse. One who does not depart from the original is called the man of Heaven, *tien jen.* One who does not depart from the true spirit is called God's man. One who does not depart from the truth is called the utmost man. The one who takes Heaven as the original, takes virtue as the fundamental, Tao as the gate, and transcends all changes, is called the sage. The one who takes jen as grace, yi (righteousness) as principle, li (rules of propriety) as guide to action, music as harmony, and to whom kindness and love come naturally and spontaneously, is called *chun tse,* a virtuous man or gentleman, in the view of Chuang.

Thus, a virtuous gentleman *chun tse* must have greatness of moral character in order to make his name consistent with moral quality revealed in his conduct. Confucius once asserted that a virtuous gentleman merely worries about his lack of abilities, not about being unknown to others. In Chinese tradition, death as an end to existence has not been a cause of sadness for the elderly. What really causes them anxiety is whether they are capable of doing enough good for their families, their society, their country, and the world at large. So the solicitude constantly confronting them has always been the problem of self-cultivation and attainment of virtuousness. Should they be regarded as famous, they will continuously try to live up to expectations of virtuous conduct. Thus their usefulness to the younger generation is in the form of sustained good example.

There are other philosophical concepts in Chinese tradition that offer comfort to the Chinese aged, when the end of their life is approaching. The Taoist philosophy, as revealed in the (*Tao Te Ching*) *Book of Lao Tse,* maintains that all things return to their roots. The return to roots is called quiescence. It is also known as reverting to destiny. Reverting to destiny is called the constant or eternal. To understand the eternal is called enlightenment. Not knowing the eternal, the *Tao Te Ching* tells us, one acts blindly, leading one to disaster. It is also said that knowing the eternal is all-embracing and tolerating, leading to oneness with all others. Being in oneness with all others is to ascend like a king and to be in accord with Heaven. To be in accordance with Heaven is to be with the Tao. The Tao is the eternal. There is, therefore, no peril when one's body dies. The real issue raised here is not death itself, but rather the enlightenment which is supposed to be achieved after thorough ontological understanding of the existence of the eternal Tao; and secondly, by the objective recognition of the fact that all things, however durable they may be, must and will one day each return to their root, namely, the Tao.

The *Tao Te Ching* pointed out that the trouble with all of us is that we possess a concept of selfness. If this notion is discarded through and through, then we have absolutely nothing to worry about. It further asserted that anyone who esteems himself or herself as much as the universe in equal love, then he or she can put the self in the trust of the universe.

Another leading Chinese Taoist philosopher, Chuang Chou, reiterated the idea of identifying one's self with the universe. He indicated in his book *Chuang Tzu,* that it is the non-action, *wu wei,* that is the key to our being and fate. The *Tao Te Ching* provides, more or less, similar explanation, when it says: "Doer will fail; holder will lose."

As we have pointed out, the philosophy of Lao Tse contended that all things originate from, and will one day return, to the Tao. This clarifies, at least from one Taoist viewpoint, the connotations of life and death. However, the theory of equalization put forward by Chuang Chou, carries with it an even more profound ontological implication. Chuang's theory illustrates the validity of the theory of relativity, and also dialectic logic at work. He argued that unending change is the most essential ontological property of all things. Of course, this idea of change was advocated in the early antiquity by the *Yi Ching,* the *Book of Change.* According to the

Explanation of Hexagrams, shuo-guah-chuan, the creation of hexagrams was primarily based upon the observation of changes of yin and yang, the positive and negative elements of the universe. It is the Tao, the Primordial Principle, of Heaven, that manifests in the permanent condition of change in the universe.

Chuang Chou repeatedly questioned the validity of all contrasting concepts, ideas, values, and judgments. He also had serious doubts about the emotional outbursts associated with the occurrence of events, including birth and death. There was no difference, to him, between them. Therefore, it was groundless to find joy or sorrow in either one. To him, as for some phenomenologists, birth and death are only different modes of being in change. He maintained that only when the past and present are forsaken may we enter where there was no death or birth. He asserted that death and birth are man's fate, just as the coming of night and day, which are the nature of Heaven. He also told us that to gain, as in being born, was merely a matter of timing; and to lose, as in death, was merely passing along; and that if we took both of them in their suchness then neither sorrow nor joy would get into us. Chuang Tse argued further that the true man of old, *jeng jen,* did not know either to like birth or dislike death. Therefore, his coming out was not done in order to please; his going in was not something to be refused. Silently, there he went; silently, here he came. He was not forgetful of his beginning; nor did he beg to hasten his ending. This was what he called doing no harm to Tao with one's mind. Such a man was called the true man.

The notion of mindlessness was advocated among Chinese Zen Buddhists, such as Hui-Neng of the eighth century. His teaching of no-mind was not to deny the existence of reality, *per se.* In the *Tan Ching,* a book of his collected sayings by his disciple Fa-Hai, he stated that to depart from the phenomenon within phenomena meant possessing no phenomenon; and that to have no thought in thoughts meant possessing no thought. Not being tied up, he added, meant non-remaining. This is to say that there should never be any mindful attachment to any worldly situation in which one happens to be. He contended that a person's mind must never be influenced or possessed in any way, by any event or phenomenon. This is what he called no-mind. He reminded us that all emotional troubles of man were due to remaining in or being possessed by what was encountered or experienced. The so-called Buddhahood that is actually an enlightenment of mind, can be achieved by transcending the phenomenal world, without denying its existence. This is to say that enlightenment, emancipation from one's anxieties and other emotional states, or gaining complete independence from all attachments in the phenomenal world, without repudiating being within it, is quite attainable by any one of us.

So from Chinese Buddhist point of view, death is not something that should cause anxiety or distress. The right understanding of the eight-fold path advocated by Buddha himself is what will lead all of us, as we age, to eventual liberation from suffering of all kinds. Thus, the Buddhist tradition offers the elderly Chinese people a way to see the future and meaning of life with exceptional equanimity.

4. A Brief Reflection

Today as always, things are endlessly changing, as perceived by the ancient wisdom of the *Yi Ching,* Lao-Tse, Chuang-Tse, and the scriptures of the Buddhists such as the *Ta Chang Ching.* However, the goal of attaining virtuousness still remains in the mind of Chinese people. It has been, and will always be the life-long ambition for their old and young. They understand that peace and security of our world, the orderliness of a nation and a society could never be achieved without the soundness of family life in general. The latter is indisputably linked to the integrity, in strong moral sense, of every and each member of a family, particularly that of parents and grandparents.

Filial piety is still firmly believed and commonly practiced by Chinese people everywhere. This is the tradition that ties up the cordial relationships of members of all families. It has been counted on in the past for the stability of their society, and it is hoped that it will be so in the future. It also has been traditional that elderly Chinese carry on continuously their duty to guide and assist in every way, the younger generation in self-improvement and social development. The elderly are always expected to give good example. They recognize that the ubiquity of change is, and always will be, the unending way of the universe. They also perceive without any delusion that both death and birth are merely modes of being in this changing phenomenal world which, in its own nothingness, is not different from all things in it perceived by the mirror of mind. To the Buddhists, the mind we have merely reflects the image of anything that comes or goes by without being attached, coloured, or possessed in any way, including mind itself. The attainment of enlightenment of this sort will lead to union with the prevailing

Whatness that no word is adequate to describe. But this prevailing Whatness has long been named and even worshipped by people through all ages.

In Chinese tradition, the union with the non-describable Whatness has been regarded as the integration of Heaven and man by Confucian philosophers, as returning to Tao by the Taoists; as entering nirvana by the Buddhists; as union with God by the Christians; and with the self-evident truth by philosophers. The Chinese elder who sees the meaning of this oneness should have a positive attitude toward his or her own life; and the love he or she cherishes should be extended to all under Heaven.

Bibliography

1. Chuang-Tzu. *Inner Chapters.* Translated by Gia-fu Feng and Jane English. New York: Random House, 1974.
2. Chung, Albert C. 1970. "The Principle of Rectification of Confucius, Plato, and Aristotle." *Chinese Culture* XI (1970):4: 69-76.
3. Chung, Albert C. *Essays on Yi Ching Studies.* Taipei: Autobiographical Literature Press, 1980.
4. Confucius. *Analects.* Translated by Arthur Waley. New York: Random House, 1966.
5. Hsi, Chu. *The Philosophy of Human Nature.* New York: Gordon Press, 1976.
6. *I Ching: Book of Changes.* Translated by James Legge. Citadel Press, 1974.
7. Lao-Tzu. *Tao te Ching.* Translated by Gia-fu Feng and Jane English. New York: Random House, 1972.
8. Mencius. *Works of Mencius.* Translated by James Legge. Magnolia, MA: Peter Smith, Publisher, Inc.

The Place and Role of the Aged in the Hindu Perspective

John B. Chethimattam

Recently it was reported that a petty official in an Indian village, who had neglected to buy any medicine for his seriously ill wife, after her death mortgaged his whole property to procure money for performing funeral rites for her. When questioned about this shocking behavior his explanation was that as long as she was alive it was her's to decide what she wanted; and that when she was gone it was his duty to perform the prescribed rites for the departed. This extreme case in a way summarizes the Hindu attitude towards the elderly and the dying: The elderly and the dying are not mere objects of pity to be dealt with delicately and condescendingly by others, but conscious human persons responsible for their own life and future, and should, therefore, be respected and allowed to fulfill their special role in society. Hence a Hindu does not hesitate to take a dying person out of the sick bed and lay him on bare ground so that he may pass to the next life in intimate contact with Mother Earth doing penance for his sins. Besides, in a gerontocractic social set up as that of India, where the elderly are in control of matters until their death both in the family and in the society, it is difficult to think of the aged as isolated and underprivileged. Instead of focusing attention on the physical weakness and other natural inadequacies of the elderly, the Hindu tradition places the whole emphasis on their spiritual maturity and wisdom which command respect and obedience from all and shows them forth as models of an authentic human life engaged in the disinterested service of all humanity.

A Sociology of Generosity

Perhaps the basis for this unique approach to the elderly has to be found in the Indian sociological conception which even from ancient times thought of the human society not as a place of conflict of divergent interests, rights, and privileges, a happy balance among which has to be achieved through compromise, but as an organic whole created by the generosity of all concerned. All sections of the social organism receive from the one and the same ultimate and absolute Real, and each one has to give to others according to one's own gifts and talents. Besides, man should not allow economic conditions and the state of bodily health to determine his spiritual life, but should rather dominate them and make them appropriate expressions of his own spirit. According to the *RgVeda,* the earliest religious text of Hinduism, dating from the 2nd millenium B.C., the authentic field of human creativity is spiritual, the dominant and intuitive exercise of the human mind. The distinctive character of man is that he acts primarily by his intelligence and only secondarily by his body. The body is only an outward extension of the spirit. "Do by intelligence," and "Do truth by intelligence" are often repeated expressions in this ancient religious classic. It must be remembered that for this ancient people, which found itself in a geographical situation of natural plenty, the main problems were not economical or social but psychological. For them religious thought did not start in wonder at the external world as for the Greeks, but from their internal experience of suffering mainly located in ignorance, and in bondage to external needs. For them human community was not formed by a sort of pact to face together external challenges, but by a sort of fellowship in the Word, which was primarily found in the heart of the sage, and the different orders and classes were formed by their respective duties in the service of the divine Word.

But this does not mean that the ancient Hindu sages were not aware of the ravages of time, the debilitating effect of old age. Time for them was the deity of Death. But the Hindu scriptures try to show that death cannot be eluded by purely physical means, but only through penance and wisdom. The corroding effect of time is counteracted by the religious sublimation of days, months, seasons and the year itself, through ritual and meditation. One important Vedic prayer says:

"From the unreal lead me to the Real;
From darkness lead me to light;
From death lead me to immortality."

But this immortality is not something awaited only after death. Like reality and light, which are only synonyms for the changeless, immortality also has to be attained in this life itself. It is the duty of each one to reach stabiity and changlessness through the process of growth. Hence old age stands for this state of maturity.

In this sociology, therefore, duties do not correspond to rights and needs of others. Duty is what one owes to oneself, to one's particular stage in life and the position one holds in the social whole. Hindu Scriptures, especially the law books, constantly insist on the duty of the young to respect and support the elderly, of children to show respect to their parents and teachers and to make offerings to them when they have departed from life. But this is not so much a response to the latter's needs, as something intrinsic to their position as children, even though often it is hinted that the departed will profit from the right offerings made by the surviving relatives or suffer bad consequences from bad offerings.

Old Age and Death

The tragic condition of man leading to old age and death was the main concern which led Siddhartha Gautama Buddha in his search for liberation from the bondage of life characterized by suffering. Hinduism, on the other hand, shows an almost total lack of concern about death. *Rg Veda* speaks of death as a sort of vacation trip to the land of King Yama, lord of death. It tells the dying man:

Depart, depart along those ancient pathways,
On which have passed away our former fathers.
There thou shall see rejoicing in libations,
The two kings, Varuna the god, and Yama.

For, after enjoying "thy good works' reward in heaven, return home; leaving all imperfections you will unite with your own body, full of vigor." (*Rg Veda X*, 14, 7-8). Death is not a tragedy, but only a passing over to the land of joy. Hence the prayer to Rudra, the final savior of beings is: "Preserve me from death until, like a ripe cucumber falling from its stalk, I attain immortality." (*Rg Veda*, VII, 59, 12). House of Death is also the school of life. *Rg Veda* recounts the story of Naciketas who is sent to Death by his angry father, but is instructed by Yama, the god of death and sent *with boons* back to life. (RV X, 135). In the *Bhagavad Gita*, Krishna, the divine incarnation, tells Arjuna, the warrior, who is worried about the death of his kinsmen who will be killed in battle:

You sorrow for men who do not need your sorrow
. . . Wise men do not sorrow for the living or the
dead . . . Just as in this body, the embodied self must
pass through childhood, youth and old age, so too at
death it will assume another body: in this a thoughtful
man is not perplexed." (*Gita*, II, 11.13)

The Individual Stands Alone

In the Hindu perspective the main emphasis is on the individual and his responsibility, and all approach to others can come only through one's own self rooted in the one Self of all selves. The individual stands alone. *Manusmriti*, the classical law book of Hinduism solemnly states this fact:

Single is each being born; single it dies; single it enjoys
the reward of its virtue, single it suffers the punishment
of its sin. (*Law of Manu,* IV, 240)

Father or mother or any other relative will not accompany one
into the next world. "Leaving the dead body on the ground like a
log of wood, or a clod of earth, the relatives depart with averted
faces. Only spiritual merit follows a person." (IV, 241). As an
individual being man has to conform to *Rta,* a term which literally
means 'course,' indicating the uniformity of nature or the cosmic
order of things. But it is not an impersonal order since the gods are
its guardians, who care not only for the physical order of the world
but also for the moral order of human actions. Varuna, the thousand eyed God of heaven reads even the thoughts of men, and
punishes those who violate his laws. (*Atharva Veda,* IV, 16). Man
should please the gods not only by offering them sacrifices but
especially by leading a morally pure life.

Hence man does not pass through life as an isolated individual.
He has to conform to the course of nature by fulfilling what is
called his *rna* or indebtedness to the different classes of beings. He
must offer worship and sacrifice to the Gods, pay his debt to the
sages of old by devoutly studying the Scriptures that enshrine their
wisdom, and discharge his duty to the ancestors by begetting sons
to continue the observance of traditional ritual and to preserve the
race. (*Taitt. Samhita* VI, iii, 10, 5). These debts are elaborated also
by the *Law of Manu* into five sacrifices or five fires, study of
Scripture to the sages, offering of water and food to the departed,
burnt oblation to the Gods, hospitality to the guests, offerings
even to the cosmic beings, and food to birds, cattle and even ants.
(*Manu* III, 69-84). These obligations, again, are not the rights and
demands of those beings, but rather something required for the
well-being of the individual offerer concerned. The implication is
that one who is truly attuned to the cosmic course of things should
manifest that harmony through his active relationship with the
various sections of the cosmos, by showing it through the ritual of
sacrifice. Sacrifice has a moral meaning since through it man gives
this material universe a sacral existence. Thus according to *Rg Veda*
the altar of sacrifice is the boundary of this earth and sacrifice itself
is the center of the universe.

Old Age as the Symbol and Climax of Growth

What gives special significance to old age in this highly personalistic moral perspective is the growth and maturity it stands for.

According to Manu, respect and honour are due to the teacher, the father, the mother and the elder brother, for the teacher is the image of Brahman, the supreme deity, the father the image of Prajapati the creator of all things, the mother the image of Mother Earth, and the elder brother the image of oneself. (II, 231). Apart from the duty of gratitude toward these persons, obedience to father, mother and teacher, is said to be the best form of penance and sacrifice for the young, and they are said to symbolize the three fires required for ritual sacrifice. But mere age does not provide respectability. A man is not venerable merely because his head is grey. Of the four castes or classes of Hindu society, "the seniority of Brahmanas is from sacred knowledge, that of Kshatriyas (the kingly class) from valor, that of Vaisyas (the agricultural class) from wealth, and only that of the Sudras (the menial class) purely from age." (*Manu* II, 155).

The Hindu conception of the growth and stages of human life is somewhat parallel to those of the universe itself. Time is both cyclic and also linear. It is cyclic since an era of creation is followed by an equal period of dissolution. But the linear conception is not of an ever continuing progress, but of progress as well as of regress. In each period of creation there are four ages, with steadily decreasing levels of spiritual vitality and righteousness. Similarly in a man's life there are four stages, student life, stage of the householder, period of retirement from active life, and the final stage of the ascetic, with an ever-increasing loss of vigor and vitality. But both in the universe and in man there is a redeeming divine principle: the divine incarnations in the universe and the maturing divine Self in the human person. As the clock of cosmic time winds down with an ever decreasing level of righteousness, the divine incarnations appear again and again in the world of the living encountering creation on its own level, assuming an ever increasing control over the course of events. Since life starts in water, Vishnu, the God of incarnations, appears first as a fish, then slowly moves to land as a tortoise, then in the increasing gradations of life as a boar, a man-lion, a miniature man, jungle man, country fellow, petty chieftain, a small king Rama, the peace-maker king Krishna, and will finally appear as the king of justice, Kalki. In a sort of analogous manner, as the biological vitality of the individual decreases the physiognomy and role of his spiritual self appears more and more divine, leading towards final identification with the Supreme Self.

The linear measure of human life is ideally conceived by the Hinda Scriptures as a hundred years. This is roughly divided into four stages, studentship, family life, retirement in the forest, and the final stage of the ascetic in renunciation. There are also four goals of human life: wealth, pleasure, righteousness and liberation. Wealth stands for the full development of human creative potential, acquisition and exercise of various theoretical and practical branches of knowledge and earning of material wealth for the proper sustenance of life. The goal of pleasure calls for a happy married life, righteousness for the realization and practice of the ethical and especially spiritual values of human existence, and liberation is the unhindered passage from the bondage of ignorance and suffering to final happiness. Along with these should be counted also the three paths towards spiritual maturity: action, knowledge and devotion. Among these different stages of life, goals, and paths there is no superiority and inferiority since they are all considered normal aspects of human life. Each is best for those who are at that particular stage, or aim at that particular goal or follow that definite path. The only dynamic element in them is that of growth according to which one passes from one stage to the next or shifts emphasis from one particular goal to another, or adopts one path in the place of another. Thus if life can be divided into two unequal parts the earlier longer part is characterized by a predominance of action and endeavour, while the latter part emphasizes knowledge and devotion.

Even studentship is not a mere preparation for anything but a definite and complete state with its own proper perspective and obligations extending over a sufficiently long period of time laying the full responsibility for its success or failure on the individual himself. It is called *Brahmacarya,* walking the path of the Lord. Its main function is gaining the knowledge and practice of the various duties proper to one's own class: For a Brahmana it is study of Scriptures, for a Kshatriya it means instruction in military arts, for the Vaisya initiation in business and agriculture while for the Sudras it is the humble service done to others which is their lot for their whole life. Once an individual has established himself as a fully conscious and responsible person he enters the state of married life. Manu says: "Having dwelt with a teacher during the fourth part of a man's life a Brahmana shall live during the second quarter of his existence in his house after he has wedded a wife." (IV, 1). Here he takes on his all round social responsibilities, including his duties to the gods, ancestors, fellow human beings and even animals. He must support himself and his family by his own labor. Even a Brahmana cannot take advantage of others' generosity. Manu states: "Those foolish householders who constantly seek to live on the food of others, become in consequence of that baseness, after death, the cattle of those who give them food." (III, 104). On his own part, however, a householder should show hospitality to all his guests according to his means and their respective position in the caste ladder. The ideal of moral life in the state of the householder is tersely stated by Manu thus:

> Giving no pain to any creature let one slowly accumulate spiritual merit, for the sake of acquiring a companion to the next world. For in the next world neither father, nor mother, nor wife nor sons, nor relations stay to be his companions; spiritual merit alone remains with him. (IV, 238-39)

Even a householder's life is only a passage to the late adulthood of retirement from external occupations so that one can be authentically human in his own self-realization. "When a householder sees his skin wrinkled and his hair white, and the sons of his sons, then he may resort to the forest," says Manu (VI, 2). This retirement into the forests has mostly remained an ideal for people to look up to than any strict legal prescription to be carried out practically. It simply defines the place and role of the elderly. The aged should transcend all temporal care and the needs that cause the temporal preoccupations. Thus he is instructed to abandon all his belongings and to abstain from all food raised by cultivation. He may entrust his wife to the care of his sons or allow her to accompany him. He should not receive any gifts. But he is not dispensed from the social and ritual obligations. He must continue to fulfill his five debts to the gods, the manes, men, animals and other beings, and tend the sacrificial fires. He must be industrious in the study of the Scriptures, patient in suffering hardships, friendly towards all, liberal and compassionate towards all living creatures, always remaining recollected in mind. Sustaining himself as far as possible with what is naturally provided by the earth, he must concentrate his whole attention to what is properly rational and human, leaving behind or at least reducing to a minimum what is common with the animal world. His sole aim should be to follow the example of the great sages, study their texts, observe their spiritual practices in order to attain a complete union with

God, the supreme Self. Since man is man not by his physical strength or material achievements but rather by the life of the spirit, those who have achieved the limited scope and restricted fulfillment of the biological and emotional aspects of their human existence in their youth and early adulthood, must concentrate on the rational and spiritual fields which have no such limitations. In spite of physical weakness the spirit can achieve a fullness of life both in personal fulfillment through mental concentration and God-realization, and service of other men through love, generosity and compassion.

The Personality of the Guru

The emphasis on the spiritual personality of the elderly is brought out clearly in the concept of the Guru. This term which literally means "weighty" was first applied to one's parents and teachers who were supposed to be important and weighty by their wisdom. Then it was extended to and often transferred to those who had attained self-realization as to be guides of other people. John Spiers states: "The India of the great search is remote from bazaars. It is always the India of the Guru mountain, with that clear-cut bare peak up there, calling to the Indian soul. It is the India of the yogi, of the contemplative, and nobody can deny this is the central and distinctive quality of the Indian." (*The Guru* p. 9).

Those who betake themselves to a retired life in their old age do not end their life there. Having renounced the world they come back to the world as impartial witnesses with a heightened authority of their own personal sanctity. The normal and natural culmination of human life is in this authentic sanctity that exerts a salutary influence on the people. Manu states: "Having passed the third part of life in the forest one may live as an ascetic during the fourth part of his existence, after abandoning all attachment to worldly objects." (VI, 33).

The special character of this stage in life is that it goes beyond all distinctions of color and race and caste. The earlier stages depended very much on and were conditioned by distinctions of caste and social position. At the stage of renunciation such distinctions do not hold good, since the main concern is to see unity in all things. Hence one who adopted *sannyasa* or the life of an ascetic even earlier in life was supposed to lose thereby his caste affiliation. Going beyond caste and class obligations the true Guru shows forth the spiritual values common to all men. In that way he is almost divine since he provides for men a focus outside their own selves to gather up and concentrate their own dissipated powers.

Thus human life is divided into two halves, the first characterized by action and life in the world, the second by renunciation of the world, and the realization of the spiritual values. These are not contradictory and neatly separated concerns, but rather complementary aspects of the one and the same human life. Instead of stressing the declining strength and increasing material dependence on others of the elderly, Hindu tradition has placed the whole emphasis on their spiritual personality. Other Indian religions like Jainism and Buddhism also agree with Hinduism in stressing this spiritual maturity in bodily existence as the penultimate state before final liberation. The Jaina saint after having gone through the twelve steps of spiritual development finally becomes a Tirthankara, a guide to show people the way to go across the ocean of births and deaths. The Buddhist concept of the Bodhisattva indicates a person who has reached the penultimate state of liberation through illumination, but continues his bodily existence through his compassion for fellow beings to show them the right path.

The Modern Crisis

From what has been said so far it can be seen that the exaltation of old age as the stage of renunciation is not to show the aged as a class all apart, but rather to emphasize the dominant values of humanity itself; man has to aim at tranquillity and dispassion at all stages and conditions in life. But today there is a certain crisis brought on by modernity in the understanding of old age even in the Hindu context. Only a few attain the prestige and authority of sages and gurus. With the fast pace of modern scientific and technological progress and the ever increasing change in the style of life taking place in every corner of the global village of humanity, the wisdom and experience of elders are seen to lack relevance for the modern age. The elderly, on the other hand, want to hold on to the positions of privilege and power they secured through long effort, and consider all the traditional lip-service to their age and wisdom a clever way to shunt them off the stage and condemn them to a life of renunciation. The ever increasing lack of sufficient jobs among people seems to go particularly against the elderly forcing them to retire into inaction at an earlier age than before, giving their place to the younger generation. There is no doubt that this situation is unfair to them, since they have a right to continue working and give the benefit of their greater experience to society.

But no one can draw justification for this disadvantageous situation of the elderly from the Hindu tradition. In fact, the Hindu ideals associated with the elderly do not envisage a merely mechanical chronological division of human life, but only emphasize the values that should be upheld at all stages in life.

Righteousness and Liberation

Righteous action and liberation, though presented as characteristics of the earlier and later parts respectively of human life, are in fact the two main concerns that should be held in view at all times. Human life need not be divided into a split of orientation into action for the first half and renunciation for the second half of life. Ideally as well as practically one can be spiritually content with the scheme of four stages of life, all of which are carried in compliance with *Dharma*, which translates in practice as "disinterested action." The spirit of disinterested action is common to paths of knowledge, devotion and action, and it should be developed as a perspective on life rather than the goal of life. This perspective of detached action or *dharma* will invariably point to *moksha* or liberation. *Dharma* and *moksha*, or righteous action and liberation are not, therefore, in conflict with each other, but are complementary since the former constitutes the attitude and the latter its consequence. Wherever there is *dharma*, there is *moksha*, irrespective of the nature of the path, knowledge, devotion or action.

The Advaita (non-dualist) school of Sankara which ascribed superiority to knowledge over action and devotion, and to renunciation over action, is, perhaps, the source of the popular belief that reserves disinterested action as the ideal of the final part of one's life as the immediate condition for liberation. But this is in no way a common Hindu understanding. Since disinterested action is the ideal undercurrent of the human conduct in all stages of life, it need not be reserved to the second half of life. Since each stage of life is lived to attain its respective goal, disinterested action is common to all the paths and stages of life.

Exertion (the literal meaning of the word *asrama* which designates the stages in life) to one's capacity is recommended, and yet, the attitude toward the acquisition of knowledge and the reaping of its practical and spiritual benefits must be fully according to the ideals of *dharma*. The principle of "disinterested action" shapes the attitude toward the process of acquisition and its reward or punishment. For a comfortably tenacious survival through the series of success and failure in the course of the acquisition of knowledge, wealth or love, one must cautiously guard against the disastrous or suicidal reactions caused by the more or less optimum anticipation of the fruit of one's exertion. The attitude of disinterested action saves an individual from frustrations, depression, demoralization and other unhealthy conseque₁ces of the improperly channelled desire for the fruit of actions, particularly in the first two stages of life, studentship and householdership. Thus disinterested action provides a restraint in the time of youth, which is the time for passionate action. Passion and intensity of zeal are not discouraged; only the unhealthy consequence of them is to be avoided or remedied by means of the attitude of disinterested action.

It is clear, then, that Hinduism does not condemn the elderly to the renunciation of action and fruits. For the renunciatory perspective is built up gradually from the initiation of the child at the age of around six. Instead of the term 'renunciation,' which may have an undesirable connotation of impractical and pessimistic inaction, the Gita's term 'disinterested action' (*nishkama karmayoga*) may be used. Hence to one who grows up through the proper discipline of withdrawal and resignation and the program of exertion in life, old age comes as a boon. It stands for a sudden withdrawal from a complex endeavour of duties assigned to one according to his caste. The traditional dilemma between the duties assigned by caste and the duty of withdrawal from them enjoined by the stage of renunciation is only one of the choices and decisions one has to make in life.

The "Crisis"

Thus the problem of old age has a moral dimension in the realm of action. The problem is not "how" to do, but "what" to do and also what not to do. Old age thus calls for a critical power of discrimination. This crisis is not anything special for the Hindus alone, but for aged people everywhere. In view of the nature of the dramatic transition from youth to old age experienced by people we may reinterpret the word *"asrama,"* effort, as "the exertion needed to convert crisis into routine." As the Greek etymology of the word 'crisis' indicates, crisis is a state in which an individual stands for the judgment of his personality, his integrity, his worth. Old age is a crisis because the marks of this new stage throw an individual in a state which is a new sort of game, the rules of which are hitherto unknown to him, and yet, he has to stand the trial of a good, righteous performance commanded and commended for this stage. But then, is not each transition, each stage of life, each new orientation of exertion a crisis each time? Therefore, in a way, the Hindu plan of life presents realistically the journey through the four identifiable crises in life. The Hindu realism hopes for the routinisation of the critical advent of each significant stage on the part of every individual toward his moral goal of freeing himself from the fright of crisis. This freedom too is a kind of *moksha* or liberation.

The experience of crisis begins with the initiation ceremony upon which the child is required to leave his parents' home for the teacher's residence. Upon completion of the educational program by the age of twenty-five, he is to return to his parents to make their house his so that along with the house he inherits the house-holdership from them. When his children are ready to take their turn of householder's role, he acknowledges the time for another change of space for his residence, which now in the third stage, is a hermitage in the forest. Finally as an ascetic he lives in the open air under the roof of the sky. Thus, with regard to the space and environment one is to undergo critical removals at the beginning of each stage in life.

Crisis in Social Environment

As regards human interaction which builds up one's social character, again, one is faced with the dramatic change of environment and of the nature and possibility of social interaction. Until the age of six one knows only the immediate members of one's family. As an initiated student, one is to treat the teacher's family as one's own, and the members of the residential school of the teacher as one's relatives. From the stage of studentship the number of individuals one interacts with intimately dwindles progressively in the succeeding stages of life. As one settles down in the family one is bound by the restrictions of space and the duties of the household. At the stage of forest dwelling one affords only the company of the spouse with occasional visits from people. Finally the ascetic breaks all human ties at the same time as forming a universal relation of humanity with the entire world of beings. Thus one undergoes characteristically different types of social behavior, the adoption of which is a psychological crisis.

The crisis in the four stages of life lies in the apprehension of one's "adaptation to the unfamiliar" rather than the "fear of the unknown." Traditionally every Hindu *knows* what is expected of him in every stage. But knowledge bears no promise of proper praxis. What one knows and how one acts according to that knowledge ought to be morally harmonious, and this constitutes the crisis, a true test of one's skill or art of living. According to the understanding of the system of the stages in life, old age is but one of four crises in life. And yet, it is a crisis that is exaggerated so much as to require an isolated treatment of it from every generation when it is baffled with the phenomenon of the generation gap.

Complementary Approaches to the Process of Aging

The process of aging or growing up may be approached from different perspectives. Besides the linear view of progressive movement in time, and the cyclical view of the revolving stages of life through death and rebirth, one can also look at old age as a dramatic descent after the peak of youth. It is in this perspective that the first half of life is said to be characterized by action and the second half by withdrawal. What this view, in which both East and West seem to concur, points to is that old age heralds the unpredictable approaching of death. Through all these different perspectives one is trying to measure the accomplishment of the purpose of having been born. Life as a long journey may be treated then as one unit, one project whose successful completion can be measured only in the last stage. In this sense, the "last" is, indeed, not the least, since the fruit of the life-long exertion that is to be seen only at the end of life is a full stop after a steady progress. From another point of view, an old person is considered as a "child again," someone to be treated delicately and almost with sympathetic courtesy. Old age certainly brings about physical and mental feebleness, if not necessarily senility, in which case an old person realizes that he is as dependent as a child with regard to his economic as well as emotional welfare. Old age is a sort of return to childhood, thus completing the circle. This is only a true and realistic acceptance of what one's condition actually is without superimposing over it an illusory view of oneself. A seeker of truth never gives himself to the superimposition of falsehood, however palatable that falsehood appears to be. In other words, what one truly is, is indeed one's own *dharma,* which one should never deny or abandon in any predicament, or for any allurement, says the *Gita* (III, 35). One can neither hide nor cure the signs and maladies of old age. As far as possible one should try to stay fit and active, but if one simply cannot, then that state has to be acknowledged with respect for the objective truth about oneself, and this acknowledgement is symbolic of one's healthy attitude toward the reality of life. If we describe old age as a descent from the height of youth, this should be taken only as a statement of fact and not as a derogatory judgment. After all, being on the peak is neither natural nor permanent. Just as one takes trouble to climb up, one needs an equally painstaking effort to climb down in order to end the journey.

Contemporary Relevance of the Hindu Approach to Old Age

The objective knowledge and acceptance of old age does not mean that the aged should surrender to the avoidable or remediable evils of old age. Here is the positive contribution of the Hindu tradition which has its relevance in the contemporary context also. Today no one retires into a jungle life, and there are only relatively few that dedicate their life to total renunciation. Still, the Hindu attitude towards the body and the inadequacies of old age has great importance for leading a healthy human life even in this scientific age. Its basic principle is, as we have already stated, that instead of the body and its vicissitudes dictating the attitude and outlook of the spirit, man's mind and spirit should control the body. This is the essential message of Hindu Yoga and the Ayurvedic tradition of Hindu medicine.

The basic supposition of Yoga is that the body and its organic functions as well as the various other aspects of human experience are evolutions of the material principle *Prakrti,* for the benfit of the spirit. *Buddhi* or intelligence which forms a sort of dynamic link between spirit and matter can and should reverse the evolutive movement of man's psyche and bring all his faculties and body itself to a state of balance. Thus the body, instead of being an obstacle to the vision of the spirit and a dissipating burden on its energies, should be a pliable instrument of the spirit and a translucent screen allowing the light of the spirit to shine out. The yogic exercises and practices are aimed at achieving this balance between spirit and matter in man. For one who has followed the yogic practices through life, old age provides the golden opportunity with freedom from external preoccupations to enjoy the tranquillity of the spirit to his heart's content. Even the natural necessities like sleeping and eating, instead of being needs man has to fulfill to survive, become expressions of real joy the spirit allows the body to participate in. Similarly Ayurvedic medicine principally aims at achieving perfect harmony between man's body and the total organic world. Instead of being a negative battle against microbes and bacteria, it is an effort to harness the benevolent forces of the organic world in building up and maintaining a healthy human body. It is more preventive than curative in dealing with human maladies. Even though the inevitable maladies of old age can never be totally elminated, the positive attitude one faces them with radically changes the condition of the individual concerned.

Positive Approach to Leisure

The crisis of old age is exaggerated only because one sees living only as acting, and therefore retirement entails non-action and non-living. The Hindu idea of authentic action is that of leisure and play. In the *Gita* Lord Krishna points to the divine action in the world as the model for man to imitate. The divine activity is termed a *lila*, sport, since God has nothing to gain by creating and maintaining the world. The action of the spirit is more akin to leisure than to agitated activity outside. To be active an aged person has not to compete with the young in the market place or in the factory or in political arenas. For him the really enjoyable activity is within the tranquillity of his own spirit, simply being human without dissipating his vital energies in the preoccupations of this world. An eldely Hindu who has made himself through life-long exertion the subject of "evolved consciousness" as regards the purpose and the practice of life, knows what he is to do and what he is not to do during the "quaintly peaceful evening" of life. The evening of life is never a time for idle rest for one who has attained self-discipline. That is why the Hindu tradition emphasized the performance of religious ritual especially for the aged. The orientation of action embodied in the ritual schedule of the day moulds one's attitude and outlook. The religious rites performed at set hours of the day turns the whole day into a sort of joyous celebration. The imagery of the "evening" does not bring to people so engaged the notion of idle rest and relaxation with the overtone of inaction. On the contrary, the evening of life is reserved for those actions which demand no pressures of deadline, which are not to be subjected to the duty-reward mechanism.

Relaxation is not inaction; it is, in fact, the action that obeys the mastery of the eternal time, and not of that time that tends to run out of course. Hence, Hindu tradition strongly emphasizes the need for one to be governed by the rules of eternal life not only in old age but throughout all stages of life. At the break of day one takes up the actions in obedience to the rules of the divisible time, and in the evening in prayer and ritual one returns to the obeisance of eternal time. The observance of the rules of the finite and eternal time during the day and during the evening, day in and day out, familiarizes one with the concepts of the dawn and the dusk of life with the same balanced attitude towards them. Hence the imagery of the evening of life used for old age cannot depress a disciplined person with the fear of inaction, nor will it elate him with the prospect of lazying around in old age.

The advent of old age thus heralds leisure and freedom. The gain of freedom outweighs in quality the rewards of the pressing duties of youth. One who suffered the constant tension of accomplishing the set obligations finds old age as the opportunity for devoting his time and energy for accomplishing his own personal goals in life. His actions are concerted and harmonized and oriented toward one gain, the validity of which is to be judged by the criteria of inner peace and tranquillity. The realization of the complex and comprehensive oneness of one's own being now becomes an incumbent "duty" reserved for old age. The unity of being requires the unity of time, space, existence and the direction of exertion. The Hindu elder is not much worried about his material maintenance and support when he ceases to be a bread-winner, since it is taken for granted that the son who takes over his place will consider his own duty and obligation to support his parents. He is not a burden to the young man since the obligation comes from the very nature of the householder's status, and the elder is only giving him an opportunity to fulfill his responsibility and thereby gain merits for himself.

The Contemporary Idea of Moksha

An important shift in Hindu thinking in response to modernity is in the idea of *moksha* or liberation. In the past sometimes the impression was given that Hinduism was a world-denying religion and its main concern was to liberate the spiritual self of man from the body and the material world. But even in classical times, some schools of Hindu thought, such as the Advaita system of Sankara, had upheld the possibility of *jivanmukti* or liberation even while one is in bodily existence. Separation from the body and the world as a necessary condition for the liberation of man is something incongruous and annoying for people in this age of fast scientific and technological progress. The great importance given to the *Bhagavad Gita* as a manual of Hinduism and the great publicity given to its positive message as a call to selfless action in the world by the Indian national leaders, especially Mahatma Mohandas Gandi during the long struggle for political independence, brought to the forefront a concept of liberation as not necessarily from the body or the world but from selfishness, greed and anger.

The earlier conception stressed *moksha* as the fourth goal of human life after acquisition of wealth, enjoyment of pleasure, and living a righteous life, all equally important and reserved for the respective stages of life. So liberation was closely allied to renunciation and leaving of the body and of the world. The *Gita,* on the other hand, subordinates both wealth and pleasure as goals auxiliary to *dharma,* and stresses disinterested action as the guiding principle of life. In this perspective liberation appears as the fullness and culmination of *dharma* or righteous action.

This shift of emphasis in the conception of *dharma* has a positive impact on the crisis of old age. In the former perspective the crisis of old age is more marked and acute since it is not only the reality about and around the aged that becomes drastically new, but also and especially the reality within them that has to be changed drastically and that suddenly, without any planning or preparation. One has to make a total departure from the previous stage and enter into a totally new world without the body and without the world. It was supposed that the point of saturation of one stage should naturally lead to the next, wealth to pleasure, and pleasure to morality, and moral observance to liberation from all particular observances and duties in total renunciation. It could almost be the sense of disgust with one stage that pushes one to the next. But in the *Gita's* perspective such a sense of saturation and disgust will never come since at every stage one has to act with detachment.

It is not *what* one strives after that makes one happy or unhappy but *why* one strives after any goal. In order to be truly happy, happiness should be understood and pursued in its total sense as corresponding to the whole being of man. Only such a goal of happiness will define the path. Hence happiness cannot be measured exclusively in terms of matter or spirit, action or renunciation, acquisition or giving up. This is why the *Gita* speaks not simply about action, but about the yoga of action as the ideal of human life. One should strive always, even in old age to seek happiness of body, mind and intellect in unison, for which constant and conscious exertion is needed. Since the particular mode of pursuit has to be determined according to the condition of the individual, an aged person may very well devote himself to the continuation of his life-long career if the bodily health and mental fitness permit, or adjust his activities according to the changing conditions of health and his own personal preference. What matters is his motive and whole-hearted dedication to the service of God and of mankind.

In this context we may point out that the scheme of four stages is devised in the Hindu tradition basically for and by the Brahmins, though it is by extension adopted by the *Kshatriyas* (warrior class) and the *Vaisyas* (agriculturists and businessmen) who also have the formal ceremony of initiation. But the *Sudras* (menial class) as well as women of all classes are excluded from it. How then may women and low castes plan their life and orient themselves to their goal, especially in view of old age? These are excluded only for ritual reasons, since they do not have the formal initiation according to the Hindu Scriptures. There is no doubt that the principles concerning the development of personality underlying the system of *asramas* apply universally to all irrespective of caste, religion, sex, culture and the like. In fact, women were permitted to accompany their husbands to retirement in the forest life. Some of the important personalities in the Upanishads who draw attention to the need to focus on the attainment of immortality moving away from temporal concerns are women, like Kaikeyi, the wife of sage Yajnavalkya, and Garghi Vacaknavi. The *Vishnu Purana* states in one context that the special role of women and of Sudras is to emphasize the excellence of selfless service rendered to their husbands and to their masters respectively which gain for them a rightful share in the merit of the ritual performances.

Old Age and Social Concern

Another ambiguous point in the Hindu tradition regarding old age seems to be the exclusive emphasis on the personal liberation of the individual concerned. Since even the responsibility for their support is placed on their sons they seem to lead a purely self-centered life. But in the perspective of the *Gita,* service of God and service of men, which even old people have to continue, imply an essentially social orientation. This is called by the *Gita* "lokasamgraha" — a taking hold of the whole world in one's concern, a path of social enjoyment which indeed can take care of the problems of old age such as isolation, loneliness, feeling of inadequacy and a sense of uselessness. This does not mean that one has to be a self-employed social worker. One simply needs to embody the spirit of rewardless service to the immediate members of one's family living under the common roof, to one's neighbors and acquaintances. His great contribution to society is to present a model of a happy combination of the strange paradoxes and challenges of human life. He can be a care-free and yet responsible member of the family and the society. He is playful and yet serious rather than frivolous. He is generous in help and advice without imposing himself on others. He is social and yet happy if he is left alone. He delights in everything, but desires nothing. This is truly the attitude of disinterested action recommended by the *Gita*.

What is emphasized in this vision of old age is not simply a negative renunciation but the spirit of sacrifice, described by *Gita* as *yajnacakrapravartana,* the continuous cycle of sacrifice in the physical universe. Just as the activities of nature are promoted to conserve the cosmic routine and energy, the human cosmos too conserves human energy through regulation of the routine. This routine may be called *dharma,* which consists of the communitarian and class duties collectively and the personal duties of the individual according to his stage and position in life. Unlike the physical universe, the human cosmos runs with the responsible agency of human beings, for it defies the mechanical causal elements. To avoid chaos and maintain the universe in the realm of human action, the principle of sacrifice is introduced and internalized by human beings. Sacrifice, according to the *Gita,* does not entail a total denial of anything, but only a certain offering up and sublimation of it. Every sacrifice is compensated invariably in the scheme of the cosmos whether physical or human. The consequence of the eternal exchange of sacrifice is the cyclical reaping of the benefits of all the sacrifices performed in the universe.

The sacrifice in the physical universe is mandatory or automatic, whereas in the human cosmos it is voluntary. Hindu tradition believes in the built-in mechanism of sacrifice and its reward in both the physical and human cosmos. This faith in the cosmic justice underlying sacrifice is what enables a Hindu to adopt the course of disinterested action when the passionate, intensive course of action for maximum reward is either impossible or only possible in a restricted way. Sacrifice transcends both these eventualities and assures the survival of all who share in the functioning of their universe with some amount of self-sacrifice. It is not question of the survival only of the fittest. Everyone benefits from the course of the universe of beings to the extent each one participates in through sacrifice in the great common cosmic sacrifice.

This principle of sacrifice is manifest also in the stages of human life. A human self that journeys, according to Hindu tradition, through the cycles of birth and death, and within human life through the stages of childhood, youth and old age, sacrifices each previous stage, leaving it to others and receives the new stage and its obligations. This attitude of sacrifice is helpful for the development of the body-mind-intellect organism of the human self and it makes humanity reap the reward of a guaranteed cooperation in the predetermined cosmic way. This vision of the cooperative cosmos implicit in the *Gita's* depiction of the cosmic cycle of sacrifice is useful especially today when our societies are faced with problems such as forced retirement, a lack of opportunities for entering into a suitable career, unemployment, and the tension and anxiety created by such problems. Old people should, therefore, accept in the spirit of cosmic sacrifice their passage from ordinary activities of human life to the leisure and tranquillity of retirement.

Conclusion: The Hindu Vision of the Future

Perhaps what is most significant and most reassuring in the Hindu approach to the aged is its vision of the future. It removes the anxiety regarding the future: You will be what you are now, and that is your unchanging and unchangeable rootedness in the one eternal Self. All that you can do is to realize more and more deeply that one Self whom you can never lose. Hinduism has no eschatology, the anxious expectation of what is going to happen at the end. The "eschaton" is already here. All that is asked of man is to pull down the walls that obstruct the light of the self from shining out. The bondage of man is like that of a lamp hidden under a bushel basket. The light shines underneath; it will become visible only when the cover is removed. Hence human perfection and achievement is not measured by having, but by being; not by all the things, positions, roles one can attain and possess, but by what one is in oneself and how one realizes one's own authentic self.

The real saintliness of an aged person is measured by the Hindus generally by the peace and tranquillity of his face, the calmness and assurance of his behavior, and the equanimity with which he views all things. A man beset with the problems of daily existence, filled with remorse about his past, and over-anxious about his own future gives evidence that he has not realized his own authentic self, the ground of his own being. The attitude of a mature old person is not one of resignation to the inevitable, but a confident satisfaction that he has finally realized the meaning of his life and of all things in the world in the light of the one true Self.

In brief, the whole Hindu view of old age may be summarized in the confident statement of the dying person presented by both the Brihadaranyaka and Isa Upanishads:

> The face of truth is covered with a golden disc. Unveil it O Pushan (Sun), so that I who love the truth may see it. O Sun, offspring of Prajapati, gather up your radiant light so that I may look at the loveliest form beyond you. Whosoever is that person yonder, that am I. Let this body end in ashes, but may this life enter into the Immortal Breath. (*Brih. Up.* V, 15, 1-3; *Isa Up.* 15-17)

Old age is not something that calls for our concern, pity and condescending help, but utmost veneration and profound respect. The aged stand alone, confident about their own identity, role and position in the overarching perspective of human life. Others should consider it their privilege and a great honor that they have an opportunity to serve them and minister to their material needs.

Buddhism and Aging

Buddhadasa P. Kirthisinghe

Introduction

Buddhism is a philosophy, a way of life and a religion. There are many sects and schools of Buddhism, but the basic teachings of the Buddha are common to all of them. While the Theravadins have stuck to the early teachings of Buddha, accepting them *in toto,* without any change, the Mahayanists, while not deviating from the master's teachings, have expanded on some of his teachings, such as Sunyata (Emptiness).

However, there have been minor deviations, as when Buddhism was accepted by an alien culture that did not give up its existing primitive religious traditions, but incorporated them into it. In Tibet, where her ancient Bon religion was assimilated with the tantric practices borrowed from the Indus civilization to form a new school of Buddhism called Vajrayana, they formed the new fabric of her unique culture. Yet in spite of these assimilations Tibetan Buddhism has within it the basic teachings of the Buddha. This is true of all others, e.g. *Dhyana* (Sanskrit) or *Ch'an* (Chinese) Buddhism, and when it reached Japan it blossomed into Zen Buddhism. It is claimed that Zen Buddhism enriched the Japanese culture, and yet it has basic Buddhism within it.

Definition of Aging Process

Aging or decay affects all parts of the universe, inanimate and animate. In our planet a bacterial cell may live a few minutes, while some trees live for centuries, such as the Redwood trees of California or some species of the plant genus Ficus. The oldest historical tree planted in the 3rd century B.C. at Anuradhapura, Sri Lanka, grows to this day. A branch of the tree (*Ficus religosa*), under which Gautama Buddha attained Supreme Enlightenment (*Samsambodhi*) at Buddha Gaya, Bihar, India, was sent to Ceylon by the 3rd century B.C. Buddhist Emperor Asoka.

Today, due to modern health sciences, man may attain an age of 80 to 100 years. Aging, more or less, begins about the 40th to 50th year of life, when glandular functioning becomes less and less efficient and secretion of hormones and enzymes becomes less and less. This leads to the physiological and anatomical weakening of the body, which is called "aging." This process of aging is faster in some while it is slow in others, for some unknown reasons. In

Buddhism, as stated before, all component things in the whole Universe are subject to change and decay with age; this is called Annica (impermanence).

Buddhism does not conceive of a Universe of its life processes as a static phenomenon, but as an ever changing structure. Buddhism maintains that something cannot be created from nothing.

The whole cosmos functions according to the universal law of cause and effect, and the law in Buddhism is termed "Kamma" (Karma) and constitutes the cosmic law called "Dhamma" (Dharma) which governs the Universe.

In the science of biology, life processes are studied mainly by observation, experiment and induction. With the advancement of biological sciences such as bio-chemistry, biophysics, and genetics, it was affirmed that the world functions in accordance with the law of cause and effect. This is, indeed, one of the principal tenets of Buddhism.

According to Buddhism all things animate or inanimate are subject to change. There is no soul (anatta) in men or animals. Nothing is permanent, all things come into being and pass away and, hence, there is no permanent entity in the form of a soul or self existing in man or in anything else.

All life on earth is interdependent and does not function in isolation. Therefore, man and animals are not self-sufficient and all biological phenomena are impermanent and undergo continuous change and are in continuous flux (*anicca*) and each is conditioned by environmental factors. Everywhere we find conflicts, and these conflicts indicate the unsatisfactory nature of life, or, to use a Buddhist technical term, are *duhkha* (suffering).

The new field of biology known as molecular biology could affirm the often cited Buddhist word *sunya,* that is the emptiness of all worldly phenomena. When an atom or molecule of organic or inorganic material is destroyed it dissipates into energy. Without energy there can be no life or functioning of the world or the universe.

Man and other animal or even plant life begins with the fusion of ovum and sperm (pollen and ovary in plants) and with the establishment of consciousness (Vinna) in the foetus a new life begins. This process is fully explained in Buddhism in its law of dependent origination (Pattica Samuppada). This is a fundamental law in Buddhist philosophy and has its parallel in some respects in Western scientific thinking.

In the Buddhist view life goes on in a cycle which is called "Wheel of Life" (Chakra). This is a very important principle in Buddhism, with birth, adulthood, old age, and finally death and rebirth. Thus aging is a part of life and continues from life to life. It is always governed by the cosmic law of Kamma (Karma).

Of course, this cycle of birth which is included in the Buddhist philosophy as "Duhkha" (unsatisfactoriness) can be overcome by recognizing the four noble truths, and following the Eightfold Noble Path to achieve Nirvanic bliss in this life or thereafter, when birth, aging and death ends. Then man or woman becomes fully emancipated to a state of immortality.

Thus in the study of aging in Buddhism one has to study the four aspects of it: (1) The Wheel of Life; (2) Evolution of Life; (3) Life as it occurs in our world, with particular reference to humans; (4) The Cosmos. Buddha's instructions to his followers on lay life, social duties and respect for elders and parents, have had *profound* influence on Buddhist civilizations and even on Hindu life.

Buddhism created the greatest period of Indian history — the Asoken era from the 3rd century B.C. to about 7th century After Christ. Although Buddhism was more or less absorbed into Hinduism after the 8th century in India, a leader called Sankaracarya assiduously worked and transformed old Vedic Hinduism by assimilating Buddhist tenets to form modern Hinduism.

In contrast to Hindu tradition, the Buddha asserted that:

No man is noble by birth,
No man is ignoble by birth,
Man is noble by his own action,
Man is ignoble by his own action.

Vasala Sutta.

In keeping with Buddhist traditions in Sri Lanka (Ceylon), South East Asia and far East Asia, there were no caste distinctions, but a class system, as the Buddha asserted strongly against caste. In far East Asia, Mongolia, China, Korea, and Japan, family ties were governed both by Confucian ethics and Buddhist thought, where elders and parents were deeply respected. The teachers were equally respected. The Indian caste system did not stand against peoples' duties to parents and elders in their society.

Kamma (Karma)

The theory of Kamma is the theory of cause and effect, of action and reaction; it is a natural law, which has nothing to do with the idea of justice or reward or punishment. Every volitional action produces its effects or results. If a good action produces good effects, and a bad action bad effects, it is not justice or reward, or punishment meted out by anybody or any power sitting in judgment on your action, but it is by virtue of its own nature, its own law.

The law of Kamma, unlike the laws of physics, chemistry, etc., is intangible, immeasurable, and unpredictable. Since it is an imperceptible law, it cannot be demonstrated by scientific experiments.

According to the teaching of Kamma and rebirth, deeds — whether good or bad — have their retribution sometime, somewhere. According to the law of Kamma, the circumstances and conditions that make up the destiny of a being come into existence without a previous cause and the presence of appropriate conditions. Just as, for example, from a rotten mango seed there never will come a healthy mango-tree with healthy and sweet fruits, just so the evil, volitional actions or Kamma produced in former births, are the seed or root causes of evil destiny in a later birth.

The only reasonable and sound explanation for the inequality among men is found in the doctrine of Kamma and rebirth. Kamma and rebirth offer a rational, consistent explanation that intends to satisfy unbiased and impartial thinkers.

The doctrine that rebirth occurs conditioned by Kamma was accepted by the Indian teachers of old who preceded the Buddha. It is incorporated in the teachings of the Upanishads and Vedas, and in the Bhagavad Gita. The teaching is that rebirth is conditioned by the good and evil that one has acquired in this and in previous lives. As this process of rebirth and death is fraught with much suffering, emancipation from this cycle of births and deaths is the goal of all Indian systems of philosophy. The Buddha taught: "Owners and heirs of their actions are beings, their actions divide beings into high and low."

How rebirth occurs has been fully explained by the Buddha in the *Paticca Samuppada.*

The Law of Dependent Origination

This is a very important concept in Buddhism and is called in Pali *paticca-samuppada.* In a way it is fundamental to Buddhist thinking and certainly cannot be ignored in any treatment of Buddhist philosophy. At the same time it has its parallels in some respects in Western scientific thinking.

In Western science the law of cause and effect has been for very long the guiding principle in all of its investigations almost from the beginnings of scientific thought until recently, when relativity and the discoveries in connection with the submolecular structure of reality and its functions made it necessary to formulate certain qualifications. Still, the tracing of events to their antecedents or what went before remains an indispensable objective in all scientific investigations.

Now, if there is an antecedent to everything and to every process in the universe, thre must be a tremendous network of processes, one cutting across another, intersecting with still another, and perhaps doing so repeatedly in the course of time. This one process is only one of an unimaginable number of processes, each one following the same pattern or a similar one. The total number of intersections, not to mention the total number of processes, is simply staggering and cannot possibly be expressed by any rational number no matter how great. It follows that there is nothing in the universe which is isolated, nothing that can be considered isolatedly or even as enmeshed in a few simple relationships. Isolation of any process or of any thing is not only an impossibility; but if the thing or process is considered more or less in isolation or with but few connections, it must be a falsification of the workings of nature itself.

Such a state of affairs may be startling to realize in the immensity of its implications in the world of nature and of society where even the minutest of occurrences is in interdependence with everything else. The scientist, of course, treats it as a problem of statistics and thus avoids frustration.

For example, a person is born. This is a very involved process in itself and has lots of antecedents, such as two people falling in love, meeting and so on and so forth. We do not take any of these factors into consideration but merely record the fact that a being is born. To be sure, we know that this is a complicated physiological and biological process "beginning" with cell division or mytosis. But let it be so simple for the time being. The person does emerge as a seemingly "independent" physiological unit, and we call him, highly inappropriately, an "individual." He is not independent at all, as a matter of fact, nothing about him is independent. It is an interesting thought, by the way, that the more we progress in civilization the less independent a newborn baby is in comparison with the animal born in the natural state who finds its way about quite readily in most of the species known.

To pursue the thought still further, the human being is born into a family, has parents and "relations," takes in food processed in a million different ways by society that has been industrialized and institutionalized, to mention only two important developments, is cared for by virtue of psychological, economic, environmental, financial and economic factors involving the parents, and so on and so forth. There is no use going into details, for we would lose ourselves in an inextricable maze of influences and factors both physical and subtle. What we want to stress is how completely interdependent a newborn human being is. Whatever action that being will manifest, it will be the result not of spontaneity but because of millions of influences and antecedents. He is, as it were, in the middle of a huge network of influences, environmental factors, causes and effects reaching back into the past and presently impinging on him. Add to this the fact that the child is alive and thus represents possibilities of altering any of these factors.

As the child develops, many of the macrobiological and other factors affect us and we set about to channel them. We keep him in health, tend him when he is sick, get a knowledgeable physician to diagnose what is "wrong" with him, and mold him into the pattern of a child of the late twentieth century. The microbiological factors escape our notice almost completely. True, we speak of love, rejection, adjusting, training and the like. We seek out the "right environment," employ psychologists and psychiatrists, and come up with judgments such as: "he is the offspring of a broken home," without being able to do much about it. What the process was that caused the broken home to emerge in an associable or other type of behavior is quite mysterious, and equally "mysterious" elements, such as "love" and "understanding" are to remedy what is diagnosed as a deviation in behavior and attitude.

We find ourselves in the middle of a situation which we try to remedy largely by guesswork and speculation, not fact. Thus we leave the realm of science and approach imagination and sometimes fantasy. True, there is much that has been experimented with and scientifically established, but there remains a mountain of work to be done. We can deal only in generalities and can be only selective as far as the individual is concerned in our determining causes and effect in his past and those applicable to the present situation. In times gone by men *hoped* and *prayed,* nowadays they *expect,* but are often deceived in their expectations.

If the astrologer is called in, as he still is in many ancient cultures of the world, and says the behavior of the child is due to a constellation of heavenly bodies under which he was born, the sophisticated reject such a statement, for they cannot conceive that the sun, the moon and other far more remote bodies could exert an influence on a human being, leave alone their aspects as they are called, for we have no visible or experimental evidence. It is adjudged purely belief, irrational belief at that, and imaginary. Still people get moody when the sun does not shine and insane asylums anticipate trouble when the moon is full. While there is an explanation for the latter, the scientist does not bother to investigate the influences of the other bodies that are entered in the astrologer's chart, and the judgment is rendered categorically: there is no cause-effect relationship here between the heavenly bodies and the behavior of a human being.

Yet, on the basis of what we said above, there must be *some* connection in the vast reticulation of interdependencies, for no thing, no process, is isolated in the universe. We may reject certain assertions as fantastic, but in the final analysis are they so? Are they even probable? Is not the scientist overstepping the bounds of his realm when he unequivocally asserts there is not and there cannot be any connection between certain processes or things?

This interdependence of things and events is not even fully appreciated as a general principle in the universe. Of course, it cannot be proven to the full satisfaction of the scientist. The complications are too staggering even to imagine, as we said, and it is basically our indolence which designates certain things as accidents and fortuitous. Yet, who would deny that certain people are "accident-prone?" Great fears and economic crises promote strange behavior, the idiosyncrasies of mass behavior are well-known and can be tested by each one of us even though there is no provable or demonstrable cause-effect relationship here.

One of the reasons — a strange one, indeed — why so-called chance events are accepted in the Western world view even though it may be convinced of the fact that nothing happens fortuitously, is that integrating remotely connected or totally unconnected, "coincidental" events does not "fit" into the modern scheme of things. Our world view has been slowly developed on the basis of scientific findings that can be demonstrated or, by logic, can be related. When logic or demonstrated connection fail, then the scientist is in general inclined to leave well enough alone and even deny that there is a possible connection. In other words, the world image as fashioned by science should not be disturbed.

If experimentalists have demonstrated again and again the likelihood, if not certainty, of ESP or extra-sensory perception under the most rigid testing conditions, its existence is denied by conservative scientists because it does not fit into the scientific world image constructed by science. At the most they are willing to re-examine the laws of chance and possibly revise them. Everything is tried first before the possibility of ESP is admitted. This may be well and good and appear stubborn, but admitting possibilities should be one of the basic attitudes of a scientist. Without it science is limited in its progress. In our case, the probability in question is that of an influence of thought on action and behavior or extended capabilities of our sensory apparatus, possibly undetected sense capabilities.

It is, perhaps, into this class of phenomena that the Buddha's *pratitya-samutpada,* as it is termed in Sanskrit, belongs. The usual translation of this technical term is "dependent origination." For it contains elements which must be classed as untraceable in their inter-relatedness in the context of our present-day world view.

No explanation is needed for the word "dependent." Anything dependent cannot exist alone. It must lean on something else or be supported by something else, in the natural world as well as in the mental world. The something else is, thus, an essential adjunct or even ingredient of the thing or process under consideration. Cause and effect may, thus, be considered to be "dependent" one on the other, or the cause may be looked upon as an ingredient of the effect. As far as "origination" is concerned, the concept is fairly clear, so long as we do not probe more deeply into the matter semantically or metaphysically. Something coming into existence may be said to originate, coming from a source, coming out of something that "is," *ex*istence. That source may, of course, also be understood as a cause, and that which originates, *ex*-ists as an effect.

Now, not every cause is of the nature of a force or power, a pushing, pulling or whatever, and not every effect is something brought about by an overt action or force. A condition in the surrounding world may act as a cause. Because of its presence a certain "effect" may be noticeable, or, certain conditions show themselves to be present at all times. Thus, the two conditions are interrelated and may be said to be interdependent. The Greeks distinguished an efficient and a material "cause." It is easily understood what is meant by an efficient cause, something which affects or brings about something else. This is the ordinary use of the word cause. But a material cause is something more passive, as it were, something that brings about an effect simply by its proximity, by its being there at the same place or the same time, as the case may be. Thus, certain biological phenomena are in existence, such as some trees and epiphites in a rain forest because of the geographic and climatic conditions offered by a rain forest.

Enzymes are another good example. They are there and by their very presence cause certain reactions to take place in matter quite different from themselves. The enzyme did not "cause" in the sense of pushing the other elements into a sort of action or adjustment, and neither do the geographic and meteorological conditions "produce," that is, bring forth the plants or "make" them grow in superabundance. To be sure, the heat of the sun and the humidity promote chemico-biological activity, but they alone or even other elements that may be present, are not solely responsible. There are the plants themselves which contribute to the possibility of an interaction, of certain "causes" to be activated. Location, presence of certain factors are necessary for the phenomenon of a rain forest to make itself manifest. It is in somewhat the same fashion that we have to imagine that the *paticca-samuppada* works.

We should have little difficulty in imagining and comprehending the interdependence of everything in the physical sphere, in nature as well as in society. However, certain traditional views get in our way, especially when it comes to man and the sphere of his activity and influence. Though the theory of evolution has taught us a certain humbleness and to consider man as an extension of the animal world, man, by virtue of his astounding abilities, thinks and knows himself to be superior to every other living thing, except some of the elements, like fire and water and submolecular forces which he is trying to control. He has every right to be proud, but no right to be haughty on that account. The humility of the strong who know their strength would be a better and more appropriate attitude.

The supposed discontinuity of man with nature which Darwin's *Origin of Species* tried to do away with over a hundred years ago, naturally interferes with a conception such as the interdependence of all things and beings and processes. It is difficult for man even at the present time with all the ado that is made about living together in society, organizing, co-operating, sharing, or whatever the phrase may be, to adjust himself to other human beings. "Individuality" which is so highly prized, and various other concepts, like competition and the appeal to excellence, vitiate an appreciation of interdependence of mankind. It starts with man and wife who seek divorce, of organizations which split up and try to achieve separate ends, religions which go out to make converts, and nations that make wars.

All these do not spell interdependence but separateness. *Yet* they illustrate more forcefully than anything else that there is such a thing as interdependence, and that it is more desirable because living under the conditions of individuality (wrongly conceived) is our unhappy lot, and the voices are gaining which call for a revision of these so greatly advertised virtues and the institutions that foster them. In other words, the recognition of a universal interdependence in the sense in which the Buddha perceived it, presents a truer picture of reality and a saner and happier one.

Thus, from every point of view the concept of *paticca-samuppada* is indeed a compelling point of view. If man has not only a physique superior to the animals which he has developed in the course of time, but also an intelligence which gave him absolute superiority over the animal world, and all processes are natural ones, then intelligence too is a natural product and is involved in the entire interdependence of all events through cause-effect relationships. Life, death, personality and all the rest are not other than nature, but nature herself in a novel aspect.

Man's thinking also, and his destiny, are involved in the dependent origination in which all else in the universe is involved. The concept of dependent origination, thus, turns out to be a grand picture of a universal integrative development which does not make artificial distinctions between man's body and his spirit or mind, but considers both in a psychophysical unity developing and interdependent with the rest of nature.

It is not possible to exhaust in the short space of a chapter the range of meaning and implication of the concept of *paticca-samuppada*. As in everything else, and Buddhism is no exception, there may be disagreement among Buddhists with our interpretation of this important concept, especially since we have raised it to such a universal status while in the application of early Buddhists the psychological interpretation was the dominant one. Still we seem to be justified in our position for even when the concept is applied narrowly psychologically it transcends the bounds of the psychophysical and relates to man's physical being which is an object of nature. We have placed emphasis on the universal aspect first so we can treat the application to the special case of man's evolution from birth to death and birth again as a special case.

We have reference here to the well-known Buddhist concept of the *nidanas* which are a masterpiece of Buddhist logic and constructionism. This concept was evolved by the Buddha himself as he was sitting by the River Neranjala. There, in the depth of night, as is reported to us in Buddhist scriptures, the vast reticulation of cause-effect relationships, the vast interdependency of states and processes, with particular reference to man whose release from sorrow and suffering he sought, was revealed to him — not supernaturally but in reasoning. It was a process of ratiocination, not a vision or a revelation as commonly understood.

That it was an insight developed through close thinking and deduction is proven by the fact that the interdependence of all states was conceived by him as not having a definite beginning and end, but could be tackled, as it were, from either end or in the middle, if you wish. For in a continuous process which is cyclical, as birth and death are in the Hindu and Buddhist conception, there is no true beginning, suggesting at the same time that extrication from this universal interdependency lies in a different realm than adapting an expedient measure to stop the process at this or that point. If by interference is meant the stopping of a particular state or process, this is quite impossible and would have to be relegated to the miraculous and supernatural which the Buddha did not expound, playing down all references to it.

The significance of the Buddha's approach to the problem of dependent origination lies in the fact that he did not start with something objectively given, but with what is given immediately, and that is man's consciousness or awareness. He searched his own mind, as it were. He used the idealistic approach which lies in the search for meaning in one's own mind. The concept of dependent origination itself is imbedded as an *a priori* principle in the human mind. It is not as such objectively verifiable but impresses its form upon all reality. When we were speaking above about the fact that everything is cause-effect interwoven and tried to bring home the universal presence of interconnectedness we already made use of the *a priori* principle to explain the processes of the universe, we looked upon them from the point of view of a principle that needs no justification by pointing to individual cases of interdependence. Rather, interdependence or *paticca-samuppada* is the very principle of explanation itself which makes us understand what is going on in the world and in man.

It is, thus, very significant and bears out our interpretation of the principle as an *a priori* one when we find that the Buddha himself began his explanation of the *nidanas* not with a description of something objectively given, but with the subjectively given intelligence as the foundation of all explanation.

But in a characteristically Oriental fashion he starts with a negatively apprehended reality, with *avidya,* or ignorance, lack of knowledge. However, we must guard against taking *avidya* merely in the sense of not knowing a particular thing, let us say, the name of a certain person, but with ignorance as a fundamental condition of our everyday existence. It, thus, has nothing to do with information or the lack of it. It is the very basis of our existence in which the Buddha's major problem appears, namely the fact of sorrow and suffering and its elimination. Before we begin to analyze further this concept of *paticca-samuppada,* it may be necessary to call attention to one other factor which also clearly shows that we are dealing here with a fundamental character of the phenomenal world in which dependent origination operates as an element of understanding. It is the problem of freedom and necessity which is raised in this connection.

Being caught up in the universal interdependency on all levels of experience is not and cannot be a very cheerful business. It means that we are not free, that we have no choice, that untold threads pull on us from every direction and enmesh us still further with every moment of existence. Indian philosophy in general has recognized this absolute inter-connectedness of every process by describing our existence as one of bondage, and the entire aim of Indian philosophy is to free us from these bonds. The state of freedom is called *moksha* or *mukti.* This too is the objective of Buddha's teachings to guarantee us perfect freedom or *nirvana.* Before we are ready for that we must have a thorough understanding of the state of bondage, of dependent origination itself in order finally to overcome it.

In the Hindu context, this bondage is usually referred to as *samsara,* the round of birth and rebirth, literally the rat-race, in which we are all involved.

In order to achieve release you must first understand that there is no escape within the field of operation of *samsara,* just as there is no *nirvana* in the field of *paticca-samuppada.* Here, of course, lies the difference between the scientific view which is completely absorbed in the study, explanation and exploration of the interdependence within the limits indicated above, without recognizing that there is an alternative to that principle. It is Buddhism which points up this alternative most clearly in and by the very explanation of the *nidanas* and by associating with it *avidya,* or nescience, the negative approach, while the Hindu points to *vidya* or *jnana,* insight and realization, as a positive approach.

The Buddha was a great psychologist. He made the round of birth and death, *samsara,* far more distasteful in its interminableness than the Hindus did, in that he illuminates with great clarity the entanglements of the *nidanas* which he pursues with relentlessly cold logic, driving home the point that we are, indeed, tied up in a knot by the very attitudes, desires and practices which we engage in habitually. The Hindu appeals more to the attractiveness of an eternal reality and the great joy of realization, while the Buddha belabours almost to nausea the unpleasant consequences of being ensnared on all sides so that complete rejection of the principle of *paticca-samuppada* is the natural reaction and consequence, whereby the very rejection of this principle spells freedom and happiness. Had he done otherwise his own method could have rightly been labelled an escapism, especially since he followed the negative approach. In Hinduism, likewise, the implication of escapism was avoided by introducing the depth category of insight and realization.

The reverse order of the *paticca-samuppada* will make the matter clear:

Old age and death are only possible in and with a corporeal organism, that is to say, a six-sense machine. Such an organism must be born, which presupposes birth. But birth is the inevitable result of past Kamma or action which is conditioned by attachment to craving. Such craving appears when sensation arises. Sensation is the outcome of contact between the senses and sense objects. Hence the organs of sense cannot exist without mind and body. Mind originates with a rebirth-consciousness which is due to ignorance of things as they truly are.

This process of birth and death continues *ad infinitum*. A beginning of this process cannot be determined as it is impossible to conceive of a time when this life-flux was not encompassed by ignorance. But when this ignorance is replaced by wisdom and the life-flux realizes Nibbana (Nirvana), then only does the rebirth process terminate.

The Wheel of Life

If man were free, completely so, there would not be any need of religion, even though the literal interpretation of religion is often given as that which binds. But binds to what? To God, is the usual answer. In other words, religion joins the human soul to God, trying to re-establish an ancient bond which was in effect before man disobeyed the commands of God, became willful and rebellious, and hence was expelled from God's grace. Obedience, religious observances and faith, then, restored the original oneness in spirit with God, and man is "saved." Thus goes the story of man's search for freedom basically in popular Christianity.

Now the Buddha, being a man, a Prince of a royal house of ancient India, also searched for freedom. But instead of searching for the source of freedom without, in some conditions of the world, in some superhuman or supernatural being, sought freedom within himself.

Whatever people believed or thought he had sympathy with and he never told them to give up their belief, as even today a Buddhist will not do so in confrontation with representatives of various religions. He never disparaged any of the beliefs, but at the same time he did not foster beliefs. He employed a different technique, that is, the method of searching for causes in order to analyze and diagnose the situation that presents a problem. His overriding problem was: why do human beings suffer? Perhaps formulated more precisely he asked what are the conditions for suffering and the lack of happiness, human unhappiness and so-called bondage? We shall follow him in that reasoning because we live in a scientific age in which problems are being solved not by faith, hearsay, assumptions and authoritative means, but by earnestly looking for the causes and conditions and their subsequent treatment, be it elimination, transformation, sublimation, or any other form of alteration suitable to produce desirable instead of undesirable results.

If it is maintained that the scrutiny of all the factors making for bondage which we shall presently mention will make a person sad and frustrated, let it be remembered that any analysis or diagnosis of an unpleasant situation or a disease is a necessary step in therapy. The cancer has to be discovered, thoroughly studied before a course of action can be devised. So, likewise, in the case of the twelve *nidanas*. They must be thoroughly understood, each one singly and all of them collectively.

That is why this section had to be preceded by comments on the *paticca-samuppada*. For it has taught us that we cannot expect a satisfactory answer to a problem unless at least the most obvious and nearest complicated threads in a whole reticulation of causes and effects have been disentangled and held up to view clearly for us to see and scrutinize. By the same token it will be understood by now that not one single factor or cause is responsible for any particular situation, pleasant or unpleasant as it may be, but a whole conglomeration of factors.

The West often makes things look too simple, at least in the popular view (the scientist is well acquainted with the large number of variables that may spoil his experiment), by thinking in terms of series of causes, a sort of linear sequence, of one thing leading to another and so forth *ad infinitum*.

In the Eastern view the circular theory seeks to overcome this simplification of events. It is the eternal return, in which all will return to the origins. While not completely satisfying and remedying the difficulties of a linear view, at least it conveys very graphically the interrelatedness of all happenings and relates a later event to a cause which seems to have vanished long since, makes it reappear and exert its influence right along in a particular situation.

The Buddha's analysis, thus, was prompted by his unrelenting search for causes of human unhappiness, that is certain. However, he could not have discovered it in any one item in the network of human activities, volitions, desires, habits or whatever. Just as the latest thinking among medical men is that an ulcer, a weak heart, arthritis, is not caused by one particular irregularity or abnormality or injury, but that the whole man with his innumerable facets of bodily or somatic and psychical and hereditary factors is the cause, in belief, the constitution of the man.

Theoretically, no cure, no remedy, no real alleviation can be effected, then, unless you make over the *entire* person. This clearly is impossible, medically speaking, and so you confine youself to either a symptomatic treatment or to isolating the focus of infection or problem and try to remedy the situation in that way. Thus, the Buddha could not have been satisfied with a symptomatic treatment of the problem of sorrow and suffering, or by singling out one particular aspect of the human being and attacking it as the root cause of the malfunction. *He went for the whole person.* This he could do only after he had been enlightened, that is, after he had gained the complete view, achieved full integration on all levels.

This is one of the important results of our study of the *nidanas* that we should realize that they do not, singly or collectively, offer a solution to the problem of sorrow and suffering, *even if alleviated* (let us say, if old age is delayed or death is eased). The remedy transcends these twelve factors and lies in a different realm.

The meaning of *nidana,* a Sanskrit and Pali word, is very suggestive. It is something that holds us down, like a fetter, a rope that ties us down, a chain that restricts us, a snare. The Buddha mentioned twelve of them. They are the ones that cause us trouble, tribulation, sorrow, suffering, unhappiness and all the painful experiences that human flesh and spirit fall heir to. What are they?

Not having the proper knowledge, nescience, or non-knowledge, is the most serious element in human bondage. By knowledge, however, as has been stated, is not meant information, for if that were the case then learning Webster, the various encyclopedias, the telephone books of all cities, would be tantamount to great happiness and contentment and the solution of all of our troubles. Knowledge must, therefore, be understood as wisdom, intelligence, true understanding, and nescience or *avidya* the lack of it. That would make sense, of course. For both intelligence, insight and realization do have a measure of "saving" power, if only of the soothing kind. But in the absence of *vidya* we can expect all sorts of frustrations, inabilities, incomprehensibles, troubles, wrong analyses, imperfect appraisals and what not, all of which ensnare us in a world of illusions, unrealities, inappropriateness and the like that will forebode no good.

Indeed, these undesirable and bothersome qualities will lead directly to the second *nidana* which holds us down in a world of confused values. This second *nidana* is called in Sanskrit *samskara,* in Pali *sankara.* This is a most difficult word to translate by any one word into English, and Western scholars have tried to do so often with feeble results.

Think of the innumerable complications that absence of knowledge and downright ignorance can cause, and you have an idea as to the second *nidana,* the innumerable chains that hold us confined in the imaginings, illusions, unrealities. Each example of nescience complicates the whole picture of the world about us. It is a melee of irrational, unintelligent and visionary things. To be in the thrall of such a world is, indeed, not only not pleasant in the long run, though perhaps tolerable and enjoyable for the time being, but may turn out to be disastrous.

What are the consequences of *sankara?* *(Vijnana* in Sanskrit, *vinnana* in Pali.) Being confronted with, or what is worse, operating in the mess produced by nescience or *avidya,* we now try to make our way as well as we can. We use discrimination, intelligent choice, if you like. In this we are helped by everyone, by our parents, educators, and the whole array of instructional material with which we are presented. At first we are merely cognitive, make no clear distinction of what is real and what is nominal. This leads us then, to the fourth *nidana,* that of *namo-rupa,* or name and form. When we are confronted with something we distinguish readily enough, a form, that is, a shape, the thingness, "something there." Before it becomes a real element in our experience, before we can range it into the rest of "things" that our world is composed of, and to make it meaningful, we have to form a concept of it, we must name it.

Without a name, the world is not particularly meaningful to us and if we were to relate anything or any experience to anyone else we would have difficulty in doing so because we could not designate the various elements that entered our experience. When we name them, when we have the proper concept, then others will know what we are talking about. But intimately connected with this is the fifth *nidana* which bears the odd name of *salayatana* in Pali or *sadayatana* in Sanskrit. The word *ayatana* means a region, compass, area, sphere in many contexts and thus the word is translated as the "six spheres," which makes little sense. What is meant are the activities of the senses, which are five in number, and of the mind which is often regarded as the sixth "sense."

As in all Indian literature, so also in Buddhist literature, all of our senses are not considered physiological complexes that are located in the human body and are passive, receiving all impressions, as they are called, from the outside, but as powers that assert themselves through the sense organs. This gives a wholly different slant to physiology and philosophy as well. The mind is the co-ordinator of all these powers which in Hindu literature are compared to strong-willed steeds which must be reined in by the mind and kept under control. Thus we might translate the Pali word as the six powers, that is, the five senses in the meaning just explained, and the mind. These collaborate in working over the names and forms and fashion our perceptible world by their action. In doing this, they further strengthen the bond we were speaking about above, tying us to the world that was originally conceived in nescience.

We can well see how the chains are forged more and more, because now we are specializing in our perception of the world which depends on the actions of eye, ear, tongue, nose and tactile organs, guided or misguided by the mind. We know only too well how unreliable all of our senses are to realize how false and erroneous our whole involvement in the world is liable to become.

In following through with the peculiar understanding in the East of mental and psychological activity it is but natural to assume that another element or *nidana* is needed, in fact several *nidanas.* Thus we get "touch" or *phassa* in Pali, *sparsa* in Sanskrit. If sensation is an activity, not a passive waiting of sense-organs for something to strike them, then sense is endowed with the ability to make contact and this leads directly to the seventh *nidana,* namely sensation. This is called *vedana.* This hardly requires explanation as it seemingly coincides with our understanding of the process of sensation when, as we say, sense-organs are brought in contact with objects. But soon thereupon develops another characteristic tendency which has in its train clinching the formation of fetters, and that is *tanha* in Pali, or *trana* in Sanskrit.

Now, the literal translation of this term if "thirst." Of course, in the world of sensations with stimulus-response activity going on incessantly and bodily and other needs crying for fulfillment, there is thirst for the objects of this world, thirst being but a metaphor. Perhaps, longing for, desire, grasping would be a more appropriate Western term. At any rate, the irresistible is brought home to us in the term "thirst," possibly also its inexhaustibleness and complete dependence or interdependence of man with his environment which now becomes almost complete and only lacks the next *nidana,* which is *upadana,* or "seizing." Upon "seizing" follows becoming, *bhava.* The objectivization, to speak technically, has now attained its full realization in that what was at first the object of desire or thirst, has been taken to oneself. Complete identification has been achieved and the process of becoming been initiated. The more abstract initial *nidanas* have led to a concretization in a world which is full of change.

Whether the next *nidana,* which is *jati* or birth, is to be taken in the literal sense or as a further development of becoming which has in its train the coming to the fore of new elements and productions, is not quite clear from the context. If taken in the literal sense, then the next and final *nidana, jara-marana,* old age and death, is the logical conclusion, for whatever is born suffers and ends in death. We have thus arrived at the end of a development which is the lot of mankind the alleviation of which the Buddha had made his primary concern. He, thus, had finished his search for the causes of sorrow and suffering; his analysis was complete. Yet, quite unlike the Western proclivity to regard death as an ultimate, a finale to life, the whole process starts all over again. There is no escape, just as the Hindu in Brahmanism could see no way out of *samsara* and became despondent over this endless cycle of rebirth and death.

The Buddha's solution is the famous fourth Noble Truth which consists in the Noble Eightfold Path. Backed up with the analysis of the twelve *nidanas,* this Path has a philosophic and logical basis in that it clearly shows that the way out from our involvement in existence cannot lie in any of the factors that constitute the involvement. To seek salvation in feeling, emotion, pleasure, enjoyment, and even death which some people seek in order to achieve "freedom," offers no solution for the problem of true freedom and happiness. These must lie in a different sphere altogether, in a way of life that is moral, ethical and dedicated to a contemplation of transcendent values.

The Four Noble Truths

The Buddha said: "It is through not understanding, not realizing the four things that I, disciples, and you, had to wander so long through this round of births. What are these four? They are:
    (1) The Noble Truth of Suffering (dukka);
    (2) The Noble Truth of the origin of suffering (dukka-niroda);
    (3) The Noble Truth of the Path that leads to the extinction of suffering (dukka-nirodha-gamini-pathipada).
    As long as the absolutely true knowledge and insight regarding these four Noble Truths was not clear to me, I was not sure that I had won that supreme Enlightenment which is surpassed in all the world with its heavenly beings, evil spirits and Devas (higher beings), amongst all the hosts of ascetics and monks, other higher beings and men. But when the four Noble Truths had become perfectly clear to me, there arose in me the assurance that I had won the Supreme Enlightenment (samma-sam-bodhi) unsurpassed.

The three characteristics of existence are:
All formations are transient (annica).
All formations are subject to suffering (dukka).
All things are without self (anatta).

The fourth Noble Truth is the path that leads to the extinction of suffering.

The two extremes and middle path: To give oneself up to indulgence in sensual pleasure, the base, common, vulgar, unholy, unprofitable; to give oneself up to self-mortification, the painful, unholy, unprofitable. Both these two extremes the Buddha has avoided and found the Middle Path (madhiyana pratipada), which one has both to see and to know, and which leads to peace, to discernment, to enlightenment, to Nibbana.

The Noble Eightfold Path (Arya attanga Marga) that leads to the extinction of suffering, namely:

> Wisdom (Panna)

(1) Right understanding (samma-ditthi)
(2) Right thought (samma-sankappa)

> Morality

(3) Right speech (samma-vaca)
(4) Right action (samma-kammanti)
(5) Right livelihood (samma-ajiva)

> Concentration (Samadhi)(Meditation)

(6) Right effort (samma-vajama)
(7) Right mindfulness (samma sati)
(8) Right concentration (samma-samadhi)

This is the Middle Path which the Buddha has found out, which makes one see and know, and which leads to peace, to discernment, and to enlightenment (Bodhi), to Nibbana. When one becomes enlightened, escape is possible from the world of the born, the originated and formed. Thus when one has achieved complete emancipation there is no birth, no aging and death. This is not nihilism, but the achievement of immortality.

Buddhism and Society

Influence of the Buddha's teachings is felt in all walks of life in Buddhist civilizations. This impact began early in the third century B.C. when Emperor Asoka Muraya adopted Buddhism as his religion, which eventually became the state religion of India. Subsequently his missionaries carried these sublime teachings all over the world from Antioch to Japan.

By adopting Buddhism as his guide Emperor Asoka built a just and moral society. He deeply respected the Buddha's ethical teachings. The Buddha's message to mankind was for his spiritual and social ascendence. He called on man for cheerful services to others and love for all life, and restraint from all irrational desires. His path was both intellectual and spiritual, and his goal can be attained by self discipline, plain living, and noble thinking.

Sigalovada-Sutta (the layman's Code of Discipline) is a famous sutta of the Buddha. Here he proclaims the duties of parents to children, children to parents, pupil to teacher, teacher to pupil, wife to husband, and vice versa.

Commenting on this teaching, the Sigalovada-Sutta, which is based on social ethics, the well-known British Buddhist scholar, Professor Rhys David, Chairman of the Department of Comparative Religion, Manchester University, says: "Happy would have been the village or the clan on the banks of the Ganges, when people were of kindly spirits and fellow feelings; the noble spirit of justice is shown through these naive and simple sayings." He adds: "Not less happy would be the village on the banks of the Thames today, of which this could be said."

He continues: "The Buddha's doctrine of love and goodwill between man and man is here set forth in domestic social ethics with more comprehensive detail than elsewhere, and truly we may say even now in this Vinaya or Code of Discipline, so fundamental in human interests involved, so sane and wide is the wisdom that envisages them, that the utterances are as fresh and practically as binding today as they were then, at Rajaraha, India, in the 6th century B.C."

In the Mahamangala-Sutta, which is highly cherished in all Buddhist lands, is a comprehensive summary of Buddhist ethics. Here the support of the mother and father, wife and children, is greatly stressed by the Buddha.

Here are three of twelve verses that make his views clear. The English translation from Pali is the work of Dr. R. L. Soni of Burma:

> With the fools no company keeping,
> With the wise ever consorting,
> To the worthy homage meeting;
> This, the Highest Blessing.
> Mother, father aptly serving,
> Children, wife duly cherishing,
> Life's business cooly attending
> This, the Highest Blessing.
> Acts of charity, righteous life,
> From all alarms the kins protecting,
> Blameless pursuits fully rife,
> This, the Highest Blessing.

The verses indicate why problems of old age are not so acute in Buddhist lands, as people look after their parents in their old age. Elders are respected even today in Hindu-Buddhist lands. They are never addressed by name. Parents in their old age are cared for by one of their children, particularly by a married daughter, others giving a helping hand.

Conclusion
In modern Buddhist lands there is still a sense of security regarding old age, as the Buddha once admonished his followers to treat parents as a living Buddha.

Homes are provided by the municipal city government for the elderly destitute and poor, and also for the crippled and handicapped. Things may not be perfect, where poverty, exploitation, and illiteracy exist. Still, most of the people are keen to take care of their elders with respect and pride.

The invasion of television in Hindu-Buddhist lands should be viewed with deep concern, unless it is channelled for moral and spiritual upliftment and guidance of the people; otherwise commercialism, crime and violence, and breakdown of family life will be the devastating consequences. Devoted family life is the backbone of a civilization. The abnormally high divorce rate in the West is a danger to society and civilized life. When families are divorced, and the people in such broken families live in hate and fear, the children are neglected and grow up in unethical and hateful surroundings. In such cruel circumstances, people have no time to think of love and affection to their elders, particularly their dear parents.

Civilizations rise and fall. When the elite of a civilization becomes creative, that civilization shines in the annals of human history, as in India from 6th century B.C. to 8th century A.D. With the domination of the cruel caste exploitation, India declined thereafter. The well known British writer and economist, Dr. Barbara Ward, states that the greatest periods of human history are periods of moral excellence rather than periods of military grandeur. Thus in our Buddhist lands, we shall strive to keep up the Buddhistic principles and uphold moral excellence. Our ancient traditions to respect the teachers, our elders, parents, uncles, and others, would be continued. Thereby the problems of old age in our societies will not be as acute as in the West.

All along in the history of Buddhist lands elders have played creative roles in assisting to build dynamic societies. Buddhist sages like the Buddha, Asoka, Vasabandhu, Asanga (India); Padmasambhava, Saint Milarepa (Tibet); Prince Shohotu, Saint Honen, Saint Nichiren (Japan); Ba Chin, Chan Toon, Mahai Sayadaw (Burma); Sri Buddhasukh, H.S.H. Princess Pismai Diskul (Thailand); Miss Pitt Chin Hui, J.P. (Singapore); Ven. Dhammananda (Malaysia); Dr. Nat Vahn Thich (Vietnam); Ven. Dharmapala (Ceylon and India); Bodhisattva Olcott (Ceylon and India); Ven. Buddhagosa (Ceylon and India), have helped to uplift their fellow humans to sublime heights.

In the present situation the elders, who are blessed with both knowledge and wisdom, would be an asset. They could use their sagely wisdom to find some solutions to problems man has to face today and in the future.

Bibliography

1. *Buddhism and Age of Science.* U. Chan Htoon. Buddhist Publication Society, Sri Lanka.
2. *Buddhism in the Atomic Age.* Dr. Wu Shu. Hong Kong.
3. *Buddhism and Science.* K. N. Jayatilleke. B.P.S. Ceylon.
4. *The Message of the Buddha.* K. N. Jayatilleke. McMillan Book.
5. *The Supreme Science of the Buddha.* Egerton Baptist. Maha Bodhi Press (Ceylon).
6. *Pattica Samuppada.* Egerton Baptist. Maha Bodhi Press.
7. *The Word of the Buddha.* Nyanantiloka. B.P.S. (Ceylon).
8. *The Maha Mangala Sutta (Life's Highest Blessings).* Dr. R. L. Soni. B.P.S. (Ceylon).
9. *Aspects of Social Philosophy.* K. N. Jayatilleke. B.P.S. Kandy.
10. *Everymans' Ethics.* Narada Maha Thera. B.P.S. (Ceylon).
11. *The Light of Asia.* Sir Edwin Arnold. B.P.S. (Ceylon).
12. *Democracy and Buddhism.* Dr. K. Leidecker and B. P. Kirthisinghe. B.P.S. (Ceylon).

Editorial Conclusion: The Aged In Buddhism

Having examined the depths of philosophical inquiry opened up by the Buddha's experience of enlightenment, we may well consider the applicability to fundamentally "awakened" insight to the aging person per se.

Aging is not a phenomenon in isolation; it is linked up to all the vast, interconnected processes of cosmic evolvement. The aging of human persons is a phenomenon that points beyond itself since, in the traditional Buddhist view, a human birth is a precious confluence of evolutionary events. It is a situation particularly favorable in relation to the streams of karmic energy flowing through the universe. Human birth, co-arising with a variety of circumstances is itself the condition for the possibility of enlightenment, of awakening to the inner Buddha-nature that is present everywhere and which energizes its own self-discovery as an Absolute.

Yet human birth is also ambiguous. It is a fundamentally open category of existence in which the process of enlightenment may be hindered or advanced in the temporal dimension. Of course, in an absolute sense, it is impossible to "hinder" the ultimate reality that is enlightenment or Buddha-nature. In the Mahayana teachings, samsara (ordinary life experienced as dissatisfaction and suffering) *is* nirvana (absolute reality, full awakening). The joy of human existence is the accessibility of each moment to the power of enlightenment. All that is necessary is that we open our "inner eye" and recognize what the Zen koan calls "our original face before we were born."

Since *all* processes are in motion, and hence *all* existence is in constant flux, it would be only a partial perspective on reality to make a distinction between the world of flux and phenomena and some posited "ground" that is static and eternal. In the Buddhist view, especially in the Prajnaparamita scriptures, the nature of the "ground" is "emptiness" (sunyata). Sunyata is perhaps best characterized for explanatory purposes as absolute openness or freedom. Things in their essence are radically free, formless, neither dependent nor independent. Thus we can avoid the negative connotations of terms like "emptiness" or "void" by balancing them with a more challenging definition for the experience of sunyata in Buddhist meditation practice. There is no boundary between the great void (maha-sunyata) and the "ten-thousand things." The Mahayana vision of wholeness includes in one sweeping embrace the radical freedom and insubstantiality of all forms and, at the same time, the ultimate importance and value of each person, object, event, moment, and form.

Hence, aging itself takes on a profound value for the Buddhist. Aging is the bodily record of the passing of time. The body is a recording of a lifetime of experience. For the Buddhist, aging is not a diminishment, but an increase, a movement toward fullness, toward "more" life. It is not a downward spiral toward death and dissolution. However, it is not at the same time a triumphal procession to fame, glory and immortality, either. The scrawl of aging on our faces and bodies is either the writing of egolessness or of bondage. Our life-record is itself a judgment on us. There is no need for an external judge; in the practice of sitting meditation one comes to confront in oneself the truth of judgment, the truth about ourselves. It is in sitting practice ("right meditation" — one of the Eightfold Path taught by the Buddha himself) that we meet the ways of the mind and make friends with all that we are within. It is meditation that is the magic thread by which Theseus can find his way back through the labyrinth after finding and slaying the Minotaur. Those who have neither entered the labyrinth nor met the Minotaur remain bound to the wheel of return, blindly following in the course of cosmic process.

The Buddha himself, while a young prince, would make furtive forays out of his palace in order to discover the conditions under which humans lived in the world. His entire way of thinking and of viewing the world was challenged by the sight of an old man by the wayside. This sight — of old age — was the first glimmer of light cutting through the illusory world of pleasure and gratification in which the Buddha, as a prince of the Sakya clan, had been raised. Thus, he began to hunger for an answer to the riddle of human suffering. Subsequently, he was to come upon a sick man, a corpse, and a monk — each a milestone on the spiritual path, each in its way a guru cutting through the bonds of illusion and opening the young prince to his own inner hunger.

Aging is a record and an invitation to truth, to confrontation with the deepest quest of the self. As such, for the Buddhist, even the debilitating effects of aging are a "gift" and a source of gratefulness because they put us in direct contact with the truth of our existence, which is the only source of our enlightenment.

A watercolor by the Zen Abbot Hakuin (1685-1768) depicts blind persons groping their way across a bridge in the manner of the aged. The painting was the Abbot's way of portraying the fundamental human condition to his novices. These blind, groping elders represent all of us who are subject to the inescapable fact of mortality and are therefore cast back upon the nakedness of human existence. They long to be carried across the raging stream to eternity, but the only route is a precariously swaying bridge —perhaps symbolizing the human body, which is full of danger, susceptible to illness and fragile, able only to creep toilsomely over the bridge of life, all-too-close to death at every step. The proximity of human life to eternal death is a warning to keep one's heart pure in the midst of life. It warns us against the illusion of bodily immortality, even if our creams and massages may delay the irksome message of the mirror. In aging, the enlightened Abbot is like the unenlightened vagabond, the Westerner is like the Easterner. Hakuin's painting is offered as the wisdom of old age, a spiritual wisdom that states: "Let the groping of blind men crossing a bridge be a symbol for the life of the aged" — an image that unites all humans in one common experience, grounded in bodily decline, but suggestive of an encounter with the Absolute.[1] This radical openness of the enlightened person is the very essence of "the wisdom of old age" in Buddhism. It is wisdom combined with "skillful means" (upaya) which knows where it is going and how to get there in very realistic, human-centered ways. This wisdom overcomes our fears about the precariousness of our situation and suggests the joy of discovery and confidence that Buddhist realism transmits to the world wherever there are seekers on the spiritual path.

[1]Georg Siegmund: *Buddhism and Christianity: A Preface to Dialogue.* University of Alabama Press, 1980. p. 129.

Aging: The Jewish Perspective

Asher Finkel

Introduction

The Biblical Tradition, Judaism and Israel
Judaism has developed out of a biblical tradition, a tradition that also affected Christianity directly and Islam indirectly. These three movements are historically revealed religions with a collection of holy writings that are based on prophetic reception of revealed knowledge. Judaism views Moses in the time of Egyptian Bondage (13th Century B.C.E.) as the father of the movement of prophets ending in the Persian period (5th Century B.C.E.). It preserves and transmits a canonical tradition of inspired Scriptures (the Old Testament) with which successive generations of Jews, whether in their land or in diaspora, continue to have a dynamic dialogue in faith and in practice.

In order to deal with the Jewish perspective on aging, one must first determine the meaning and its scope from precisely those determinants affecting a biblical orientation as the frame of thought for the emergent Judaism. The particular attitudes, value judgments and practical measures about aging, after all, flow from a perception of life itself. Responses to critical events and the period of aging are governed by a human consciousness of oneself (the intrapersonal), of a Being transcending oneself (the transpersonal) and of others who are either persons (the interpersonal) or non-persons (the subpersonal). These four human relationships embrace the total experience of living and they receive meaning and guidance from the religious system. The biblical tradition indeed has revolutionized human consciousness with its distinctive view of the four realms of relationship. The Bible establishes a sacred cosmos for Judaism as a religious system and offers a constructed world order for the Jewish society evolving in history, within which one lives and finds significance.

The Jewish orientation grew out of an earlier prophetic movement which challenged and negated the polytheistic religious expression and their mythopoeic frame of thought in the prevailing Near Eastern civilizations of Old Testament times. The classical prophets offered a new religious orientation of monotheism and a historical framework for human salvific development. It took many centuries from early amphictyonic times to the end of the Judean monarchy (12th Century—6th Century B.C.E.) for the Israelite society to emerge out of its struggle and tension with the dominant forms of nature worship and with the polytheistic expression of the Near Eastern world.

After the Exile (6th Century B.C.E.), the monotheistic community of returned Judeans accepted the Pentateuchal canon as its constitution (Nehemiah 8-10). The transmitted prophetic works and other religious writings that came to reflect and support the Mosaic tradition were edited and included to form the authoritative texts for the historical community of Jews. The canonical Scriptures became the guide for the Jewish state in its self-determination, when complete freedom from Hellenistic Greek rule was enjoyed in the days of the Maccabean rulers (163-142 B.C.E.). The biblically oriented society adopted a theocratic model for living which produced different interpretative parties. All these sects shared in the common acknowledgement of an allegiance to the Bible but they differed on its application to daily life. The hermeneutical differences resulted in the teachings of conservative and liberal Pharisees among the people, as well as in the practice of the priestly Sadducees in the Temple and that of the stricter Essenes.

After the fall of Jerusalem, Judaism emerged as the rabbinic interpretation of a "way of life" without sacrifice and Temple. It adopted the liberal Pharisaic teachings and their hermeneutics. The diasporean situation became the historical setting for the developing rabbinic system. It began especially after the defeat of Bar-Kochba, the false national messiah, and after the edict of Hadrian forbidding the return of Jews to Jerusalem and to biblical life (135 C.E.). Judaism lived apart from Judea and has developed its legislation and socio-religious model in Galilee and in Babylonia. The rabbinic system spread into the European continent, North African countries and the Persian Gulf where Jews lived. In these lands, Judaism remained under constant threat of forcible conversion and extinction by the dominant faiths of Christianity and Islam. It learned how to cope with its precarious situation with an abiding hope of return to its homeland.

In 1948, following the genocidal action against European Jews by Nazi Germany, the world through the United Nations organization recognized the independence of Israel. This recent event in Jewish history offered for the first time since the Maccabees the opportunity for the creation of a Jewish state. Israel, despite its

hostile neighbors, is free to develop its own institutions and legislation which will remain within the bounds and be conscious of its
biblically oriented tradition. The diasporean Jewry which faces
assimilation maintains newer forms developed out of an adjustment
with a modern philosophical and cultural setting. The contemporary phenomenon of Judaism as the religio-cultural expression of
an independent democratic state and as a socio-religious community
in dispersed lands is analogous to the historical times following the
Babylonian Exile and during the Hasmonean rule. The two separate
existences for the Jewish people give rise to forms recently studied
with regard to aging and they will be considered in the conclusion.

This brief account of a long history of Jewish civilization with its
roots in biblical times indicates dynamic cycles of growth. It is a
human story of a collective body of Jewish people living with long
memories of their former history of birth and decline. These events
are recalled affectively in religious celebrations and fast days of
remembrance. The Feast of Passover for exodus and the Fast Day
for the destruction of the Temple, for example, deepen the commitment to human freedom and to the land of Israel and religious
culture, respectively. Due to its biblical orientation, the Jewish
people are moved by a historical awareness and corporate consciousness. They relate to one another as an organic whole, both
extratemporally — a dynamic link with past and future generations
— and extrapatially — a reciprocal concern for Jews of different
countries in the present. The vertical and horizontal dimensions of
history are affectively imprinted in Jewish consciousness which
relates the person to the collective body of his people.

Person-Nation and Imagery of Aging
Our study, therefore, cannot ignore the correspondence of person
and nation in relation to Jewish reflections on aging. Already the
prophets, in their dramatic use of the parabolic word, depict the
people of Israel as a living person. The idea of people convenanted
to God was expressed projectively from the human experiential
setting of marriage (Hos. 1-3). The nation began as an abandoned
female infant who was adopted by God and then entered into a
mystical covenant with God (Ezek. 16). It grew out of an affec-
tionately remembered national period of youth (Jer. 2:2). Alas, as
Israel grew older she became estranged from her transcendental
mate. Israel in exile after the destruction of the Temple is depicted
as a separated or widowed old woman (Jer. 3:1; Lam. 1:2). The

prophets of exile echo the nation's self-image of reaching old age when aloneness and deterioration set in. Yet Israel can continue to live meaningfully in embracing a prophetic conception of life and prospect for the future. On the one hand, the prophets call for national renewal of life in history through the human act of genuine return to God (Jer. 4:1, 2; Ezek. 18). On the other hand, prophetic vision depicts a collective resurrection after death through God's act of creative restoration (Ezek. 37). Both prophetic messages were introduced with reference to the nation's existence in days of destruction and exile.

Pharisaic teaching and rabbinic Judaism have translated these messages into pillars of Jewish faith for the individual. The rabbis insisted on the genuine act of repentance that can be performed anytime during one's life span. In their view, it becomes necessary to gain a new lease on life as one faces death daily. They also declared that resurrection is a biblical doctrine. In their view, personal life even after death is the ultimate heavenly reward. The strength of the biblical tradition depends on its ability to offer dignity and worth to the individual person and to the historical society he belongs. For the human society is, in the last resort, persons banded together in the face of death. The earthly experience of repentance comes to renew purposeful life and the heavenly promise of personal resurrection overcomes the emptiness of death. In turn, they deepen a concern for dignified life that is filled with doing good in recognition of human work. Thus, repentance and resurrection are linked with the eschatological prospect of human life free from evil. The prophets and later the rabbis speak of the renewal of human personality, which eliminated either its heart of stone or evil inclination respectively. Such a psycho-axiological linkage in Judaism seems to deepen the meaning of aging as the crown of life when rebirth is possible and resurrection is promised.

The person-nation correspondence also reflects a psycho-historical understanding of the Jewish people. The aging nation in history was recently resurrected in its homeland when Jewry in the European diaspora faced death. The Jews in Israel see themselves collectively as an old man returning home to be reborn. He was threatened with annihilation due to antisemitism in Christian countries, but now he must prove himself in a struggle for existence and recognition by Islamic neighbors. He knows the experience of aloneness as an old man, but he must endure the pangs of birth as a new nation.

The Approach

This study focuses on the Jewish perspective on aging of the individual living in society. It is limited to an exploration of the rabbinic tradition as it is rooted in the biblical frame of thought. The perimeters of the tradition have shifted from time to time but the organic system of religion was preserved. In dealing with Jewish attitude and practice, as maintained through the ages, one must view the frame in order to understand the orientation. The way the Jewish society relates to the aged and the way the older Jew relates to himself can be properly evaluated if one sees the interrelatedness of conceptions of the self and the other, of God and life.

The first part presents the structure of biblical thought as it is determined by a particular human response in living due to a transpersonal relationship. Such a religious orientation affects the scope of interpersonal relationship and in turn determines the human attitude towards the older generation of parents, teachers and the aged. The Jewish attitude as reflected in the rabbinic sources will be discussed in the second part. The third part explores aging within the general concept of life. Since it relates to the terminal period of life, two intrapersonal views may result. Either one sees a developmental opportunity for life fulfillment or one may be negatively affected by a period of deterioration. This concluding part is devoted to how the Jewish tradition deals with these opposite possibilities. The three parts of the study flow from selected biblical text(s) which come(s) to capture the basic themes of exploration. All texts from the original sources are translated afresh in comparison with standard works.

Part I

"Even unto old age I am (present) and unto hoary time
I bear (your presence). For I have created and I sustain;
I bear and will deliver" (Isaiah 46:4).

Distinctiveness of the Biblical Tradition

The biblically oriented tradition is rooted in the human response to God's presence: God has manifested in the acts of creation; he reveals himself in the history of mankind and he holds the promise of salvation. The whole person relates to the wholly Other (the numinous) as a creator who existed prior to and apart from the cosmos. This awareness flows out of a deep sense of being a creature. "I am nothing but dust and ashes" (Genesis 18:27). As a mortal creature, the person lives in the awareness that he shares this fate with a created world of other persons and non-persons.

Biblical faith is predicated on this crucial distinction between the transpersonal relationship and the subpersonal one. For in the ancient world of nature worship an identity between the two realms prevailed. An affective personalistic response to nature as the arena for the manifestation of divine wills and minds governed the mythopoeic expression of ancient religions. It is found in the drama of the sacrificial rituals and the recitation of creation-myths. Near Eastern myths related how the present cosmic order emerged out of chaos in the birth of gods battling for supremacy and control. God of the Hebrew Bible, however, stands apart from nature as its author. He was not born out of a chaotic world but existed apart as the creator of all. He endures beyond time and sustains all life in time. God can make his presence known to man throughout time but remains the abiding source of deliverance beyond temporal existence.

In mythological thought the sacred cosmos emerged out of chaos and continues to confront the latter as its terrible contrary. Nature itself is determined by a fixed order of seasonal cycles. Myth and ritual come to express verbally and dramatically the account of gods who gave rise to such an order from the beginning. In accordance with this view, society is embedded in nature, whose human members must preserve the cosmic order and social solidarity in the face of chaos. The human being is thus enslaved to an imposed mythical order of gods in nature and to the socio-political order in which he lives. To be in good relationship with the sacred cosmos and the human order will shield the person against the terror of chaos and *anomie*. To fall out of such relationship is to be abandoned on the edge of the abyss of meaninglessness and nothingness. The power of polytheistic nature religion was rooted in the dread of return to pre-creation state of chaos and darkness. To die is to journey into the netherworld, the realm of demonic monstrosities. Biblical thought has emancipated the person from subjugation to the cosmic order and from the dread of chaos. The human creature is a free being who can choose and shape a course of life. It was God's intent to create the person in his image and thereby to bestow upon him the intellectual abilities to shape and to control the subpersonal realm.

Human freedom means responsibility for personal decision and action to do good in the world of persons and non-persons. The biblical tradition, therefore, pays close attention to the growth of human personality that is beset by inner tension between egoistic and altruistic drives. The intrapersonal realm becomes the unique focus of early biblical code ("Thou shalt not covet," Exod. 20:17) and it is the ethical concern of the prophetic teaching. This concern for individual freedom was lacking in the mythopoeic world of thought and precisely Israel's genesis as a biblical people resulted from the event of liberation from human bondage. Through the experience of freedom, Israel became open to a radical new orientation so apodictically expressed in the Mosaic Decalogue.

The Decalogue and the Four Relationships

The earliest code of the Bible reflects a new orientation as regards four human relationships. The transpersonal relationship is established on the negation of hierarchical gods in the three realms of the cosmos. "Thou shalt not have other gods in my presence . . . those are in the heavens above or those are in the earth below or those are in the waters under the earth" (Exod. 20:3, 4). The cosmos is God's creation. "For God created the heavens and the earth, the sea and all that is in them" (20:11). This creator is not an otiose god but is ever present in the human world. His providential presence was experienced in the historical event of exodus. "I am the Lord your God who took you out of the land of Egypt" (20:2). A holy day is set apart weekly to be open to God's presence. On the Sabbath, human life can enjoy sanctified rest in the abstention from daily work and its problems. The person deepens the sense of "imago dei" (being in the image of God) in the witness to God of creation. For the biblical notion of "imago dei" is linked with God's intent of human stewardship for the world He created (Gen. 1:28). The rabbis explain that the human being entered into a partnership with God in the work of creation. Thus, the subpersonal relationship as distinct from the transpersonal one is legislatively linked with the human concern for restful existence of the animal kingdom. "It is a Sabbath to the Lord your God . . . for you . . . and your cattle" (Exod. 20:10). The rabbis teach (Babylonian Talmud), therefore, that causing pain to animals is biblically prohibited.

The interpersonal realm is likewise affected by the transpersonal relationship. The Sabbath promotes a human concern for the subjugated people. This lesson is particularly stressed in the

Deuteronomic version of the Decalogue. "In order that your manservant and your maidservant may rest as well as you. For you shall remember that you were a servant in the land of Egypt" (Deut. 5:15). The interpersonal commandments are also linked with the transpersonal ones in the Decalogue. They are unconditional prohibitions to promote the sanctity of life. "Thou shalt not murder" (Exod. 20:13). For "whoever sheds blood is considered as the one who abnegates the 'imago dei'" (Mekhilta ad loc.). The rabbis teach that anyone who destroys a human life is seen as if he destroyed the entire cosmos (see Part 3).

In a unique way the Decalogue ushers in the interpersonal legislation with the predicate that the blessing of long life rests in the human show of respect to the older parent, father or mother (Exod. 20:12). For a society that honors its aged values human life and is therefore blessed with longevity. In the Decalogue the biblical prescription of filial piety governs the social ethics. Like its counterpart of transpersonal demands, it reveals a new orientation for Israel. For the Decalogue concludes with the climactic law governing intrapersonal realm: "Thou shalt not covet." The rabbis consider this principle as the core of the biblical legislation. For it focuses on the inner world of the person, on his drives, intentions and thoughts. The Decalogue links the intrapersonal concern with the interpersonal laws. The Mosaic legislation guides the inner world of the person in contrast to ancient Near Eastern culture and law.

The biblically oriented community is rendered distinct by religious motivation for social action. Thus the book of Genesis offers the historical contrast between the archetypal representative of the Mosaic faith, Abraham, with the people of Sodom and Gomorrah, the model of a depraved idolatrous society. Abraham teaches "the way of God to do righteous and justice" (Gen. 18:19). Whereas, "the cry (of the oppressed) in Sodom and Gomorrah is so great for their sinfulness is very grave" (18:20). Abraham exemplifies the biblical way of altruistic concerns coupled with a loving faith in God. His first act of prayer is an intercession for the others, the sinful community. "Will the judge of the universe perform an injustice?" (18:23-32). The question of theodicy expressed in terms of the human predicament, which reveals the affective faith of the biblical person in relating the transpersonal encounter with the interpersonal concern. Thus, the social world becomes the arena for translating the biblical consciousness of God's presence. So did Jesus the Jew teach and likewise it was advanced by the contemporary Hillel and the later Akiba, the pillars of rabbinic legislation. A show of love in human relations is the governing principle of the Bible.

God's Presence and Human Response

The biblical tradition is theocentric and it is governed by a theology of Presence. To live in God's presence dictates the way one conducts himself in the other relationships. Human consciousness can be open affectively to the awe-inspiring experience of God's apartness or can be deepened by the soul yearning for God's nearness. The way of awe and the way of love relate to the anthropological view of the Bible. On the one hand, the person is a mortal creature conscious of his finitude and perishability ("nothing but dust and ashes"). On the other hand, the person senses a creative partnership with God in the cosmos ("a little lower than God," Ps. 8:6). The biblically oriented individual aspires towards a fulfillment of his partnership with God through responsible actions of concern and love for both the interpersonal and subpersonal realms. In this manner, the person gains dignity and worth as an earthly creature ("crowned with glory and honor"). Egoistic aggrandizement is therefore the gravest intrapersonal sin in prophetic thought. Its folly becomes clear in the human awareness of creaturehood limited by death. "For when his death comes, he cannot take anything away; his glory cannot go down after him" (Ps. 49:17).

The biblically oriented personality, whether an individual or a collective group, is shaped by a covenantal awareness. It relates to God's presence out of an attitude of awe and love. This motivates the person to develop a similar attitude of reverence and respect in the realm of human interaction. Furthermore, the person aspires to imitate God in his way of love and pathos. Thus, one elevates the meaning of life by the principle, "You are holy as I am holy, the Lord your God" (Lev. 19:1). "Imitatio dei" (imitation of God's way) governs the ethical laws of Leviticus including the interpersonal commandment to "love thy neighbor."

The drama of life in the relationship of marriage and family, in the attitude towards judges or kings provide imagery to describe a transpersonal relationship. In prayer, God is addressed as "father" in his attribute of love and as "king" in his attribute of awesomeness.

Thus, the ethical response demanded in interpersonal relationships also opens the person to the reflection on the meaning of relationship to God. In light of this biblical frame, the traditional Jewish perspective on aging can be evaluated meaningfully as it is reflected in attitude and in practice.

Part II

"Honor thy father and thy mother that your days may be long" (Exod. 20:12). "Each person shall revere his mother and his father" (Lev. 19:3). "Before the hoary head rise up and respect the presence of an old man, so you shall be in awe of your God" (Lev. 19:32).

Awe of God

The pedagogical principle of the Hebrew Bible is that the awe of God is the beginning of human knowledge (Prov. 1:7; Ps. 111:10). It is legislated apodictically in the Deuteronomic tradition: "Be in awe of the Lord your God and Him you shall serve" (Deut. 6:13). This religious attitude of "let there be heavenly awe upon you" guides the Pharisaic theology. The common worshippers and priests in the Temple concluded the daily intercessory prayer with the above Deuteronomic injunction. Early Christianity of the Second Temple period pointed to Jesus repelling the Satanic temptation of world domination. His scriptural response ushers in his own ministry with the same principle (Matt. 4:10 — Luke 4:8). For biblical faith is rooted in the human response of awe in God's presence and such response is the biblical expression for religion (Gen. 20:11).

To be in awe is not to experience fear from external threats to one's own existence — feelings that promote superstition and magic. It is a response of creature feeling from within oneself. Through this inner conviction one senses the overwhelming presence of the "mysterium," which affects the person internally in the tension of "tremendum et fascinans."

The rabbis (Babylonian Talmud) explain that one does not stand in awe of the Temple or its magnificent buildings but in awe of God for whose presence the structure is commanded. According to the rabbinic code (Mishnah Berakhot and Tosefta), the biblical prescription of awe posture in God's Temple (Lev. 19:30) signifies in the pilgrim's life an abstention from monetary items and the minimization of material goods. For apostolic dedication to Kingdom of God is to be experienced on the road as a sacred pilgrimage in God's presence.

To be in awe of God, therefore, can be translated into a religious consciousness affecting all aspects of life. All realms of human relationship are so governed and the verbal response of prayer is so affected. According to the rabbinic tradition one lives by placing God's presence constantly in mind (Ps. 16:8). Such an attitude governs the rabbinic prescriptions of blessings in all areas of life: the consumption of food, the performance of daily tasks, the witnessing of natural events and the pleasure of the senses. One also relates to God in reverential speech and the careful use of language. The excessive use of attributions and appellations in prayer is prohibited. Human designations for a transcendental reality are not to be applied lightly. Even when they are used, the qualifier, "as if it is possible," is introduced in the description. Speech before God must reflect the genuine thought and intention of the person. The standing posture assumed in Jewish prayer reflects attentive and reverent awareness of God. The gestures of bowing, kneeling and prostrating are clearly added to denote creature's humbleness.

Honor and Reverence

The forms of reverential posture, respectful speech and affective attitude come to reflect awe of God. The similar corresponding forms are introduced in the interpersonal realm in relating to older persons. The younger generation relates to the parents, teachers, the learned and the elderly. The rabbis have observed that the biblical commandment regarding children and their parents is phrased in the same terms as the transpersonal commandment, namely to honor and to revere. Furthermore, they maintain that the attitude towards the teachers and the sages must flow from the same expression of awe before God. The elderly are to be acknowledged with a standing posture and respectful speech. One acknowledges the dignity and worth of the aged as he receives God's presence.

The apocryphal Ben-Sira, continuing the Jewish wisdom tradition in early times, commented on the linkage among expressions of awe for elders and for God: "The fearer of God honors his father. He honors his parents as masters" (3:6). To honor one's parents expresses a sense of awe and results in filial service. The similarity between service of a son and a servant is clearly reflected in the rabbinic code. The concrete translation of honor into action begins with maintenance and personal service. "Honor means one must give food and drink, dress and cover him and accompany him in and out." However, the attitude of awe towards a parent as a servant before a master expands personal services to "washing his face, hands and feet . . . anointing him and putting on his shoes."

Stories are told of the rabbis to show how far one must translate the fifth commandment into action.

"The mother of Rabbi Tarfon went walking in the courtyard one Sabbath day and her shoe tore and came off. Rabbi Tarfon came and placed his hands under her feet and she walked in this manner until she reached the couch. Once when he fell ill and the sages came to visit him, his mother said to them: 'Pray for my son Rabbi Tarfon, for he serves me with excessive honor.' They said to her, 'What did he do for you?' She told them what had happened. They responded, 'Were he to do that a thousand times, he has not yet bestowed half the honor demanded by the Bible.'"

This incident is often cited in Jewish literature as a model of Jewish filial piety. The climactic response of the sages indicates that the concrete expression of honor does not exhaust the infinite possibilities inspired by reverential love.

The rabbis focus on reverential love as the attitude motivating filial responsibility. The biblically prescribed responses towards parents are not rooted in loving acts but in the categories of honor and reverence. These categories embrace the feeling of awe. The behavioral attitude towards older parents should not be limited to their mutual feeling of love only. For when love is lacking and the situation produces tension and abuse, the sense of heavenly awe must guide the filial response. Maimonides, the authoritative codifier of Jewish law, explains:

"How far must one accord honor to one's parents? Even if they took his wallet full of gold pieces and threw it into the sea before his very eyes, he must not shame them, show pain before them or display anger to them, but he must accept the decree of Scripture and be silent."

"How far must one show reverence to them? Even if he is dressed in precious clothes and is sitting in an honored place before many people and his parents come and tear his clothes, hitting him in the head and spitting in his face, he may not shame them but remain silent and be in awe of the King of Kings who commanded him thus."

Both love and reverence for parents take as their model love and reverence for God. Heartfelt reverence in the presence of God, the internalizing of honor, must fuel the behavioral commitment. One whose filial relationship grows out of reverential love can check the inner anger provoked by his parents' behavior. Reverential love promotes, on the one hand, patient response and attentive service, the rabbinic formulation for "honoring the parents." On the other hand, it demands response of reverence, the complimentary biblical prescription. Reverential attitude is cultivated through a respectful awareness of parents' presence even though they may not be present.

The fundamental expression of honor implies parental support but it must be accorded in view of their dignity and worth. The rabbis illustrate with the case of a rich man feeding his father well but with contempt.

"There was a man who always fed his father fattened hens. Once the father inquired, 'Son, where do you get these hens?' The son replied, 'Old man, grind and be silent, just as dogs eat and are quiet.'"

The older teachers are viewed as parents and served in an attitude of honor and of reverence. So teaches Rabbi Joshua son of Levi, "a disciple must serve his teacher in all the ways that a servant serves his master." The disciples would, for example, put the sandals on the feet of the master. The master is revered in respectful address ("my master and my teacher"), in conscious posture ("not standing nor sitting in his place") and in consideration of his position ("not to contradict his words"). A contempt for his teaching through scheming, show of anger and conflict with the master are seen by the rabbis (Babylonian Sanhedrin) as the rejection of God's presence. The person appears in their view to have suppressed the inner force governing religious life, namely the creature's feeling of awe. For the teachers' task in the first place was to instill a reverential attitude toward God in seeking knowledge. The master in the rabbinic code therefore is given preference over the parent, because "one's father brought him into this world while one's teacher brought him to the future world." The teacher relates to the disciples as his sons in whom he fathered wisdom and love of God. The relationship to God in reverential love is developed through the pedagogical association. The transpersonal realm serves as a ground to deepen the response of honor and reverence towards one's parents. Thus, the rabbinic law (Mishnah Baba Mesia 'a) directs the disciples to prefer the needs and honor of his master to those of his own parent, should the two conflict.

The learned and the aged demand likewise from the person a show of reverence. Filial piety is restricted to biological and spiritual parents and therefore it is limited to one's immediate circle. However, the presence of the sage, may he be younger or older, is acknowledged by the person unbeknown to him. The sage elicits reverential response, for he himself personifies a life in God's awe. Similarly respect shown to the aged relates to a stage of life embracing all human beings. Therefore, the elderly are to be acknowledged respectfully whether they are Jewish or not. For their presence points to a human being full of life experiences on the road to death, triggering in us creature feeling and the sense of heavenly awe.

Parents, Teachers, the Learned and the Elderly

The presence of the aged in human life evokes an existential response to one's own physical being, to his intellectual quality and to the experience of living. One relates to parents by the fact of birth, to his teachers and the learned by his reception of wisdom and to the aged by their achievement of experiential knowledge.

Professor Gerald Blidstein in his study of filial responsibility explains that "parents are creators and the recognition of human creators forms a continuum with the recognition of God as the creator." There is a partnership of God and parents to be acknowledged in the biblically oriented society. The rabbis maintain that the sacramental union of husband and wife invites God's presence in marriage. Life within the family was charged with near numinous significance. This religious attitude prompts Rabbi Joseph (Bab. Talmud Kiddushin) to say upon hearing his mother's footsteps, "Let me rise before God's presence that is approaching."

Just as filial respect for parents has its model human reverence of God who created him, so does devotion to one's teacher have its model in devotion to God, the supreme teacher. The rabbinic imagery of God who revealed his Torah on Mount Sinai is that of a sage teaching in the academy.

In a similar way, old persons personify the living tradition and they are to be honored because of the many changes that they witnessed in a long life. They transmit to the younger generation the experiential lessons of the past as a living testimony to God's presence. "Remember the days of old, consider the years of many generations. Ask your father and he will tell you, your old men and they will inform you" (Deut. 32:7). Thus, the older generation points to God who acts in history, the fundamental view of biblical faith. Accordingly, the apocalyptic imagery of God is that of "ancient of days" (Dan. 7:9), whose presence endures beyond the existence of the four world empires in history (7:3-8, 17).

Authority and Theodicy

The parent, the teacher, the sage and the aged provide the child with a sense of authority. As he grows older the person relates in depth to the ultimate source of authority. A society that develops a reverential framework for its family, school and the elderly instills in its citizens a sense of heavenly awe as the principal deterrent in interpersonal relationships.

The disturbing concern of human appeal to God is the problem of theodicy. So was it first posed by Abraham in prayer, "Will the judge of the entire world commit injustice?" So did the prophets and the psalmists classically phrase the question, "Why do the righteous suffer while the wicked prosper?" Its very formulation reflects how the person projects his questioning of human authority that avoids justice. One indeed is free to protest the wrong committed to his person even by his parents, teachers or older people. Moreover, if their demands conflict with God's commandments, the person is instructed to avoid the former. In rabbinic view, the very answer to theodical inquiry lies in the attempt to project a sense of justice in human realm upon God. For it falls short in the face of creation revealing the awesomeness of the creator God. This awareness becomes the dramatic ending to the agonizing dialogue on theodicy in the book of Job.

Authority and retributive justice are essential to the structure of society and as such it is first encountered in the home. The family unit is the essential basis of social organization and moral system. These are maintained and developed by its educational institution. Then, the attitude assumed towards the older parent and teacher will advance the well being of the society. Such is the biblical link between honoring the parents and the reward of long life. Correspondingly in biblical thought, "The awe of God prolongs life" (Prov. 10:27). For a society that allows for the family and educational structures to disintegrate invites its own demise.

From Awe to Love

The criterion of heavenly awe is singled out as the fundamental demand of the biblical orientation on life. "Now Israel what does the Lord your God require of you but only to stand in awe of the Lord your God" (Deut. 10:12). Rabbi Hanina explains, "all is in the hands of Heaven except heavenly awe." For the principle of human freedom serves the individual best in choosing to live by the sense of awe. It is a path that one takes first out of fear of heavenly retribution, the case of Job. He offers the model for gentile fearers of God, the semi-proselytes in rabbinic law. However, this religious path must be accompanied by "walking in God's ways, to love him and to serve him with all your heart and with all your soul" (the continuation of Deut. 10:12). Climactically it is manifested in total commitment even unto martyrdom. Rabbi Akiba, who faced this ordeal in Roman times, sets the example for Jewish generations of martyrs with the teaching: "Love the Lord your God with all your heart and with all your soul" (Deut. 6:5) means even if your soul is taken away.

Abraham demonstrates his loving faith in bringing his beloved son as sacrifice and only then he is acknowledged as "one who fears God" (Gen. 22:12). The rabbis explain (e.g. Midrash Hagadol to Gen. 22:12) that the deeper meaning of the biblical account is not the divine approval of the event but that Abraham's act of faith caused other people to acknowledge the full dimension of heavenly awe. In the example of Abraham not only was the transpersonal relationship motivated by loving awe, but it was effectively demonstrated and applied in the interpersonal realm. The love of the person is linked with the love of God in a dynamic way, thereby promoting the idea of rehabilitating justice.

The symbiotic attitude of love of God and love of person results in the rabbinic explanation that a show of love for God is actually found in the personal conduct of one's life. For he sets an example for others to follow.

The Jewish tradition locates the love for parent and teacher in the reverential attitude. Moreover, it is deeply manifested in the way of life of the older parent or teacher. Their lives are continuously valued and emulated by the younger generation. This leads to a loving acknowledgement by the community, which verbalizes its praise for the parent and the teacher as well as accords them proper station in life. Even after their death, their presence is recalled in loving memory and in praise, the common Jewish practice on the anniversary day of their death. Reverential love towards the older generation dynamically builds a bridge with the younger generation, whose attitudes and actions will be forged by the sense of heavenly awe.

Part III

> "A crown of glory is hoary age, in the way of righteousness it can be attained"(Prov. 16:31). "Do not cast me off in the period of aging, forsake me not when my strength is spent" (Prov. 71:9).

The Image of God and Imitation of God

The social attitude towards the older person is determined by the impact of the transpersonal relationship. Likewise the intrapersonal attitude of how one relates to aging himself is reflected in the personal view of God. Finally, theistic consciousness corresponds to the way the society and the individual relate to each other. For the content of meaningful life finds expression in the social setting. The person will be charged with a sense of fulfillment in growing old when the interpersonal realm generates altruistic love and reverential response to his being. These social attitudes evoke inner feelings of human dignity and worth, the force making life meaningful.

Life itself in the biblical tradition is perceived as something that transcends purely biological and material existence. It flows from the loving God and His numinous spirit, "who has crowned (the person) with 'kabod' and 'hadar' " (Ps. 8:6). (glory and honor) However, these attributes convey phenomenologically dignified presence (weightiness) and manifested worth (splendor) respectively. Thus, the society that is guided by the biblical responses of "kabod" to older parents and teacher as well as of "hadar" to older persons, promote a numinous view of life for the individual.

The focus of the above Psalm is on the biblical notion of person created in the image of God, namely, a being bestowed with dignity and worth. As such, the concern is with the development of the human personality that achieves purposeful living. To be conscious of life is integral to human existence. Consciousness is deepened by the numinous quality placed on the content of life. The biblically oriented rabbinic tradition speaks of a human consciousness that strives to imitate God's way in the world of man and nature. In order to achieve dignity and worth, the person must elevate himself through "imitatio dei" and thereby he transcends a merely biological existence.

The person is not perceived dualistically in the biblical tradition. In contrast to Greek thought, he is not a living composition of an alien immortal soul residing in an earthly body. The rabbinic system is grounded in a monistic view of the person, whose personality is affected by different drives, qualities and faculties. There is an heavenly aspect of his existence which can develop an earthbound personality into a divine image. Yet the preservation of the body affected by a biological process is highly valued when it conflicts with the lofty transpersonal demands. For "to save life or to do good" are governed by the same ethical demand of "imitatio dei." What motivates the respect and care of the physical body is not simply the esthetic or hygienic outlook on the human body but the reverence for the dignity and worth of life.

The shedding of blood was reckoned as if one destroyed God's image. The great potential in human life to reproduce physically and to affect creatively or destructively successive generations of people is captured by the biblical archetype Adam in rabbinic thought. This conception was formulated as an admonition to witnesses in Jewish courts dealing with capital cases, for the alleged criminal was facing the sentence of death. The theocratic court of the Second Temple period would address them thusly:

> Know that capital cases are not like civil cases, when money is paid and the person is forgiven. However, in capital cases, his blood and the blood of his offspring depend upon us until the end of time . . . . Therefore, Adam was created singularly to demonstrate that anyone who destroys one life is considered in the Scriptures as if he destroyed an entire world.
>
> (*Mishna Sanhedrin*)

Rabbi Akiba, the pillar of rabbinic code, teaches that the person assumes special significance because he was created in the image of God and lives by that sense. Such a view promotes essentially an attitude of respect and concern for the living to be translated by the imperative of altruistic love. The same Rabbi Akiba maintains that the commandment "to love thy neighbor as thyself" (Lev. 19:19) is the main principle of the biblical law.

The Jewish tradition, therefore, stresses a show of love especially to those who live in the face of suffering and death, namely, the infirm and the elderly. For the rabbis (Sifra to Lev. 19:19) extend the show of love to the other, even to the one who is condemned to death. One should not abuse him or cause him humiliating pain. Life is precious because it flows from the Giver of life and all moments or stages of life are equally sacred. Thus, the period of deterioration in aging deserves special concern. To be cut off (karet) while still young is the gravest divine punishment. It is therefore a crime to take one's life and the high court (Mishnah Makkot 1:10) must refrain from administering death penalties. How much more is the concern for those who live into old age or are facing death. Every step must be taken to preserve their life but surely to preserve it with dignity and worth. This legal and social understanding, as well as the historical practice of personal and medical care in Judaism, has been adopted by the modern state of Israel. This development from rabbinic times until now seems to be rooted in a constant biblical image of life as a divine gift.

The Gift of Life and Eternal Life

Aging is a process of life beginning in the womb and ending in the tomb. One can view life towards death as the candle burning out or as the dry withered leaf. The recent concept of aging is a reflection on biological time as deterioration sets in. The symbols become the emptying hourglass, sunset or the winter season. Two opposite images of aging emerge. On the one hand, there is the image of a conflict between inner forces of health and decay ending in damaging defeat. On the other hand, there is the image of the renewal of life symbolized by the seed growing from a dry decaying shell or the reptile shedding its outer skin. These images are reflected and dramatized in myth and ritual. The former points to a constant war between good and evil powers and the latter points to the idea of resurrection.

The biblical tradition has drawn on similar images but its meaning is captured by the idea of "gift" (Pss. 36:10; 66:9; 139:13). "God gives and God takes; let the name of the Lord be blessed" (Job 1:21). This becomes the classical Jewish response to the event of death. The human community acknowledges gratefully the gift of their life in the proclamation of "God's righteousness". Each morning in thankful acknowledgement a person recites upon awaking the blessing of "God who restores the souls to dead bodies." The person is a recipient of a gift, which makes him responsible for his life throughout the time he is in conscious control. Each day is perceived as it may be the last as well as all periods of life are equally significant. One relates therefore to aging in Judaism as Rabbi Abraham Heschel so eloquently addressed the White House Conference on Aging in 1961. He spoke of contemporary criticism and of a constructive religious vision. Old age need not be "defeat," "punishment," "a disease," "irreversible decline." Growing older is an opportunity for achieving significant being. Aging can mean growth, a celebration, the sanctification of time, an opportunity once again for experiencing the presence which makes us truly human.

Most important for a constructive understanding of life is the parallelism developed in biblical thought between life on earth and life beyond. Life on earth is bound by the grave, "to earth you will return" (Gen. 3:19). Yet, "many of those who sleep in the earth shall awake, some to everlasting life and some to denigration and everlasting contempt" (Dan. 12:2). In rabbinic thought, therefore, life on earth assumes cosmic significance for it holds the promise of renewal beyond the grave. The period of one's life offers the opportunity for eternal life. This is a central concern for fulfilling on earth the teachings of God. The Jews acknowledge upon being called to a Sabbath reading of Scriptures, an old and continuous custom for the collective reception of and commitment to the biblical tradition. "God gave us a Torah of truth and has planted in us eternal life." To gain eternal life is to fill the content of earthly life with Torah consciousness and righteous deeds in imitation of God.

The Glory of Aging, Elders and the Sages

Old age becomes a crown of glory when one pursues the path of righteousness in imitation of God. The biblical model is Abraham who pursued and taught "the way of justice and righteousness" in an altruistic concern for others. In light of this understanding, the rabbis claim (Gen. Rabba 65,4 to 27:1) that it was Abraham who achieved the glory of old age and God himself accorded him honor. The manifestations of turning old were given as desired gift to Abraham to be the indicators of increased worth and status. Gray hair became a crown of glory and the disappearance of youthful visage marks growth and maturity. Of particular importance in this respect was Israel's institution of the elders. It is true that old men were not necessarily equated with elders. The focus was upon a person who has acquired wisdom, namely, the sage.

However, the ideal leadership in biblical and rabbinic times was entrusted to the elderly sage, as exemplified by Moses and Rabbi Yohanan ben Zakkai respectively. They attained inspired leadership with four scores of years. Psychologist Harvey Lehman in his classical study of *Age and Achievement* describes the accomplishments of older thinkers who did notable creative work late in life.

Wisdom and experiential knowledge were highly respected in Israelite society. The periodization of life in rabbinic thought points to the biblical association of forty years with creative understanding and fifty years with projective advice. This span of life corresponds to late adulthood, which is characteristic of reflective awareness. The optimum constructive age in antiquity was seventy years. Such achievement in the circle of the sages was acclaimed with inspired reverence. For the rabbinic community views the older teachers with dignity and worth in seeking their mature knowledge and testimony to life. Moreover, it is a biblically oriented society that promotes the way of righteousness to fill life with meaning. As such it seeks the elders and the sages who pursue the way of righteousness in actual living to exercise a central creative role in the life of Israel. For beyond the principle of strict justice one must prove his worth by doing "that which is right and good" (Deut. 6:18). This guided the rabbinic academy and its decisions. The sages would renounce title even to that which they could legally claim as their own for the sake of other's needs.

This is illustrated by the example of Rabbah son of Rabbi Hana, who was asked by his rabbinic colleagues to return the garments he seized for the damage done to his property by some poor porters. After he had returned their garments, the porters said, "We are poor men and have worked all day and are in need. Are we to get nothing?" "Go and pay them," was the reply of the court, "for it is written, 'keep to the path of righteousness.' "

The sages remained the pillars of the Jewish community throughout the ages as the lawmakers and models of piety. The institution of the sages in the academy came to replace the biblical movement of the prophets. The older person either opted for a life of good deeds engaging in public affairs or for a life of Torah study promoting ethical values. The test of the sage was whether and to what extent his actions and conduct led to the sanctification of God's presence or to its profanation. All consideration of honor and station had to be disregarded where there was any fear of desecration or rejection of God. The lives of the sages were, therefore, marked by constant preoccupation with the Bible and the Way of God. The sages became the reprovers, guides and teachers of the people for they demonstrated altruistic love and piety while living in awe of God.

Aging and Deterioration
The older person is afflicted with the disabilities of age. The author of Ecclesiastes (12:3-7) draws a dramatic picture of those anguished days. "When the keepers of the house (the feet) tremble and the soldiers (the hands) are bent and the grinders (the teeth) cease because they are few and the windows of the chimneys (eyes) become dim . . . For the person departs to his eternal abode (the cemetery) . . . Then the dust (body) returns to the earth as it was and the spirit to God who gave it." These conditions are painful as well as distressing in light of impending death.

The process of letting go has been described as the stages of dying - from shock and denial to acceptance and fulfillment. Accepting the fact that one is going to die can liberate a person so that he can really be free to live, to see each moment as a possibility for concern, for care and for love. It is most important to offer older people, even the terminally ill, the opportunity to translate their time into righteous acts. Food and medicine may keep the aged alive, but only respect for their usefulness and experiential knowledge will make their lives worth living.

Louis J. Novick recently described the specific practices of traditional Judaism in filling important psychological and social needs in later years. It is the diasporean community today that answers the needs of the aged to play socially significant roles, to experience warm relationship with others and to utilize time in a socially fulfilling manner. The person hallows life by performing ordinary activities of daily life and thus is occupied with the fulfillment of God's commandments during all of his waking hours. The traditional community draws together older people in the fellowship of Torah study and the practice of righteous deeds. Thus the older Jew with a biblical orientation feels himself to be surrounded by God's love and human fellowship.

In contrast, Yonina Talman has analyzed the influence of ideological factors on aging in collective settlements (kibbutz) in Israel. The older people on the secular kibbutz generally maintained productive roles in the economy as long as possible but retire gradually as full members of a cohesive community. Nevertheless,

many experience aging as a difficult and painful process of re-
orientation. The deceased professor of sociology at the Hebrew
University of Jerusalem pointed out that the kibbutz is a future
oriented and youth centered society in which the major rewards
are given for hard physical labor and productivity. These values
make it difficult for older persons to maintain feelings of worth.
This contrast with traditional Judaism is also apparent in modern
nations of "youth worshippers," whose "Peter Pan syndrome"
contributes to the rejection of the aged. This youth orientation in
contemporary American society was correctly pointed out by
Rabbi Benjamin Blech in his article on "Judaism and Gerontology."
It is apparent that the religious response to the phenomenon of
aging is affected also by the cultural attitude of modern society.
The need is to increase sensitivity to the issues of care and justice,
reverence and human dignity, which in the Western world are
derived from the biblically oriented tradition. The case of traditional
Judaism speaks for a continued orientation, for those in diaspora
and those in Israel to develop and to deepen their responses to the
older generation.

Such is the poetic appeal of Rabbi Heschel to the modern
society:

Old men need a vision, not only recreation.
Old men need a dream, not only a memory.
It takes three things to attain a sense of significant
being.
God, a soul and a moment.
The three are always here.
Just to be is a blessing, just to live is holy.

Bibliography

The editors have selected materials in English suggested by the author.
Translations within the text have been made by the author.
1. G. Blidstein. *Honor Thy Father and Mother.* (New York: Ktav, 1976).
2. O. B. Bromley. *The Psychology of Human Aging* (Penguin, 1977).
3. *Encyclopedia Judaica* (Jerusalem, Keter, 1971). See Vol. 10 on Law.
4. Rabbi Nathan Z. Finkel (author's grandfather). *Or Hasafun,* Vol. 1 (Jerusalem:
Hofman, 1978) and D. Katz, *Tenu'at Hamussar,* Vol. 3 (Jerusalem, 1974).
5. C. and P. LeFevre. *Aging and the Human Spirit: A Reader on Religion and
Gerontology.* (Chicago: Exploration Press, 1981). See pp. 35-44.
6. Harvey Lehman. *Age and Achievement.* (Princeton University Press, 1953). pp.

200ff.

7. Mishneh Torah, Mamrim 6:7. (Translated by Hershman. Yale Judaica Series), pp. 155-56.

8. Pesiqta Rabbati 21 and Torah Shelemah, Vol. 16, ed. Kasher. (New York, 1955). (To Exodus 20:17).

9. Soncino Hebrew-English Talmud. (New York: Bloch Publ. Co.) See: Tractate Baba Kamma 6:4, et alia; Tractate Sanhedrin, etc.

10. S. Terrien. The Elusive Presence (Harper, 1978). God and His Temple, Ed. by Lawrence Frizzell (Seton Hall University, 1980). See also: Asher Finkel: The Responses to God's Presence and His Withdrawal (Seton Hall University, 1982).

11. C. Tresmontant. A Study of Hebrew Thought. (New York: Desclee, 1960). Cf. I. Pedersen, Israel, Vol. I (London, 1964) and Hans W. Wolff, Anthropology of the Old Testament (Philadelphia: Fortress Press, 1978).

12. E. E. Urbach. The Sages: Their Concepts and Beliefs (Jerusalem: Magnes Press, 1975).

13. _____ The Sages. Encyclopedia Judaica, Vol. 14.

A Christian Theology of Aging

Jose Pereira

1. Christianity, the Universal Religion

This is the religion that contains the universal way for
liberating the soul . . . This is somehow the royal way,
which alone leads to the Kingdom . . .

AUGUSTINE[1]

Christianity proclaims itself the universal religion. All faiths, it declares, culminate in itself; all the truths they contain are fulfilled in its own teaching. "Anyone who is a good Christian" remarks Augustine, perceives "that the Truth, wherever it is found, is his Lord's."[2] This assurance of uniqueness, this conviction of transcendence is not exclusive to Christianity, but is found in each of the world religions, even in the least abrasive of them, Buddhism. "Whatever is well said anywhere in the world", exclaims the Buddhist poet Matrceta in a hymn to the founder of his religion, "derives from your teaching. Faultless discourse is the Buddha's alone."[3]

Hence all teaching for the Christian, no matter what its source, is Christian when illuminated by the Christian message. Indeed the religion of Christ, from its inception, has unfailingly irradiated man's thoughts. As Newman maintains, "in the collision and conflict of opinions, in ancient times or modern, it was that Message, and not any vague or antagonist teaching, that was to succeed in purifying, assimilating, transmuting and taking into itself the many-coloured beliefs, forms of worship, codes of duty, schools of thought, through which it was ever moving. It was Grace, and it was Truth."[4]

With the passing of time Christians, pondering Christ's message, came to discover several variations in it, and to incorporate them in several denominations. But most of these denominations can be said to agree that our salvation, or final blessedness, consists in God; that this God is one Being in three Persons; that the second of these Persons, Jesus Christ, the Logos, became man, and by His death made us capable of salvation; and that to enable us to realize this salvation He instituted a body of believers, the Church.

Many of these denominations, strongly opposed by some others, further declare that the Church is a visible, priestly, and hierarchical organization, mediating the grace of salvation through visible signs of that grace, the sacraments. And one of these denominations, the Catholic Church, also maintains, not without opposition, that the Church's hierarchical structure is pyramidally unified by the authority of the Pope.

2. Sources for the Christian Understanding of Aging

Although divine and supernatural theology depends upon the divine light and on the principles revealed by God, it is also completed by human discourse and reasoning, and is therefore aided by the truths discerned through the light of nature as well.

SUAREZ[5]

It is from within the Catholic tradition (which is my own) that I shall endeavor to assess the Christian understanding on aging. The sources which already embody such an understanding, or those capable of embodying it, are of two sorts. First, those belonging to traditions ideologically and *historically* connected with Christianity, such as Judaism and Hellenism, which preceded it in time, or were contemporaneous with it, and which helped it to acquire a definitive intellectual character. Second, those belonging to traditions only *ideologically* connected with Christianity, as the Indic and Sinic religions, which, so far, have had no significant direct impact on its intellectual formation.

Of the historical sources, both Judaism and Hellenism (in its Greek substance and in its Hellenistic and Roman modes) are ambivalent in their attitude to age. They both celebrate youth, beauty and vitality, abhor the disabilities of old age, but declare longevity to be a reward bestowed by divinity — either for the accomplishments of youth and maturity, or for one's having persisted in righteousness. Among the topics concerning age discussed in the Old Testament are the positive qualities of the aged, their wisdom, dignity, and lore-retaining memory; their disabilities, picturesquely described in *Ecclesiastes,* chapter 12; and a quasi-magical quality, of uncertain value, consisting in the parents' ability to promote or blight the prosperity of their offspring by means of a blessing or curse respectively, as in the story of Isaac and Job. Part of this old age lore is found in the Old Testament's wisdom literature, some of it derived from Egypt and Mesopotamia, repositories of the secular culture of the Ancient Levant; it was this culture which provided the conceptual and mythological basis of much of ancient Hebrew thought.

This culture was supplanted by a greater one, the Hellenic, the wisdom of which, in turn, became part of the intellectual fabric of Christianity. The writers of this culture usually took a gloomy view of old age, such as is reflected in the remark of the Greek didactic poet Theognis (6th cent. B.C.) that "men are fools and children to cry for the dead, and not for the flower of youth perishing." But the philosopher Plato (c. 428-c.348 B.C.), who was 80 when he died, introduced a note of optimism into this dismal gerontophobic melody. According to his philosophy, man is formed of two elements; an essential one, the soul, an immortal spirit; and an accidental one, the body, its material adjunct. The body could be the soul's impediment or (dispensable) instrument. The soul was unaffected by the body's states; indeed, as the physical appetites and vigor decreased, so increased the spirit's freedom. Some old men, it is true, are querulous, lustful, and mournful of their lost youth. But others celebrate their liberation from sex's thraldom; old age arouses in them an immense feeling of peace and liberation. Human growth can thus be conceived as a possible rise or *ascension* toward spiritual perfection, and Plato can be identified as the first exponent of the "ascensionist" philosophy of old age in the history of Western thought.

But his pupil Aristotle (384-322 B.C..) held that human life reaches a peak of development around fifty, after which it experiences a *lapse* or decline; thus, this great herald of Scholasticism can be called the first Western proponent of the "lapsarian" philosophy of old age. According to Aristotle man is a unity of body and soul, both elements being essential to his constitution. Hence what happens to the body cannot fail to affect the soul, and old age cannot be happy unless the body remains intact, which rarely happens. To Aristotle's mind old age is an unamiable state (which he himself, however, did not experience for too long). Those who have lived long enough to feel this state have often been deceived, made mistakes, and failed in their tasks; hence they have confidence in nothing, but are reserved, fearful and hesitant. They are ill-natured and distrustful, since they suppose that everything is getting worse; they are lukewarm in their love and hatred; they are also selfish, timid, cold, shameless and contemptuous of human opinion. They live more upon memory than on hope, are garrulous about their past, and prone to sudden but feeble anger. Their apparent moderation is due to their lack of desire, and their weakness to pity, not magnanimity. They are steeped in self-pity and have forgotten how to laugh.

There was a reversion to an ascensionist philosophy in the third century B.C., when Zeno founded the Stoic philosophy, according to which all that is in keeping with nature is in its own way good (and nothing is so completely in keeping with nature than that the old should die). This principle was systematically applied to old age by the great Roman (moderate) Stoic, Cicero (106-43 B.C.), author of Graeco-Roman antiquity's most consistent portrait of aging, the *De Senectute (On Old Age,* 44 B.C.); a sketch of it is given further below. Its bright colors were later glazed with more somber tones by another great Roman (rigid) Stoic, Seneca (c. 4 B.C. - A.D. 65), within whose lifetime Christianity was born.

Proclaimed by Jesus, the new Message of salvation, pondered by the community of its first believers, the Apostolic Church, was incorporated in the New Testament (A.D. 49-120). But these believers were too preoccupied with the problems of Christ's Person and deeds, and with His imminent second coming (not to mention their own human limitations), to give every theological problem all the attention it deserved. They were hence unable to reflect much on aging, and if Scripture contains all that is necessary for salvation, then a very inadequate knowledge of aging must be taken to be necessary for salvation — which is certainly true for those who will not live to experience age.

Whatever its shortcomings, the theological reflection of the Apostolic Church on aging comprises at least three heads. First, of *age as a state of physical decline.* "When you were young," John the Evangelist makes Jesus say to Peter, "you girded yourself and walked where you would; but when you are old, you will stretch out your hands, and another will gird you and carry you where you do not wish to go."(John 21:18) Second, of *age as a state endowed with authority and worthy of honor.* Its possessors, the elders, were the community's traditional leaders in Christ's time, and parents were the models of the elderly state. "Children," counsels the apostle Paul, "obey your parents in the Lord, for this is right. 'Honor your father and mother' (this is the first commandment with a promise), 'that it may be well with you and that you may live long on the earth.' " (Ephesians 6:1-3) Elders are to be treated like parents. "Do not rebuke an older man but exhort him as you would a father," commands Paul (I Timothy 5:1). Hence, asserts the author of the First Epistle of Peter (I Peter 5:5), himself an old man, "Likewise you that are younger be subject to the elders." Third, *age as requiring an appropriate moral behavior* which renders it worthy of the honor of the young. Paul recommends: "Bid the older men be temperate, serious, sensible, sound in faith, in love and in steadfastness. Bid the older women likewise to be reverent in behavior, not to be slanderers or slaves to drink; they are to teach what is good, and so train the young women to love their husbands and children, to be sensible, chaste, domestic, kind, and submissive to their husbands, that the word of God may not be discredited." (Titus 2:2-5)

The Apostolic Church was succeeded by the Patristic Church, which initiated the intellectual structuring of Christian thought. It presided over the formation of systematics, the integrator of the various disciplines of theology, and over that of mysticism and ascesis, within which Christian insights on aging were later to be incorporated. Principal among its theologians concerned with aging are the three illustrious contemporaries, Jerome (c. 347-420), Chrysostom (347-407) and Augustine (354-430). To this triad one may add the no less illustrious Maximus the Confessor (c. 580-662), who comes at the very end of the Patristic period, and to whose thought I shall allude later. I shall here concern myself only with the three contemporaries. Of these Jerome, who lived to be 73, derives his ideas on aging more from Cicero than from his own experience. Augustine, who was 76 when he died, dwells on the trials of age (Sermo 128), observing that its foes (meaning the passions) are fewer and weaker, but that they still continue to disturb its quiet. What is new in Augustine (in relation to the Apostolic Church) is the treatment of old age as a symbol of life in contrapuntal motion, carnally wasting while spiritually waxing. Aging is treated as though it were the senescence of the carnal "old man" (that each of the regenerate are ceasing to be) coincident with the birth of a spiritual "new man" that each of them already are. Carnal youth, the early part of physical life, is a time of pleasure; carnal age, the latter part of that life, is a time of trial. On the other hand, what we may call "mystical" youth, the initiation of spiritual life, is a time of trial; mystical age, the time of spiritual fulfilment, is the time of joy. Chrysostom, the last of our triad, died at the age of 60, at the very threshold of old age. He wa concerned more with the preparation for old age, to be initiated in youth, than with old age itself. Age for him is a time of realized virtue, and is symbolized by royalty; youth, on the other hand, is a state of striving for that virtue, and is symbolized by athletics. One has to start early in the fight against vice; one who does so "erects trophies at the very start of the race, and adds victories to victories, like the champion of the Olympic contests, who from his early yearss moves to old age through cries of victory, and finally retires wreathed in numberless crowns."[6] Furthermore, "the old man is truly a king, if he wishes to be one, clothed as he is in a purple more regal (than the one worn by mundane kings) — but only if he governs the disorders of his soul, and who makes subjects of his vices. If not, let him be dragged away and thrown from his seat. Let him become a servant of money, love, and empty renown; of affected elegance and pleasures and drunkenness and anger and sensual love; let him tint his hair, and exhibit his age as dishonored by a free decision of his soul: will he not then be worthy of punishment?"[7]

The work of the Patristic Church was developed by the Romanesque Church and the Gothic Church, through the structuring of dogmatic and moral theology, in systems of surpassing architectonic power, like Bonaventurianism, Thomism and Scotism; in challenging counter-systems, like Nominalism; and through the formation of mystical theology as an independent discipline. But there was not much in the way of a theology of aging: one of the period's monographs on the subject was a sermon by Martin de Leon (Martinus Legionensis + 1203), an Augustinian monk, on *Qualiter senes ac juvenes Deo servire debeant (How the Old and the Young Ought to Serve God)*. But the remarkable medical research of later times was heralded in the work attributed to the Franciscan theologian and proto-scientist, Roger Bacon (c. 1210-1291), entitled *De retardandis senectutis accidentibus (On Slowing the Accidents of Old Age)*, where the author, who seems to have lived to be 82, recommended the pursuit of fruitful longevity through good hygiene and biological and chemical experiments. This chemical (or alchemical) search for the secret of long life was later continued, among others, by Paracelsus (1493-1541).

The Renaissance Church elaborated the Classical and Nominalist Scholastic systems of the Gothic Church, and witnessed the revival of the philosophies of antiquity, such as Platonism. Its own great contribution to religious thought was the introduction of the positive method into theology. In the time of the Renaissance

Church, arose the Scientific Revolution (to which I shall presently refer in more detail), which applied the positive method to the empirical sciences. The Renaissance Church produced two outstanding philosophers on age, both Italians, the Venetian nobleman Luigi Cornaro (or Alvise Corner, 1475-1566), and the cardinal, theologian and art critic Gabriele Paleotti (1522-1597). Cornaro, author of the *Della vita sobria (On the Sober Life,* 1558-1565), demonstrates, in a more elaborate fashion than perhaps any other writer, and taking his own life as an example, that old age needs to be prepared for earlier in life, and that a temperate youth is the best guarantee for longevity. As he approached middle age, Cornaro discovered that his mind and body had been dissipated by undisciplined living, and determined to turn his life around by a consistent use of the principle of moderation, especially through dietary control. His resource was perpetual good sense, not complex remedies and exotic medicines, though he recommended a reasonable use of "new wine." These methods enabled Cornaro to live till the age of 91, and they appear to have convinced him that the old age so attained could be superior to the ages preceding it. "I think my present age," he observed, "although it is very advanced, the pleasantest and finest of my life. I would not exchange my age and my life for the most flourishing youthfulness."

The French physician Andre' duLaurens (Laurentius, 1558-1609), author of *A Discourse of the Preservation of Sight; of Melancholy Disease; of Rheums and of Old Age* (1599), agreed with Cornaro's philosophy of moderation, but disagreed with its meliorism, maintaining that age brings nothing but pain and languishing grief, with mind and body becoming feeble, the senses dull, the judgment failing and the memory lost. Paleotti, a subtler thinker than both, wrote the *De bono senectutis (On the Good of Age,* 1595). He was one of the great Christian humanists of the Renaissance, and a disciple of Cicero in his philosophy of age, transforming the Stoic Nature into the Christian God. Paleotti held that the sadness of old age could to some extent be relieved by forms of relaxation like music, games, baths and pleasure tours. But these left the inner cause of sadness still intact, and it consisted of the awareness of diminishing time and approaching death, and the collapse of self-regard occasioned by the assault of the public's stereotypes of the aged as miserly, timid, suspicious and disagreeable. It was for the aged to realize the dignity of their state, that the "good of age" consists in the fact that reason-endowed man reaches his maturity in it. It is then that reason attains its completeness, and the free will is rendered capable of its fullest exercise. Moreover, old age is in its way the image of eternity, *senectus est velut imago quaedam aeternitatis.* Eternity is one, and simultaneously present to events that succeed one another in time, as though contemplating them all. So, too, old age is one; it seems in a way to include all the other ages: the old man retains them in his memory, and contemplates all the things he did in his youth and at other times, as though they were present events.

We turn now from the Renaissance Church to the Baroque Church, the climax of the theological achievements of the previous eras. Systematics attained an unexampled massiveness and grandeur in the work of Suárez (1548-1617), and mystical theology acquired some of the stability of systematics in the thought of Juan de la Cruz (1542-1591). Indeed, mysticism is one of the blazing achievements of the Baroque Church, its constellation of mystics outshining in brilliance other constellations in the galaxy of Catholic spirituality. I shall recall or allude to the thought of only a few of these spiritual masters, Tomé de Jesus (+ 1582), François de Sales (1567-1622), Jacques-Benigne Bossuet (1627-1704), Manuel Bernardes (1644-1710), François Fenelon (1651-1715), and Jean-Pierre de Caussade (1675-1751). From the writings of the latter, a refined synthesis of the thought of the Spanish and French mystical schools, it is possible to develop what may be called a *spirituality of afflicted aging.*

It was during this age that ascetical theology became an independent theoligical dicipline, due probably to the efforts of the Polish Franciscan, Chrysostomus Dobrosielcius (Chryzostom Dobrosielski, 1605-1676), a theologian of the Bonaventurian school. It is to ascetical theology that the spirituality of aging properly belongs, as the modern ascetical theologian Otto Zimmermann has observed. The Baroque age also produced two explicit works on the spirituality of aging. The first is the *Provisiones senectutis (Foresights of Old Age)* by the Polish Jesuit Gaspar Druzbicki (1590-1662), one of his nation's most famous preachers and ascentical theologians. The book (in 59 pages of folio size) is a well structured ascentic treatise, chiefly for the use of aged priests, and is in three parts. The first consists of foresights of a speculative nature (as for instance the thought of one's cooperation with God's grace and glory), designed to incite one of fervor and to striving for spiritual perfection. The second comprisess practical foresights, leading to the correction of past faults, and for the remedying of previous remissness in spiritual matters. The third provides stimuli for the attainment of the same perfection, according to the three ascetic ways of purification, advancement and fulfilment. But the works shows little knowledge of old age's medical, psychological, and social problems, and seems to view age as no more than the stage of life nearest to death. Druzbicki's message is that spiritual perfection, expected of all Christians, is more pressingly demaded of the aged.

The second of these works of the Baroque period is an ambitious work on aging in all its aspects, the *Academia senectutis (Academy of Age)*, by the Belgian Cistercian, Benoit de Bacquère (1613-1678). Only three of the six projected parts of the work appear to have been completed: the *Senum Salvator (The Savior of the Old, 1673)*, the *Senum medicus (The Doctor of the Old, 1675)*, and the *Senum anatomicus (The Anatomist of the Old, 1678)*. I have only seen the first of these parts, whose full title is *Senum Salvator salutaria suggerens media per quae quis de senectute bona transeat in juventutem perpetuam (The Savior of the Old Providing Salutary Means Whereby Anyone is Enable to pass from a Good Old Age to Perpetual Youth)*.

This work (like that of Druzbicki) may be described as a treatise on the spirituality of comfortable aging (as opposed to Caussade's *spirituality of afflited aging* which I shall outline later on). It too makes very little reference to the situation of the aged, except to remark that age is a wretched state and near to death. This work, of 185 pages, begins with a chapter which declares that medicine is (or will be) capable of restoring youthfulness to the old. But such a restored youthfulness will eventually decline to old age. There is another, perpetual, youth that the old must strive for, the youth of heavenly existence. This is attained by a delightful and easy method, love — of oneself (moderate), of God (absolute) and of one's neighbour (referred to God). One must also, under the mentorship of a prudent director, mediate on the Last Things (death, judgment, hell and heaven). And one must always be ready for death, and be in a state of constant prayer at the moment of death itself. Its title apart, any Christian, even the most robust youth, could use the book as a manual of Christian perfection.

Conjointly with the Renaissance church, was inaugurated the Scientific Revolution, as a study of phenomena and their laws based on exact observation, by Copernicus (1473-1543), Leonardo da Vinci (1452-1519), Galileo (1564-1642) and others. The human intelligence finally acquired a method of properly knowing its proper object, the material singular, a method which respected the object's singular, material and intelligible character at once. Up to· this time, theology had made use of one principal auxiliary discipline, philosophy, and that based chiefly on the deductive method. The new scientific method, based on induction, gave rise to new scientific disciplines that were to affect our understanding of the universe and its phenomena, including aging, profoundly. The information on old age available to the Baroque Church mainly consisted in ancient folklore and the speculative hypotheses of Galen (c.A.D. 130-c.200), whose pontifications had supplanted the more empirical approach of his predecessor Hippocrates (c.460-c.370 B.C.). Now new areas of knowledge of old age were made available to theology by the development of the physical sciences, especially chemistry; of the biological sciences; of medicine and its affiliated disciplines; and of the social sciences, like anthropology, sociology, economics, political science and psychology.

The facts, disclosed by these sciences, as relevant to the study of aging, were in the 19th century methodized in a new science, *gerontology.* The forerunners of this science may be said to be two pathologic anatomists, the Swiss Theophile Bonet (or Bonnet, 1620-1689), author of the *Sepulchretum anatomicum (Anatomical Cemetery,* 1679), based on the dissections of diseased corpses; and the Italian Giovanni-Battista Morgagni (1682-1771), disciple of Bonet, and author of *De sedibus et causis morborum per anatomen indagatis (On the Seats and Causes of Diseases as Investigated by Anatomy,* 2 volumes, 1761), which had a section on old age. Morgagni is said to have been the first to restore medicine to its true essence, pathology, and to have been among the first to demonstrate the necessity for basing diagnosis, prognosis and treatment on a knowledge of anatomical conditions. A younger contemporary of Bonet's, John Floyer (1649-1734), author of *Medicina Geronocomica, or the Galenic Art of Preserving Old Men's Healths* (1724), may be considered a forerunner of modern geriatrics, which deals with the specifically medical aspect of gerontology.

Morgagni's successors who continued to prepare the way for gerontology were the German physician Christoph Wilhelm Hufeland (1762-1836), who wrote a book on the prolonging of human life, the *Makrobiotik* (1796); the American physician and psychiatrist, Benjamin Rush (1745-1813), author of the *Medical Inquiries and Observations Upon the Diseases of the Mind* (1812); and the French physician Leon-Louis Rostan (1790-1866), discoverer, in 1817, of the relationship of asthma in the aged with a cerebral disturbance.

Then came the Belgian statistician, astronomer and sociologist, Lambert-Adolphe Jacques Quetelet (1796-1874), the reputed founder of modern gerontology, as well as of quantitative social science. Applying statistics to social phenomena, he developed the concept of the "average man," and established the theoretical foundations for the use of statistics in sociology. These ideas were incorporated in his best-known work, *Sur l'homme et le développement de ses facultés, ou Essai de statistique sociale (On Man and on the Development of His Faculties, or An Essay on Social Statistics,* 1835). Among the topics he discussed was the productivity of playwrights considered in relation to their age.

Continuing research in aging were the German physician Carl Canstatt, author of *Die Krankenheiten des Höheren Alters und Ihre Heilung (The Diseases of Advanced Old Age and Their Healing,* 1839), believed to be the first systematic treatise on the subject; and the English scientist Francis Galton (1822-1911), the founder of eugenics, who investigated factors like strength of grip in the aged, their vital capacity, visual accuracy, reaction time and loss of sensitivity in hearing. In 1868, the French neurologist and psychiatrist Jean-Martin Charcot (1825-1893), famous for his work on pathological anatomy, clinical treatment of the sick, and nervous pathology, published his *Leçons cliniques sur les maladies des vieillards et les maladies chroniques (Clinical Lessons on the Illnesses of the Aged and Chronic Illnesses),* which had a great success. In 1908 the Russian biologist Ilya Metchnikoff (1845-1916), who had coined the word "gerontology" around 1903, published his *The Prolongation of Life.* And the term "geriatrics" was coined in 1909 by the Viennese physician Ignats Leo Nascher (1863-   ), the reputed founder of the discipline in its modern form. Around this time, too, the Canadian physician William Osler (1849-1919) discovered that aging is closely related to the state of the blood vessels in the body, and that if the brain changes with age, it is through the hardening of the arteries.

Other gerontologists of this pioneering period are the American physician and pathologist George Richards Minot (1885-1950), author of *The Problems of Age, Growth and Death* (1908); the American biologist Raymond Pearl (1879-1940), author of *The Biology of Death* (1922), who demonstrated that aging is the result not of any one factor, but of multiple factors, biological, social, psychological and ecological; the Russian physiologist and experimental psychologist, Ivan Petrovich Pavlov (1849-1936), who demonstrated the importance of the central nervous system in aging, and how the mobility of the nervous process is affected in the old, with the responses sometimes becoming chaotic; and the American psychologist Granville Stanley Hall (1844-1924), author of *Senescence, the Second Half of Life* (1922), who showed how senescence, like adolescence, has physiological and psychological states proper to itself, and that the old are afraid, not so much of death as of the conditions of dying.

From its physiological foundation in pathologic anatomy, the study of aging acquired superstructures ever more spiritual, such as the economic, the sociological, and the psychological, until it was ready for a philosophical complement, enabling us to perceive the place of aging and the aged in our universe and in human existence. A philosophy to answer the question, thus phrased by Seneca: "Is the extremity of life its dregs, or its clearest and purest part?"

Such a philosophy, developing over the centuries, appears to have crystallized in our time. It considers the aged under two aspects, as individuals or as related to society. As individuals it views them again from two positions, which I shall call the "lapsarian" and "ascensionist". As related to society it examines them for still other two viewpoints, which I shall call "associationist" and "dissociationist."

Lapsarianism can be defined as the philosophy for which life progresses to a climax, biological and mental, and then "lapses" or falls into a decline. This philosophy justifies the abhorrence of age found in all societies and can be linked with "agism" (an infelicitous term for an infelicitous phenomenon). Robert Butler, who coined the term in 1968, makes it signify "a process of systematic stereotyping of and discrimination against people because they are old". A proponent of lapsarianism is William Osler, whose work was discussed above. "It is difficult," declares the eminent Canadian physician and medical historian, "to name a great and far-reaching conquest of the mind which has not been . . . done between the ages of twenty five and forty — these fifteen golden years."[9] I am unable to say how far this applies to the speaker, who was well past his golden years when he uttered those memorable words (since he was 56). A more aggressive supporter of this philosophy is Edmund Ronald Leach (1910-   ). "In a changing world," insists the well-known British anthropologist, "where machines have a very short run of life, men must not be used too long. Every one over fifty should be scrapped."[10] The speaker, who was 58 when he pronounced those words, either lacked the intelligence to perceive that he could not be an exception to the scrapping, or the modesty to imagine that he could. The lapsarian logic was enunciated more poetically by Henry de Montherlant (1896-1972). "It has always been said," remarked the French novelist and playwright, who killed himself because he feared blindness, "that a butterfly grows out of a worm. With man, it is the butterfly that grows into a worm." The divine Virgil (70 B.1C.-19 B.C.), expressed a like idea, but more poignantly. "Life's finest days," declared the noblest and saddest of poets, who died in his 52nd year, "fly first for us poor mortals; then follow diseases and sad old age and sufferings; and the unkindness of hard death snatches us away."

Ascensionism maintains that the individual, as a whole, progresses as he ages; that is "ascends" to an ever better state; there are losses, certainly, but they are outnumbered by the gains. This philosophy, again, has two variants, which may be described as the "homologous" and the "lapsarian." *Homologous ascensionism* is, so to speak, homophonic, and signifies that life progressively improves on both physical and mental levels; it seems to be the philosophy of Cornaro, discussed above. *Lapsarian ascensionism,* on the other hand, is contrapuntal; it proclaims the necessity of some biological lapse with aging, but with a distinct possibility of mental improvement or "ascension." "I am not aware," confesses Seneca modestly, that age has harmed my spirit, as it has my body." This seems to be the position of most of the Christian theologians discussed in this chapter, and the most reasonable one to hold.

Associationism, also known as "activism" or the "engagement theory", recommends the elders' continued association with or involvement in society, insisting, with two modern disciples of associationist Lillien Martin, that the truly old are not self-conscious about their happiness; rather, they are absorbed in the joy of their life-work. They are progressively achieving that which gives them happiness, mastering life with enthusiasm, and so life seems good and zestful to them until the end.

Dissociationism, also known as the "disengagement theory," and advanced in our time by Margaret Elaine Cuming (1917-) and William Henry (1913-), holds that the growing adult acquires certain interacting roles in society (such as parent, spouse, child of aging parents, homemaker, worker, user of leisure, club member, church member, friend and citizen). As adulthood changes into age, the individual and society conspire to lessen those roles and their interactions.

Associationism can seemingly be used to justify the ascensionist philosophy only, but dissociationism serves to buttress both it and the lapsarian viewpoint. It can be advanced in support of the forcible removal of the aged from their work at any arbitrary age, say 65, and thus to consign them to possible loneliness and poverty. This is especially true in achievement-oriented activist societies, where to desist from work is to invite failure. But in societies which value leisure and contemplation, and where it is possible for the aged to experience either without forced hardship, dissociationism is the right philosophy to assist the aged in their quest for spiritual perfection or rewarding and fruitful leisure.

Essence, says Suárez, is not really distinct from existence; the difference between them is mainly conceptual. Following this dictum, it is worth our striving to keep the scientific (or essential) and experiential (or existential) aspects of our inquiry into old age together, if we are to rid ourselves of the possibility of falling into the ideal hallucinations of Platonism on the one hand, and the factual imbecillities of positivism on the other. The existential aspect of our problem is best studied in the mystics and the writers (such as poets, novelists, and even philosophers). I shall refer to the mystics later. As for the writers, age had probably nowhere been so celebrated as in the work of Victor Hugo (1802-1885), whom Baudelaire considered "an ass of genius," and whom many French critics claim to be their greatest writer. To him we owe such fine lines as "old age, this august priesthood," and "one sees flame in the eyes of the young, but in the eyes of the old man, one sees fire."

Some of the other great writers of the past that have confronted the problem of aging (with hope, despair, or indifference) are Michel de Montaigne (1533-1592), William Shakespeare (1564-1616), Pierre Corneille (1606-1684), Jonathan Swift (1667-1745), Voltaire (1694-1778), Carlo Goldoni (1707-1793), Pierre-Auguste Beaumarchais (1732-1799), Johann Wolfgang von Goethe (1749-1832), François René Chateaubriand (1768-1848), Charles Dickens

(1812-1870), Ivan Turgenev (1818-1883), Walt Whitman (1818-1892), Fyodor Dostoievsky (1821-1881), Lev Tolstoy (1828-1910), and Emile Zola (1840-1902). Some more recent writers are George Bernard Shaw (1856-1950), Marcel Proust (1871-1922), Thomas Mann (1875-1955), Aldous Huxley (1894-1963), Giuseppe di Lampedusa (1896-1957), Ernest Hemingway (1899-1961), Evelyn Waugh (1903-1966), Arthur Miller (1915-   ) and Muriel Spark (1918-   ). Worthy of notice also are the philosophers John Cowper Powys (1872-1963), author of *The Art of Growing Old* (1943), and Marcel Jouhandeau (1888-   ), author of *Réflexions sur la vieillesse et la mort (Reflections on Old Age and Death,* 1956).

We have traveled far from the Baroque Church. This Church, as I suggested, was witness to the consummation of Scholasticism, the finest creation of man's speculative intellect. But in Scholasticism theology had incorporated "the principles revealed by God" into only one kind of "human discourse and reasoning," the metaphysical: the Scientific Revolution showed that many more truths can be "discerned through the light of nature." Christian thought began to make use of the new disciplines embodying these truths as they became established in their methods and acquired control over their content. For instance, the Rococo Church, successor to the Baroque Church, was strongly influenced by physics, the science which dominated the 17th and 18th centuries, especially in its Newtonian form. Among the new dimensions added to theology by the Rococo Church was the articulation of pastoral theology as an independent branch of sacred learning, as in the work of the Austrian Benedictine Stephen Rautenstrauch (1734-1785). Pastoral theology was elaborated in the following period by the Romantic Church, but I have been able to trace only one work which applied this theology to the problem of aging, J. Ehring's *Des Priesters Greisenalter (The Priest's Old Age,* 1896).

We come now to the Modern Church, which has begun to deal more fully with the problem. However, most of the religious writing on old age (that I have come across) is of a popular consumerish kind, a sort of modernized version of the old devotional writing for the masses. None of it compares in thoroughness and profundity to *La vieillesse (On Old Age,* 1970), by the existentialist philosopher Simone de Beauvoir (1908-   ). Besides the above-mentioned devotional writings, there are also cassetts whereby minor spiritual masters communicate to their disciples their reflections of this subject and on many other topics.

Among the more serious writers who treat of aging in itself, apart from its sole relationship to death, are Joseph Brugerette (Born 1863) (*L'art de vieillir/ The Art of Growing Old,* 1926); the Jesuits John LaFarge (1880-1963) (*Reflections on Growing Old,* 1963), and William Bier (1911-1980) *Aging: Its Challenge to the Individual and Society,* 1974, and *Human Life: Problems of Birth, Living and Dying,* 1977); and the religious psychologist Henri Nouwen *(Aging: the Fulfilment of Life,* 1974).

But all this holds promise for a cogently formulated gerontic spirituality. The theological disciplines, doctrinal, moral, ascetic, pastoral and mystical, have long been in a state of architectonic stability; gerontology, in its many aspects, has attained maturity, and disclosed a wealth of insights and information: it is therefore time to attempt a synthesis, to construct a many-faceted theology of aging, thus providing gerontology with its final, theological, complement. It is not for me to attempt to do this, as I lack competence in gerontology. What I have sought to be, in this chapter, is a systematic theologian, seeking to disclose, in the light of theology, the possible systematic interconnection between the various kinds of knowledge relative to aging available today.

I now turn to the sources which are connected with Christianity ideologically, not historically. As some Christians see it, the religions of the world are found to reflect one aspect or another of their Founder's message. This is especially true of those religions which developed and continue to develop certain aspects of the Christian message better, to my mind, than Christian theology itself.

One of these is Buddhism, which, like Christianity, believes suffering to be central to human existence, and release from that suffering to be salvation. This release may be attained through the efforts of a wholly altruistic being (the Buddha-to-be or Bodhisattva, in Buddhism; the Savior, in Christianity). The fundamental salvific emotion in both religions may be said to be *caring* (unqualified caring, or *love,* mainly for rational beings, in Christianity; caring for all suffering beings, rational or not, or *compassion,* in Buddhism). From the Christian viewpoint, then, Buddhism may be described, in an oversimplified manner, as the "soteriological" dimension of Christianity.

Similarly, with other religions, an attempt can be made to show how, from the Christian point of view, they constitute the several dimensions of Christianity. I shall, however, refer to one other religion, Hinduism. Like Christianity, it affirms the immortality of a human soul destined to find its supreme joy in union with a God who is one and at the same time, in some mysterious way, many. This God has also assumed human form, indeed a servile one, according to Ramanuja (1017/1056-1137),for He is "the god become mortal for the service of the world and overwhelmed by tenderness for His suppliants." Furthermore, supreme joy in God is only attained through His grace, for, as the Vedic Revelation (Katha Upanished) proclaims, "only by one whom He chooses can He be attained." Hinduism may accordingly be described, also over-simplistically, as Christianity's "theological" dimension. However, it must also be emphasized that these religions have dimensions of their own which in no way accord with Christianity.

3. Christian Strength for the Aged

> *The crown of our Monarch is a crown of thorns; the splendor which flashes from it is afflictions and sufferings. It is in the poor, it is in those who suffer, that the majesty of this spiritual kingdom abides.*
>
> BOUSSUET [11]

Is there then "a spiritual vigor, which, renewed and strengthened from day to day, does not permit the soul to feel the decrepitude of age?" Yes, replies Bossuet; "it was this interior youthfulness which sustained" the worn-out limbs of St. François de Paule (who was believed to have died at the age of 91 in 1507, "in his decrepit old age, and enabled him to continue his penance up to the end of his life."

It is the ascetic and mystical theology of the Baroque Church, perhaps better than any other in the history of Christianity, which permits us to outline a spirituality of aging — especially the teaching of Jean Pierre de Caussade, itself a synthesis of significant trends in Baroque spirituality. This teaching enables us to indicate what we may call a heroic solution to the problems of age, an element of it having to be present even in non-heroic solutions if they are to be at all effective.

The motifs of this teaching are basic to Christianity. God is all; the creature, nothing. Prevented from perceiving this truth by its blindness, the creature (meaning man) remains self-centered through an inordinate self-love. An affront to the majesty of God, this self-love is the source of the creature's suffering. This suffering is used by God to destroy its cause, self-love; the creature can best co-operate by unreserved surrender — whereby it attains interior peace and spiritual perfection.

Its emphasis on the centrality of pain in human experience and on self-love's being its basis, makes Christianity accordant with that other, and older, doctrine of universal suffering, Buddhism. The first Noble Truth of the Buddhist faith is that all is *pain:* birth is pain, aging is pain, sickness is pain, and death is pain. Its second Noble Truth is that *craving* is the cause of pain; its third Noble Truth, that the *suppression* of craving is liberation or nirvana; and its fourth Noble Truth, that the *way* towards the attainment of this suppression is the Buddha's teaching. Craving is rooted in the "self" or "soul" (or, as the Christians might put it, in "self-centeredness" or "self-love"). In the words of Santideva, the lyrical theologian of Buddhist mysticism, "one cannot do away with suffering unless one does away with the soul, just as one cannot do away with burning unless one does away with fire. So, for calming my own suffering and for quieting that of others, I shall give up my soul for them, and take them for my own soul."12

Christianity's nirvana is realized through an unqualified submission to God's will. "One thing alone is important in heaven and earth, in time and eternity," exclaims Tomé de Jesus, the Portuguese Augustinian mystic, "that the divine Will be done in everything for its honor and glory, and that one should desire this, according as one understands it, with humble submission. Here is the fountain of all the good things which we can justly hope from God, and the remedy and cure of all the evils which render human life heavy and perilous, as well as of the quieting of the human heart in all the changes and disorders of life."13

Its emphasis on unreserved trust in God (whose shared inner life is our supreme joy) makes Christianity accordant with the other, and older, doctrine of a beatifying and unreservedly trustworthy God, Hinduism. "The supreme Lord of all beings abides in the heart, Arjuna," proclaims Krsna. God incarnate, in the *Gita;* "trust Him alone with all your being, and by His grace you will attain supreme peace, the eternal state."

For both religions, God embodies humanity. But for Christianity, He also embodies human pain, since He is a God who was hung on a cross and buried in a tomb. A like pain has to be ours if we are to attain His pain-free glory. "All sensible things need the Cross", declares Maximus the Confessor, who died when he was 82, of martyrdom, not of old age; "all *sensible* things need the Cross, that is, of a state which checks their inclination towards all that is activated by the senses. And all *intelligible* things need the Tomb, that is, a total immobility in them of all that is activated by the mind. Then, in the condition where all activity and movement towards things is completely destroyed, flashes the Logos, alone, springing from among them as though coming to life from the dead."

Let us return to Caussade's teaching and examine how he varies the fundamental Christian motifs of which it is composed. Six motifs may be distinguished. First, that *God is everything, and the creature nothing.* All creation is as though obliterated by the sovereign majesty and grandeur of God. All that the creature is has issued out of the bosom of the divine plenitude, through creation, and so belongs entirely to God. It must therefore by right be returned to Him by a free act of surrender on the part of the rational creature. But the creature is unable to make this surrender without God's help, and still needs that help to thank God when the surrender has been made. Thus man's soul and his faculties are lost in the abyss of his dependence, which takes him towards his annihilation, and thus to his natural state, nothing.

Second, *the human creature, by its self-centeredness, implicitly rejects God's sole title to glory.* This self-centeredness is motivated by its self-love; it prompts the creature not to surrender, and is the cause of its unhappiness. The self-love is delicate, imperceptible, and subtly present in all the creature's actions, even in those inspired by grace itself. The poisonous root of the creature's self-complacency, self-love is a profound inner abyss of perversity, a chaos of corruption, but unseen by the creature through its blindness.

Third, *God's mercy wills to disclose this corruption to the creature through the apposite therapy of suffering.* It is the lancet (never more poignant than in age) that punctures the consuming abscess of self-love. The ensuing putridity is horrifying to the creature; it is a sight too humiliating and afflicting for any self-love and pride to withstand. The soul is plunged into a state of dryness, anguish and obscurity, and is permitted to remain so long enough to realize its own impotence, and total dependence on God. It rebels against this treatment, though still wishing God to sdanctify it (not in God's way, but according to its own ideas and taste). However, the anguish it suffers is not a sign of its rebellion, but of the greatness of its sacrifice. Through this anguish the soul dies to all the things of the sense, and arises with Christ to a new life.

Fourth, *the soul's response to this treatment has to be one of total surrender.* Blind submission to the orders of Providence are our only source of peace in this unhappy life. So the soul is not to resist God's action, but to allow itself to be humbled and annihilated. Like delirious patients we plead for an end to our painful but life-saving treatment, but God, the good doctor, pays no heed. It is therefore best to bear these trials in patience, for impatience only doubles them. These trials bring us to a state of abjection; we must love this abjection for God's sake, and that makes it a great spiritual treasure, for it keeps us in profound humility. And what are these trials? They are ailments of the body (never more afflicting than in age), and they are sometimes incurable, but they serve to detach us from ourselves; they are vexations and woes of the mind (the frequent companions of age), which restrain us from clinging to any sort of comfort derived from the senses, so that we are held to God alone in pure faith. These trials can lead us to despair, but the moment of hopelessness is one of the greatest hope, for then we can hope in nothing but in God, who never fails. Indeed, the conviction of our misery is a sign of our spiritual advancement, and a substitute, at least in part, for the unimaginably greater pains of purgatory. Yet the way of suffering is not a difficult and heroic way. It is the center of a solid peace, and gives us an unalterable repose that is proof against all reverses. We are more than well paid for the paltry sacrifices that we make for God, but as we keep making them, the need to make them ceases, for then we have nothing left to sacrifice but God —for whose sake the sacrifices were made. Also, one must not go out of one's way to seek suffering. What Providence sends suffices; all one is expected to do is to accept without complaint. Hence ordinary Christian patience, applied to life's ordinary situations, can help us achieve extraordinary perfection. Indeed, this suffering has to be undergone in an ordinary way, not grandly and courageously, but in a small and humble manner, almost as though one were about to be crushed by it. Great courage is apt to inflate one's self-love, to fill one with interior pride and presumption, instead of promoting a sense of one's smallness and frailty before God.

Fifth, *God's grace supports our surrender.* To the degree that one abandons everything for God alone, even the feeblest soul is sustained, though it may not be aware of the support. God by Himself makes up for all our sensed deficiencies, when we show any confidence in Him — a truth which is ignored by many devout people. This support does not always take the form of a cheering mental uplift. The soul is always in God's presence, but in a dry and even unconscious manner: it is then that the sense of one's inner misery begins to produce humility and a great distrust in oneself. It is then that the peace of pure suffering is attained, the peace of God which is free of fear and illusion. This peace, and the surrender and the self-annihilation which lead to it, is the best preparation for receiving the sacraments, sources of the grace that promote and sustain the surrender, especially the sacrament of Christ's own self-annihilation, the Eucharist, for it is there that He veils not only His divinity, but His humanity as well. In our surrender to God, Christ crucified is our model. He wishes to save us through our similarity to His suffering self, and sows crosses on the paths of each of us. Besides the example of Christ, the incarnate God, we have that of the Virgin Mary, the Mother of God, the most simple and abandoned of souls. The surrender expressed in her reply to the angel, "As you have spoken, so be it," is the height of mystical theology. She also exemplifies the ordinary character of the way of suffering, for it was in the most ordinary things that she recalled the works of God.

Sixth, and last, *the surrender is rewarded by divine joy.* As the creature is annihilated through being emptied of all created things, it acquires a great capacity for divine love, now lavishly poured on it. At once satiated and thirsty, the heart drinks this love at its source in long draughts, being inundated, overflowing, and inebriated by it; and set on fire by love's most pure and divine flames.

God afflicts the saints with the mystical agonies that lead to this reward at all times, but mostly in youth and maturity, since few saints have lived to be very old. While the desolateness and excruciation of body and mind experienced by God's sufferers is at least as great as that felt by the stricken aged, yet, as youths and adults, they have with them their natural faculties and powers of endurance which age, at its worst, would have deprived them. "The great part of our devotion in youth," observes Newman, who lived to be 89 and who was already experiencing physical decline at 58, "our faith, hope, cheerfulness, perseverance, is natural —or, if not natural, it is from a *euphuia* which does not resist grace, and requires very little grace to illuminate." The same grace goes much further in youth as encountering less opposition — that is, in the virtues which I have mentioned. The Greek poet (Sophocles), himself an old man, speaks (in the Chorus of the *Oedipus Coloneus*) of the unamiable state of the aged. Old men are in soul as stiff, as lean, as bloodless as their bodies, except so far as grace penetrates and softens them. And it requires a flooding of grace to do this. I more and more wonder at *old* saints. St. Aloysius (Gonzaga, 1568-1591, patron of youth, died aged 23), or St. Francis Xavier (1506-1552, died aged 46), are nothing to St. Philip (Neri, 1515-1595, founder of the Oratory, Newman's order, died aged 80). "O Philip, gain me some little portion of thy fervour. I live more and more in the past, and in hopes that the past may revive in the future."

Caussade's method of facing up to afflictions, including those of age is not, as we have seen, heroic from the viewpoint of his own exalted spirituality "illuminated by the heavenly light," which makes one "think differently from the generality of men; yet, what a source of peace, what resources does one not find in this manner of considering and envisaging things! O, how happy the saints are, and how calm their lives! And O, how miserable we are, and blind and senseless, not to wish to accustom ourselves to think like them, and to prefer to remain buried in the thick darkness of the accursed human wisdom, which makes us as unhappy as blind and culpable!"

These are the words of Caussade, as modest as he was sublime; they may not apply to him, but they do to most of us, who lack the spiritual stamina to live out our purgatory in this life. We are therefore to be permitted to live in accord with the demands of self-love, though within Christian moral bounds. And if our means, and the state of our body and mind render this task burdensome (and old age itself a painful load), then we have a right to aid from our fellows, according to Paul's command: "Help one another to carry these loads, and in this you will fulfil the law of Christ." (Gal. 6:2)

Yet, before the elderly await help from others, they must help themselves, if they are at all solicitous not to reinforce the popular view of old age as decrepit and helpless. This is especially true of our time, when there are more aged persons than in previous times. An excellent state of affairs, thinks Cicero, for, declares the great orator, speaking of his own time, "few people live to old age; but if it were otherwise, life would be better and more prudently lived. For sense and judgment and prudence are found in the old." What better way to use these excellent qualities than in the defense of one's rights, particularly as there is so little to fear if one does! "Aged of the wold," we might say, "unite, you have nothing to lose but your lives."

But the aged who are unable to help themselves have, as I said, a right to be helped by their fellows, in this case youths and adults, most of all in the matter of vindicating their rights, particularly if the helpers themselves will profit from the vindication when their own time comes. These are rights to the good things of life, familial, cultural, economical and political, rights ultimately supervised and protected by the state through the appropriation of power and the exercise of justice. However, through man's fallen nature, power is frequently corrupted and justice violated. And "with justice removed," queries Augustine, "what are states but big robberies? And indeed, what are robberies themselves, except small states?" As for the corrupted power, it gives rise to a class of people who have a greater share in it, the privileged, and to those who share less of it or none at all, the underprivileged. In the latter class fall the poor, including the aged, who have been called "the new poor."

So prone has society based on power been to corruption, that the only way to eradicate this evil seems to have been to create a society based more on concern for its members, than on power over them; a society where the underprivileged become the holders of privilege, and the privileged those deprived of it. This society is Christ's Church: it has often been false to its ideal, when corrupted by power.

Traducement of ideal in Church and State is to be owed not so much to the fallibility of the ideal itself, as to that of the human creature intended to be exalted by it. "From among the animals," exclaims Bossuet, "man is the one most made for concord; and, from among the animals, man is the one where enmity and hatred produce the bloodiest tragedies. We cannot live without society; and we cannot long endure in it." There is no way whereby an institution can guarantee that its ideals will be followed; such depends on its members' free decision. But, granting that the will to follow those ideals exists, an institution with nobler objectives can be said to exalt man more than an institution with less noble ones.

No ideal can be higher than the Church's, ordered as it is to the perfection of the spiritual life, one consisting in the exercise of the noblest of virtues, a virtue which binds us most intimately to God, charity, or love. "The perfection of anything," affirms Suarez, "is its union with its ultimate goal; but our ultimate goal is God, made known to us by faith; therefore our perfection consists in union with God." Charity, which unites us to God, is the ideal of the Church; it is also the perfection of the ideal of the State, justice, for it is, in Augustine's words, "the truest, fullest and most perfect justice".

Yet charity reverses another ideal of the state, power, the origin of political pride and privilege. The kingdom of God, the Church, was created to abrogate both, and to ensure that "the first will be last, and the last first." This was done through the kingdom being founded on the poor and the underprivileged, with its own privileges denied to those held in esteem by the world. "The graces of the New Testament," emphasizes Bossuet, "belong by right to the poor, and the rich do not receive them except through the hands of the poor." The power and pomp of the State is wholly exterior, whilst "all the glory of Holy Church is hidden and interior." "In the promises of the Gospel He no longer speaks of temporal benefits," continues Bossuet. "Jesus Christ has put afflictions and crosses in their place, and by this marvellous alteration the last have become first, and the first last." The God of the New Testament is not one who appeared in glory, but in the form of a servant; hence "the Church, His mystical body, needed to be an image of His lowness, and to bear on herself the mark of His voluntary annihilation." In this new spiritual kingdom, truly "the city of the poor," the underprivileged are the privileged ones, because of their nearness to Jesus Christ. For "it belongs to the majesty of the State and to the grandeur of its sovereign that the splendor flashing from his crown should in some fashion reflect on those that draw near him . . . The crown of our Monarch is a crown of thorns: the splendor that flashes from it is afflictions and sufferings. It is in the poor, it is among those who suffer, that the majesty of this spiritual kingdom abides."

Yet the world's underprivileged, who are no less human than its privileged ones, constantly suffer dehumanization. "What an injustice, my brothers," cries Bossuet, "that the poor bear all the burden, and that all the weight of misery should fall on their shoulders! If they complain, and if they murmur against divine Providence, Lord, permit me to say that it is with some semblance of justice. For as all of us are kneaded from the same mass, and as there cannot be much difference between mud and mud, why is it than on the one side we see gladness, favor and affluence, and on the other, sadness, despair, extreme want, and even contempt and servitude? . . . In this strange inequality could one acquit Providence of having badly managed the treasures which God places among equals if, through another way, it had not provided for the needs of the poor? It is for this reason, Christians, that He has established His Church, where He receives the rich, but on condition that they serve the poor, where He ordains that abundance make up for deficiency."

How is the Church to aid the underprivileged of society, among them the new poor, the aged? By seeking to transform society through the growth of more equitable social structures, if necessary by confrontation with the State, as has been done, with some success, in Poland and parts of Latin America. There the Church has challenged the tyranny of two of the vilest systems of oppression ever contrived for the oppression of man, communism and capitalism.

But human social structures cannot be entirely devoid of justice. The Church must therefore seek to work through them while more equitable ones are being devised. Both pastors and laity can help the Church in this task. According to the teaching of Vatican II, it is the special responsibility of the pastors clearly to enunciate the Church's teaching about the finality of creation, and about the ways in which the world is to be used (and not abused), and also to provide moral and spiritual assistance. The Christian wisdom thus enunciated has to be applied by the laity. It belongs to the lay state to be present in the temporal order, to assume its affairs, and to intervene in them directly and definitely, in accordance with the teachings of Christ and His Church.

Service to the world and to all in it can be on an individual and social level. Such service, or apostolate, originates of necessity on an individual level, from which its organized or social level of expression rises. It consists, among other things, in the Christian testimony proclaimed by one's words, and by one's life lived in its familial, professional, cultural and social functions in accord with the loftier motives of faith. But man is also social in nature. It has pleased God to proclaim salvation through the world through an organized body of believers, the Church. The apostolate is one expression of the Church's social nature, and can be exercised on the level of family, parish, diocese, nation and world.

The family starts with the conjugal partnership, the beginning and basis of human society, and the domestic sanctuary of the Church. One might almost say that to strengthen the family is to assure its members a happy old age. "Do you have a wife," inquires Chrysostom, "do you have children? What joy can compare with these?" Accordingly, a generation that leaves its children in the hands of indifferent baby sitters must not be surprised if it finds itself abandoned to the mercies of even more indifferent grandpa sitters, and perhaps of no sitters of any kind.

While the family is the cell of human society, the parish is the cell of the diocese, itself the universal Church in its local form. Gathering together the human diversity found in a further particularized area of the diocese, the parish draws it into the ambit of the universal Church. And it is with the parish as basis, but extending from it to the diocesan and national level, that the pastors and laity, in close cooperation, can best serve the aged, in whom they see Christ Himself. First, in their *economic needs,* working to assure them a decent retirement income, or, better still, ways of earning money, like part-time jobs or hobbies for profit, so that the elderly may not be more of an economic burden to society than they need to be. They must also be protected from consumer fraud and quackery. A decent income in old age will make for clean and pleasant housing which assures them some privacy, affordable, and they will be able to afford to live in institutions which will not exploit or discriminate against them. Second, in their *social needs,* such as recreation, the company of friendly visitors, and physical and psychological safeguards against crime. Third, in their *medical and psychiatric needs,* whether these require hospitalization or not, including nursing care provided by trained, motivated and supervised staff.

Fourth, and in a way the most important, in the defense of their *political rights,* whereby the fulfilment of all their other needs will be assured. Christian service will here consist in working to establish a program of adequate standardized care for the aged. This cannot be realized unless a clear political philosophy aiming to change or improve public policy on aging is evolved and generally accepted. And while it is being evolved there will be need to use legal action and moral persuasion to represent the elders grievances and needs. The formation of political organizations of the elderly will allow them to be their own best advocates. And the cogency of this advocacy will of course depend on the development of gerontological research.

From the national level Christian service, appropriately modified, must extend to the world. For, "although the human race is divided among various peoples and states," in words of Suárez, the most illustrious disciple of Francisco de Victoria (1480-1546), the founder of international law, "it always retains a certain unity which is not only specific, but also in a sense political and moral, a unity proclaimed by the natural precept of mutual love and compassion extending to all, even to strangers, and of whatever condition. Hence, though any autonomous commonwealth, republic, or kingdom is in itself a complete community, and one dependent on its own members, still, any of these political communities is also in a way a member of this world, in so far as it pertains to the human race. For they will never be individually so totally sufficient to themselves that they will not need some reciprocal aid, fellowship and communication, sometimes for a better life and greater advantage, sometimes indeed out of moral necessity and need."[14]

Such reciprocal aid, fellowship and communication cannot be attained without "professional skill, family and civic spirit, and the virtues leading to social behavior, namely, honesty, the spirit of justice, sincerity, kindness, and courage, without which there can be no true Christian life.

"The perfect example of this type of spiritual and apostolic life is the most Blessed Virgin Mary, the Queen of the Apostles. While on earth she led a life common to all persons, one filled with family cares and labors, but was always intimately in union with her Son, and cooperated in the Savior's work in an exceptionally unique way. Now that she has been assumed into heaven, 'with her maternal charity she cares for the brothers of her Son who are still on their earthly pilgrimage and are surrounded by dangers and difficulties — until they are led to their blessed fatherland' ". (Vatican II)

Notes

I dedicate this essay to my sister, Victoria Epiphania, who has devoted her life to the care of our ailing parents, Alexio Francisco and Esmeralda Rosa, now in their eighties. All translations by the author. Scripture quotes are from the Revised Standard Version.

1. Augustine. *De civitate Dei.* Lib. 10, cap. 32, n.1.
2. Augustine. *De doctrina christiana.* Lib. 2, cap. 8, n. 28.
3. Matrceta. *Varnahavarnastava.* Ch. 7, v. 17.
4. John Henry Newman. *An Essay on the Development of Christian Doctrine.* London, 1906, ch. 8, pp. 356-7.
5. Francisco Suarez. *Disputationes Metaphysicae..* Proemium.
6. John Chrysostom. *Ad oppugnatores vitae monasticae.* Migne, *PG* 47:379.
7. John Chrysostom. *In Epistolam ad Hebraeos.* Cap. 4, homilia 7. Migne, *PG* 63:66.

8. Robert M. Butler. *Why Survive? Being Old in America.* New York, 1975, p. 12.
9. *William Osler. Aequanimitas, with Other Addresses to Medical Students, Nurses, and Practitioners of Medicine.* "The Fixed Period," Third Edition, Philadelphia, 1932. pp. 381-2.
10. Leach, quoted by Simone de Beauvoir. *La vieillesse.* Paris, 1970. p. 12.
11. Bossuet. *Sermon sur l'eminente dignité des pauvres dans l'Eglise.*
12. Santideva. *Bodhicaryavatara.* ch. 8, vv. 135-36.
13. Tome de Jesus. *Trabalhos de Jesus,* Carta . . . A Nacao Portuguesa.
14. Suárez. *De legibus.* Lib. 2, cap. 19, n. 9.

The Art of Aging According to the Monastic Tradition

M. C. Cymbalista, O.S.B. and
Jean Leclercq, O.S.B.

The monastic tradition does not hold the monopoly of either the aged or a doctrine on the art of aging. Thus when we turn to this tradition for a doctrine on the subject, we must sift out from the elements common to humanity in general and Christians in particular those which are specific to the monastic way of life which aims at fostering the personal growth of individuals living the common life with a stress on asceticism and the search for God in prayer. Thus our principal source of information and reflection is to be sought in the history and literature of the past as well as in the present-day reality of monastic life. Inspiration and encouragement for all can be found in the experience being *lived* by old monks and nuns and those who care for them in the ever increasing number of monastic infirmeries. Such encouragement and inspiration will be all the greater if the facts are considered from a triple standpoint: personal, communitarian and contemplative.*

Aging in Joy

All Christians are bound to seek God in self-renunciation. But the monastic way of doing so, that is to say, monastic ascesis, is a privileged school for whoever wants to learn to age without growing old, that is, to advance in years and yet remain young. And indeed, what does it mean, essentially to be young and to remain so. It is to have some part in the eternal youth of God, He who can never grow old because He is unfailing spontaneity, the total gift of self to self, within the Trinity, and to others, to every creature —angelic, human, cosmic — which He ceaselessly brings or maintains in existence. Youthfulness is to be like God mainly through a constant effort to see everything through His eyes, and thus have the sense of an ever-springing sourcefulness, a sense of admiration and wonder. To be young is to be untireingly generous, like God, in the gift of self, open-hearted to others, relaxed and unanguished,

---

*These pages are largely inspired by the article of Reverend Mother Ma Candida Cymbalista, O.S.B., *Reflexiones sobre el enverecimiento, in Cuadernos monasticas,* ano VI, n. 29, oct-dec. 1971, p. 185-202. That is why they will be signed with her name as well as with that of the present author.

in total receptivity, with never a look to self, without calculation or fear, in an attitude of inner abandon to every possible surprise that God may have in store for us, rejoicing in the gift brought by every present, fleeting moment of time.

To live thus after a long experience of the human condition supposes being detached from the past, free from all that we once were, from all that we dreamt of being or doing, free too from all that we really have accomplished, all that we have suffered, all that we have omitted doing, free from any nostalgia, illusions or false hopes for the future, having no other perspective but God alone. This is true even though throughout life we have taken some hard knocks, and received deep wounds, some of which are more or less healed, and we have known frustrations. The art of aging is the art of going beyond all that, and if we cannot forget, at least forgive, thus retaining our *inner freedom,* our inner wholeness entirely directed to the final encounter with the one Whom we come to seek: GOD. All monastic ascetisicm is a journey and we are all travellers buoyed up by that reassuring final word of the Rule of St. Benedict: *pervenies*: you will get there.

Old Age, An Age for Love

The monastic life is lived by Christians who have freely chosen to live in this way with brothers and sisters who are not those of human kith and kin but of God who, in his love, has called each and all to live in the unity of the same community, persevering throughout life in stability of love and life. Thus it is essential to the very nature of a monastic community that young and old should live side by side. St. Benedict sums up the respective duties of these two age-groups in a single compact phrase: "respect the elders; love the young" (RB 63.10). St. Benedict knew well enough that in a monastic community, more than elsewhere, by reason of longer coexistence, there will be conflicts arising from the close proximity of different generations separated by the span of years, but destined to live together in mutual acceptance. Thus he dares to propose the utopia of a society marked by the absence of conflict between generations and where all live in reciprocal consent and service.

This presupposes that the older members be entirely integrated with the whole social framework. Such integration depends on old and young alike.

On the part of the young, it implies a deep conviction and incurs certain duties. The conviction is that the older members witness to monastic life and have a value tested by time, that they have a common destiny and grace, even though they may no longer have the same efficacy, the same type of "usefulness" as in their younger days. The temptation for the younger members is often to marginalize their older brethren, to eliminate them by tacit consent from community discussion and decisions. Old and young are of equal importance, and it requires a vision of faith on both sides. This is one of the joys of stability. The respect which St. Benedict requires the younger to show towards the elders is an attitude of religious *reverence* for the mystery of life which God gives to every human being at all stages of development, either in growth or in decline, especially, and above all in decline.

Elsewhere (ch. 37), St. Benedict asks that we have an attitude of "kind consideration" towards children and the aged. Both categories are in a state of weakness in comparison with the energy of the adult age. Since the time when the all-powerful God deigned to become poor and feeble in his incarnate Son, every human being who is in such a state witnesses to the presence of God among us. The "consideration" which St. Benedict asks for does not, as he points out in the same chapter, derive from a natural and spontaneous tendency: it is the fruit of thought and reflection in prayer in the presence of God. St. Benedict uses the word "piety" in this context. In the tradition in which he lived, "piety" meant the feeling which a child had for his parents. It entails love and affection, and in the context of St. Benedict, it also means "mercy," that is to say, *compassion*. It is something more than mere respect and has nothing to do with cold, indifferent, calculating reflection, the fruit of abstract reasoning on the relativity of time and human strength. It is a veneration which leads us to incline with our hearts towards another person, towards all others, especially those who are more dependent on their milieu.

An attitude like this is not necessarily natural, spontaneous, or easy, especially towards someone who has not been able to age harmoniously, one who is difficult and fosters friction between his own generation and the following ones. And it may even happen that the community has to discuss the problem raised by the presence of such older members. Whatever may be the situation, an effort must be made to facilitate the declining years of the aged.

On the other hand, the elders must not take advantage of their age, their seniority, experience or wisdom. They must be careful not to assert themselves, imposing upon others. That is part of their particular *ascesis,* as we have already seen. It is up to them to accept the fact that they have entered upon a stage of life in which they may suffer from physical or psychological diminishment and may thus even be a burden to others. And if by chance the contribution made by one of the older members is negative or even downright destructive, then he must be told so frankly but kindly. He in his turn must have enough humility to accept this being pointed out to him. Thus he will advance in the process of his monastic conversion.

The anonymous author of a treatise written for monastic novices wrote: "If the old do not always give you the good example you expect, go to the chapel, look at the statues, the paintings, the stained-glass windows, and there you will see saints." However, even if the elders are not always models to be imitated, they are nevertheless witnesses to fidelity in spite of many difficulties of which the mystery is known to God alone. The witness to fidelity given by an elder is one of the reasons why such a monk is often included in the group sent out to found a new monastery. He will probably not be of much help for the hard labour, but without him there would be no foundations, no roots in tradition. Benefitting by his presence, the younger founding monks will be able to build on the rock of a witness to experience and fidelity, and such a witness is of more value than their own rentability, however useful and necessary this may be.

St. Benedict writes that God often reveals to the youngest member what is the best thing to be done (ch. 3.3). This statement alone should suffice to remind the older members that they are not the only ones to have the gift of wisdom. But they too have their particular grace and the revelation of what they can do for the younger members is perhaps simply that they must show them the same *patience* that God shows to all — young and old alike — the patience which they themselves have had with life and in their milieu. The important thing in St. Benedict's eyes is that everyone, whatever his age, be for the others a *sign* of the presence of God, of his action in our existences, and in this sense each one is a sign of God's word, constantly sought after, listened to and obeyed in loving welcome as being a special call coming from God, even though it may come to us through his more humble members, even the more humiliated ones.

Such convictions, common to all, must lead to certain concrete and practical attitudes in daily life, beyond the pale and possibility of legislation, but springing up from that inventive love poured into our hearts by the Holy Spirit. Similar attitudes have been evoked in the *Beatitudes of the friends of the old* recently printed in several monastic publications:

> Blessed are they who support my uncertain steps and my paralysed hands.
>
> Blessed are they who understand that my ears can't quite catch what is said.
>
> Blessed are they who see that my eyes are dim and my mind is weakened.
>
> Blessed are they who do not see when my coffee has been spilt on the table.
>
> Blessed are they who, with a joyful smile, have time to chat for a while.
>
> Blessed are they who are not always saying 'You're telling me that for the twentieth time.'
>
> Blessed are they who know the art of remembering old days.
>
> Blessed are they who tell me with kindness that I am loved, respected and not alone.
>
> Blessed are they who can see that I am nearing the end of my strength to carry the cross.
>
> Blessed are they who make life a bit easier in our last journey, by their love.

Aging, Joy and Hope

A perfect model for those seeking to end their days in a contemplative manner is to be found in the first pages of the Gospel of St. Luke, chapter 2, verses 36-38. "There was a prophetess, Anna . . . she was of a great age . . . She was eighty-four. She did not depart from the temple, worshipping with fasting and prayer night and day . . . she gave thanks to God." And a little earlier on in this same chapter (2, 25-32) we read about the "Old man Simeon," as the Liturgy calls him. St. Luke writes that "he was looking for the consolation of Israel, and the Holy Spirit was upon him . . . and inspired by the Spirit he came into the temple."

Anna fasted. The original meaning of fasting is moderation in eating. St. Benedict recommends that the same severity in matters of food should not be applied to old people as to adults. But fasting is also, and above all, a spiritual attitude: it consists in being able to be modest, discreet, willingly passing unnoticed. I remember an old monk of whom another said "He always seemed to apologize for being alive." The spiritual attitude of fasting means renouncing every form of self-assertion, not drawing attention to one's self, not seeking to be in the limelight or to be spectacular; not affecting to be the 'wise old man,' nor pretend to have an answer to every question. There is nothing more annoying than a remark such as "Believe me: I am an old priest." Rather than take pride in our past, we must look to the future, eternity. Anna and Simeon did not take pride in relating their life story, but they were totally and solely preoccupied with the future, looking forward to HIM Who was to come, the coming one. The best witness that old people can give to the young, those who are still looking forward to an earthly future, is to encourage them to turn their eyes to true and lasting realities, which will not fade with the passing of time. This does not mean that they are to anticipate or make provision for the future. Anna and Simeon prophetised not because they announced things to come, but because they discovered God under the veil of the present. We must all be in a state of expectancy and consent to receive God's revelation of Himself at every age of life, in the midst of every weakness and frailty. Thus doing, we shall lovingly and joyfully, with simplicity submit to the laws of life with, for some of us, its ineluctable process of aging.

St. Benedict asks that we "desire eternal life with great spiritual desire" (ch. 4.46). This precept for monks applies to every Christian, but very specially to the aged who have to accept to 'pass on' in hope and in joyful expectation of death knowing that when it comes it will be for them a leap into light. They must kindle and keep alive within their hearts a burning curiosity to see at long last, Him whom they have loved and served without ever having seen: in death we shall come face to face with Him who is the Resurrection and the Life — the risen Lord, the Living One. The Church uses in her prayer this verse of psalm 103: "Send forth thy Spirit and all will be re-crated: you will renew the face of the earth." To be constantly docile to the Holy Spirit and His 'inspiration,' as were Anna and Simeon, is to grow old in a rejuvenating way. It is to believe that God alone is ALL and that He alone can fill us, for we are incapable of satisfying ourselves; to adore, in silence and admiration, to sing with praise and thanksgiving: such is *graceful* aging. Anna, Simeon, St. Benedict, all three teach us the *joy* of such aging: the happiness of advanced age, of terminal age, not merely because it is inevitable, but for the good reason that old age is one of God's many gifts to man.

An Age to Love and Be Loved

The monastic tradition reminds us that the old need more than simply material care, social security, medical doctors or experts in geriatrics. The physical and spiritual difficulties of old age must not be neglected. The old need to be consoled, encouraged, entertained, they need to feel that they are understood and that their presence among us means something to us, something that we value and cherish. If the witness of the elderly is apparently useless, it must be remembered that it is often a silent, recollected, patient and sometimes suffering presence lived in joyful acceptance of the will of God, in contemplation of His Word and His words, in prayer for the younger monks. And if these latter serve the elderly with gentle care, then all members of our great human family, young and old together, will present to God the witness of what he most desires: LOVE.[1]

[1] In order to help seniors in their life of presence to God and to aid the entire world, three monasteries of three different countries have recently published, in letters which are readable even for old eyes, a volume of "Prayers for the Third Age" (*Recueil De Prières Pour Le Troisième "Age"*) in which beautiful texts adapted to aging Christians are mixed with other ones which are valuable for all: *Prières de Toujours. Une Réalisation Des Abbayes De Clervaux, Hautecombe et Saint-André. Textes Rassemblés Par Le Frère Henri Delhougne Del'Abbaye De Clervaux,* Luxembourg (Eb. Brepols, Turnhout: Belgium, 1979).

[2] For further information, please write:
Ma Candida Cymbalista, O.S.B.
Monasterio Gaudium Mariae
5153 San Antonio di Arrerbondo
Cordoba, Rep. Aiyentina
    and
Jean Leclercq, O.S.B.
Abbaye
L. 9737. Clervaux
Luxembourg

The Aging in Islam

Muhammad Abdul-Rauf

Does Islam assign a special status to elderly people, with a special set of roles, rights and privileges? Before attempting to answer this question it is pertinent to start off with a definition of the term "Islam" as it will help in the discussion of the theme of this article.

Islam is the religion proclaimed by the Prophet Muhammad in Mecca, his own birthplace, in A.D. 610, calling for devoting worship and loyalty to the One True God, the Creator and Sustainer of all mankind. Islam also taught respect for human dignity and called for other basic rights due to each human person, man or woman. Islam also taught that this life on earth was merely transitory, and a stage or a path leading to a more meaningful and lasting life during which every person will be rewarded and graded according to his or her deeds during his or her earthly life.

Mecca, then a prosperous commercial city midway on the vital caravan route between Yemen and Syria, was the capital of Arabian polytheism with a proud aristocratic class who summarily rejected Islam and vehemently opposed its Prophet, because of the call to human equality and the insult to their ancestral idols. The stiff opposition and outrageous persecution compelled Muhammad and his followers who had dared to embrace Islam to leave Mecca after thirteen years of hard struggle and forebearance. In spite of a series of military campaigns waged against their new town, Medina, Mecca capitulated in A.D. 630, and the whole of Arabia was soon united under the banner of the new religion. Within a few decades after the death of the Prophet in 632, Islam became an empire, absorbing the territories from the Atlantic to the borders of China. The number of Muslims today is said to approach one billion.

An important thing we have to bear in mind about Islam is that it recognizes the validity of the mission of the Holy Prophets who preceded the Prophet Muhammad. Each adherent of Islam, called Muslim, has to recognize twenty-five of them by name, including Adam, Noah, Abraham, Joseph, Moses and Jesus. The Virgin Mary, Mother of Jesus, is believed to be the most virtuous and meritorious woman among all nations. Muslims also have to acknowledge past Scriptures, and particularly recognize the Torah, the Psalms and the Gospels. Jews and Christians are of a special status in Islam and are called People of the Book. To summarize the Islamic doctrine, it consists of five beliefs: God and His Attributes; belief in His Angels, His Prophets, His Scriptures and the Hereafter.

Although the earthly life is transitory and a preparatory stage to the Hereafter, it has to be filled with human activities to meet the spiritual and material needs of the individual and society. These activities, whether domestic, personal, communal, economic, political, ritual or recreational, have to comply with the guidance of Islam. In other words, no human activity should violate the divine guidance of God, since Islam is a total way of life aiming at achieving the best for humanity.

A feature of the Islamic teachings is that each person is responsible for his/her deeds only. An action of a person will be counted for him or against him alone. Obedience is a virtue, and disobedience is a sin. No concept of Original Sin is recognized in Islam.

All Islamic teachings and guidance are enshrined, explicitly or implicitly, specifically or generally, in an Islamic sacred book called *Al-Qur'an*. This Holy Book, in the Arabic tongue, was revealed by God to the Prophet Muhammad through the Archangel Gabriel. It came down in pieces over the 23-year period of the mission of the Prophet. It was revealed to him orally, word by word. The Holy Qur'an, as it exists today, is believed by all Muslims to represent the exact sounds and dictum revealed through Gabriel by the Prophet who learned them and transmitted them to his disciples, the first generation of Islam, as he learned them from Gabriel. In every Muslim generation, millions learned how to recite the holy text accurately from memory, and everyone enjoys listening to the recitation of the Word of God.

The Qur'an has thus preserved all Islamic teachings and is the acknowledged source of Islamic guidance. However, the records of the life of the Prophet himself, including his deeds and his sayings and tacit approval, provide details supportive of what exists in the Qur'an, or expanding it. This latter source is known as *Al-Hadith*; and thus Al-Qur'an and Al-Hadith are the recognized sources of all Islamic guidance. The total body of rules and verdicts guiding human conduct, which was derived from these two sources by the early leading scholars, has become known by the term *shari'ah*.

With the above details serving as a background, we return to the discussion of the main theme of this article, namely, the treatment of aging people.

The notion of human aging is related, we may say, to the total Islamic concept of the process of human life as reflected in the Holy Qur'an. The Islamic concept of the human life process recognizes all the stages of human growth from conception to death, including embryonic developments, birth, childhood, maturity and the declining stage. Let's listen to these Qur'anic words:

"God created you from dust, then from a little fluid, then He made you pairs, (male and female). No female bears or brings forth save with His (God's) knowledge. And no one grows old . . . , nor is decreased in his life except that it is recorded in a Book." *Qur'an* XXXV, 11

"He it is (God) Who created you from dust, then from a drop (of seed) then from a clot, then brings you forth as a child, then He (lets you live) to attain full strength, then (He may let you live) to become *shuyukh,* (old people) — though some of you die before — and to reach an appointed term." XL, 67

"Verily We created man from a product of wet earth; "Then placed him as a drop (of seed) in a safe lodging; "Then We fashioned the drop a clot, then fashioned the clot a little lump, then fashioned the little bones, then clothed the bones with flesh, and then produced it as another creation. So blessed be God, the Best of Creators!
"Then after that you surely die.
"Then, on the Day of Resurrection, you will be raised again." XXIII, 12-16.

And the Prophet Muhammad is related to have said,

"Each one of you is gathered (deposited) in the womb of his mother as a drop for forty days, then becomes a clot for forty days, then he becomes a little lump for forty days, then the spirit is blown into it . . . . "[1]

Thus Islam recognizes both the general stages of human growth and human declining. The latter stage we call "old age." The Qur'anic term for an aging person is *shaikh,* (fem. *shaikhah,* pl. *shuyukh*). Another term is *'ajuz.* Sarah, Abraham's wife, used both terms. On hearing the good tidings that she was conceived of a son, Isaac, she retorted:

> " . . . Woe to me! Shall I bear a child when I am *'ajuz,*
> and this my husband is *shaikh*? This is indeed a strange
> thing!" XI, 72

> "Has the story of Abraham's honored guests reached
> you, (O Muhammad)?
> "When they came in unto him and said: Peace! he
> answered: Peace! (and thought) Unknown folk (to
> me).
> "Then he went apart unto his housefolk so that they
> brought a fat calf.
> "And he set it before them, saying: Will you not eat?
> "He then conceived a fear of them. They said: Fear not!
> and gave him tidings of (the birth) of a wise son.
> "Then his wife came forward, making moan, and smote
> her face, and cried: A barren 'ajuz?
> "They said: (Even so), thus said your Lord. Verily He is
> the Wise, the Knower." LI, 24-30.

Islam, however, does not define a sharp point of time in the age
of the individual at which a person moves from one stage in his
growth to the next. Apart from birth and death, the movement
from one stage to the other is a slow invisible process, although
visible signs may exist to denote the transition. The most important
stage so denoted is the point when a person reaches majority.
Islam regards emission of semen by a male person, in a dream or
otherwise, and the female's discharge of menses as signs of reaching
majority, at which point the person, male or female, becomes a
fully responsible agent. He or she has to undertake all ritual and
other duties from then on until death so long as the person is of
sound mind. Prior to this period a person is a minor, to be trained
by his or her guardian in performing these obligations. If emission
or discharge is delayed, a person attains majority on reaching the
age of fifteen lunar years.

As for reaching the aging stage, the matter is determined by the
personal feeling of declining physical strength and advancement of
age. So health conditions such as slow steps, weak sight or weak
hearing or recurrent illness, combined with advancement in years,
qualify a person to belong to the category of "elderly people." A
physical change which does not affect the physical vigor, such as
greying hair or wrinkling, is not alone sufficient to make an aging

person. On the other hand, someone may become an aging person at the age of fifty or fifty-five if his physical strength begins to fail. However, a tradition makes the age of sixty, or somewhere between sixty and seventy, to be a Muslim's average life anticipation.

The important question now is whether Islam assigns a special role to such elderly people, or qualifies them to any special privileges? Although the full weight of regular duties and personal and social obligations may be lightened a little in the case of a person weakened by old age, an elderly Muslim person, man or woman, continues to be a fully responsible agent so long as his mental power remains sound. He or she has to continue to undertake the ritual and other obligations. For example, such a person must continue to observe the five daily prayers. If it happens that a person has become so weak as not to be able to stand in prayer, which is obligatory, he is entitled to sit, like a sick person who is not so old. Every Muslim also must fast from dawn to sunset every day during the ninth month of the lunar Islamic calendar, called Ramadan. If an elderly person cannot afford to fast, he or she is entitled not to fast but then has to feed one poor Muslim for each day he or she misses, just like a young Muslim who is burdened with an incurable disease. But a young Muslim who suffers from a curable illness on the day of Ramadan and has to break his fast, must make up for the day or days he misses. Likewise, every Muslim who has attained majority, young or old, must make pilgrimage to Mecca at least once in a lifetime if he or she can afford the trip physically and financially. A person who is forty or fifty or sixty or more years old who is strong enough to make the journey must make it if he did not do it earlier.

It is thus clear that old age in itself does not entitle for exemption from ritual (or other) duties. It is physical weakness which entails some exemption. The main criterion for *taklif,* "responsibility" is consciousness and soundness of the mental power as well as ability to deliver or to perform. A *hadith* related to the Prophet says:

"The pen, (recording of human deeds), is stopped in the case of a sleeping person until he (she) awakes; and for a minor until he (she) becomes a major, and from a person of unsound mental powers until he (she) recovers."[2]

If ritual duties continue to apply in old age with some consideration to physical fitness, all non-ritual obligations similarly continue so long as the person's mind is sound. There is no reason for a person who is sixty or seventy, but is physically fit, to stop his productive role, or give up his domestic, economic or other activities. True, a person has to take into consideration the degree of his forbearance. If, on account of his age and physical condition a person cannot work eight hours a day, let him reduce the period of his activities. After all, an hour of work with so much experience and long training may be equal to several hours of work by a person not so experienced or trained. In fact the idea of formal retirement is not a tradition in Islam. On the other hand, to exert oneself beyond what one can bear is forbidden in Islam. The Prophet criticized a group of his disciples who were overheard undertaking to fast every day, to stay up praying all night, and to shun sexual activities. He said,

> "As for me, I fast some days and do not fast some other days; I only celebrate a portion of the night in prayer and rest the other portion; and I do not keep away from women."

He also wondered when he saw an elderly man walking in pilgrimage supported by his sons on both sides. He was told that the old man was fulfilling a vow to make pilgrimage on foot. He said,

> "Let the man ride; God has no need for his suffering."

The Prophet also said,

> "A traveller who continues his journey and does not give his riding beast a break to rest, neither reaches his destination nor does he spare his (valuable) vehicle!"

The merit of productive activities in Islam can be gained from the Qur'anic command praising work as does the following:

> "And say (unto them): Act! God will behold your actions, (and so will) His Messenger and the believers, and you will be brought back to the Knower of the invisible and the visible, and He will tell you what you used to do." IX, 105.

In our time, some people seem to have been intoxicated with the rhetoric of social justice, and to have become preoccupied in utopian fantasies, forgetting the fact that you cannot distribute fairly when you suffer shortage. Equal emphasis should be laid on the significance of productive work. Islam provides such a stimulus, as we have seen in the Qur'anic text just quoted. The Prophet also emphasized it. He said,

"It is meritorious and charitable to plant anything
from the fruit of which a person or an animal can be fed."

He once asked one of his disciples, after shaking his hand, why his
hand was so rough. On hearing that it was because of handling the
axe in tilling the land, the Prophet almost kissed the hand and said,

"Such a hand that sweats in labor shall not suffer
burning in the Hellfire."

The point I wish to emphasize here is that the Islamic praise of
hard work and the emphasis laid on the merits of labor and
perfection of one's product for God's sake is not limited to productivity at the time of prime age. The call is extended to all stages of
life so long as a person remains responsible and of some physical
fitness. We also have to bear in mind that productivity is not
confined to hard economic goods, but includes important services
which do not require much physical exertion, such as education
and investing one's experiences and knowledge in extending advice
and counselling. The ancient Arab tribes, and tribal societies in
general, invested the wisdom of their elderly members in such
pursuits.

In short, Islam looks at elderly people as responsible individuals
with an economic and social role which takes note of their health
condition so long as they are mentally and physically fit. On the
other hand, to condemn them to isolated idleness, depriving them
of the affectionate attention and emotional tenderness of their kin
is unfair and exceedingly harmful.

In other words, old age in itself does not grant relief from the
regular duties incumbent upon a person, nor does it automatically
make him an immediate liability, so long as he remains of sound
mind and can afford to undertake responsibilities. Only in the case
of lack of physical fitness can relief be granted; but this is also true
in the case of a young person incapacitated by illness. There is no
reason in Islam to exempt a fit person because of his age from the
regular obligations . . . social, religious, economic, domestic
. . . which are incumbent upon ordinary people, so long as he
remains healthy enough. All potentials, all energies . . . all God's
bounties . . . within man and around, are to be duly invested and
should not be wasted. Ayesha, the renowned widow of the Prophet,
said that she did not count as part of her age any day that should
pass without earning some means of living or gaining some knowledge. And the Prophet Muhammad, peace and blessings be upon
him, warned:

"The feet of the son of Adam will not cross the Path, (the bridge over the Hellfire, connecting the site of Resurrection and the gate to Paradise) unless he has satisfactorily answered to the questions as to how he spent his life-time, how he used his youthful energy, how he earned his wealth and how he disposed of it."

If it is desirable in our organized society for a person to retire at a given point in time in his age in order to give a chance to the rising generation, it does not necessarily mean that he should take leave from all worldly activities or depend entirely on his pension. God, according to the Islamic belief, wishes us to be always productive and to work not only for our own needs, but also to contribute, in some degree, to the needs of society.

In short, elderly people should be encouraged to continue to invest whatever energy they have so long as they can do so. Their wisdom should be sought appreciatively, and they should continue to play a role in life. They should not unnecessarily be condemned to isolated existence in an "old age home" to consume the remaining period of their life waiting to die! This type of treatment would most likely lead to senility, loss of self-esteem and rapid mental and physical decline. Self-esteem and confidence can be maintained and enhanced so long as a person feels that he is still important and helpful in any degree, not when he is abandoned and made to feel useless and a burden on others. To remain close to their offspring, or members of their extended family, sharing their pains and pleasures, would make life more tolerable. Traditionally, elderly people who were treated with awe and respect and regarded as unfathomable sources of wisdom, radiated dignity, grace and serenity and maintained their mental vigor, if not also their physical strength. So, to waste the resources of the aging members of society is a loss, and waste is a sin in Islam; and to continue to invest their energy according to their health condition is in the best interest of all, and will be in keeping with the spirit and letter of Islam.

Although Islam does not exempt an elderly person from continuing to play a role within his capacity, Islam recognizes that his declining physique may reduce his economic productivity, and at some time of his life he may become in need of support. Here Islam does not immediately make such a dependent person the burden of society but the responsibility of the nearest of his kin. In Islam, a person moves in three circles, so to speak: his own circle, the circle of his consanguinous group, and the circle of the *ummah,* "nation." So long as the individual can manage, his needs are his own responsibility. He even has to provide for the maintenance of his wife, and his children until puberty. At this point a male, healthy child, has to provide for his own needs, according to the shari'a law of Islam. Only a daughter's maintenance continues to be her father's burden up to marriage, as well as that of a handicapped son. Needy parents' cost of living is the responsibility of their son or sons, or son's son, or a brother. Only in the absence of such a close relative able to bear the cost of maintenance of his needy parents, grandparents or brother, may the burden be thrown on to society. The Prophet, peace be upon him, said:

"I am the guardian of him who is with no guardian."
and "The state is the guardian of whoever has no guardian."

State responsibility for the needs of those without other resources is due to all citizens, Muslims and non-Muslims. The second Caliph of Islam, Umar Ibn al-Khattab, on seeing an elderly Jew begging in the streets of Medina ordered that he should be taken care of by the Treasury of the Muslim state, saying: "How can we use his taxes when he was younger and neglect him when he became old?"

Whether an elderly person is economically dependent or independent, the Islamic religion accords him a special place of honor. He is to be treated kindly and respectfully; and should be listened to when he talks; and his requests should be promptly answered. The Prophet, peace and blessings be upon him, said:

"Whosoever does not treat our elders with respect and the young among us with sympathy is not worthy of being counted one among our members."

"A youth who has treated an elderly person with honor and respect for the sake of God, God shall cause people to treat him likewise in his own old age."

"Those who sympathize toward the weak shall be blessed by the Merciful God. So be merciful to those on earth, so that He Who is in heaven may be merciful unto you!"

And when Abu Bakr, the most senior one among the disciples of the Prophet, brought his own father to proclaim his conversion to Islam before the Prophet, the Prophet said:

"I wish you had let the shaikh rest at home!"
which means that the Holy Prophet would have gone to him in
respect of his age!

Honor and respect due to elderly people is more seriously
emphasized in the case of a person toward his aging parents,
especially his mother. It is not enough to fulfil their material needs.
They are to be treated with care, affection and tenderness. The
Holy Qur'an reads:

> "And your Lord has decreed that you should not
> worship (anything) save Him, and that you should
> treat the parents most kindly. If one of them or both
> attain old age with you, say not "Fie" unto them nor
> repulse them, but speak to them in a noble way. And
> lower unto them the wing of humility through mercy;
> and pray: My Lord! Bestow Your mercy upon them
> both, as they did care for me when I was a helpless little
> one." XVII, 23-24.

> "And We have enjoined upon man to treat his parents
> well . . . his mother bore him in weakness upon weak-
> ness, and his weaning is in two years . . . (command-
> ing) Give thanks unto Me and unto your parents. Unto
> Me shall be your return.

> "Yet, if they strive with you to make you ascribe to
> Me as partner in that of which you have no knowledge,
> then obey them not, but seek to live with them in this
> earthly world in peace and kindly . . . . "XXXI, 14-15.
> Cf. XLVI, 15.

And the Prophet, peace be upon him, in answer to a question:
"Who among all people deserve my best treatment?" replied:
"Your mother." The person who put the question to the Prophet
asked: "And who is next?" The Prophet answered, "Your mother."
When the inquirer repeated: "And who is next?" the reply came:
"Your mother." The question asked again, "And who is next?"
And the Prophet said, "Your father."

In another haditb, the Prophet, peace be upon him, related the
story of three men who sought refuge from a storm in a cave, but
soon a huge stone rolled over from above and rested at the mouth
of the cave, thus closing it completely. The three men could not by
any means move the large stone one inch, and they realized that
unless something miraculous should happen, the cave was going to

be their grave! So, they thought that the best thing they should do was to pray to the Almighty God for deliverance, appealing to Him each on account of a specially meritorious action each done in the past for the sake of God. So each began to recall and relate an event while the other two listened. At the end of the prayer of each one of them, they saw the huge stone slowly moving, first allowing some light to penetrate, and then moving a little more making a narrow but insufficient gap, and by the end of the third prayer the gap became sufficient for them to file through! The prayer of the first person, which is relevant to our theme, ran as follows:

"You know, our Lord, that on my way home at the end of my daily pasturing work, I stopped every day with my sheep at the home of my parent to deliver milk to them before I could go to my own children. One day, You know my Lord, I found my parent already asleep. I decided, for Your sake, my Lord, not to disturb them, and waited at the step of their room all the night long until they woke up in the morning. I milked the sheep for them, and then proceeded on my way to my children.

"Almighty God! If You know that I did all this truly and sincerely for Your sake, please, our Lord, relieve us from this disaster!"

Old age itself is praised and honored if it is put to good use. The Holy Prophet, peace and blessings be upon him, said:
"The best among you is the one who is blessed with long life which he invests in good deeds."

And seniority in age was regarded an asset and treated as an additional qualification for high posts. When the Prophet Muhammad died in 632 without having named a *caliph*, "successor" to undertake the temporal responsibilities of the state, the community elected Abu Bakr for the high office. He was of almost the same age as the Prophet. The closest in blood to the Prophet among all his Companions, Ali Ibn Abu Talib, his cousin and son-in-law, a man of great valor and wisdom, and with noble records in serving Islam, was passed over, even later when for the second and third times the post became vacant. Only twenty-four years later he was elected to that position. His age at the time of the Prophet's death was about thirty years, and was apparently the major factor in delaying his nomination to that post.

Respect for the seniority of age, however, should not be pushed so far as to overshadow other virtues. It is related that a tribal delegation paid a visit to Umar Ibn Abd al-Aziz, the Eighth Century Umayyad Caliph in Damascus, then seat of the capital of the Muslim Empire. The delegation included a bright youth who proceeded to address the Caliph on behalf of the delegates, among whom were elderly members. The Caliph interrupted the speaker, saying: "The elders! The elders!" Then the youth said: "O you Commander of the Faithful; were seniority of age to reign supreme there would have been many people in this nation much older than you!" Upon which the Caliph lent his ear to the youth and asked him to proceed. The youth said: "We have come neither as a delegation of demand nor as a delegation of fear," (meaning that they had not gone to ask for a favor or to plead for forgiveness) "but we are a delegation of gratitude. We have come to convey to you our grateful appreciation and then return to our camp."

Moreover, an elderly person should himself respect the status of his age and rise above mean acts. He should particularly shun forbidden acts and obscene behavior. The Prophet, peace and blessings be upon him, warned of severe punishment awaiting an adulterous *shaikh;* and he criticized unworthy inclinations among many a person : the older he becomes the more he clings to life and wealth!

---

1. *Footnotes giving references to sources of quotations inaccessible in English translation have been eliminated.*

III. AGING AS FULFILLMENT

The Paradigm of Aging

John Borelli

Everyone, everywhere and at all times, is aging gradually, unnoticeably — except for those stark moments of self-confrontation when we experience ourselves as helpless bystanders to the movement of time through our lives. As a boy, who, like most other children, looked forward to Saturdays, I would experience a distinct feeling of transiency on Saturday evenings when I realized that the day would not last much longer. The sullen mood of a child does not match the poignancy of the confrontation with old age which T. S. Eliot's J. Alfred Prufrock expressed: "I grow old . . . I grow old . . . I shall wear the bottoms of my trousers rolled." But there is much in common, too, for Prufrock's pain arose as he considered that he would deteriorate before he could ever leave his mark in human society. I remember quite clearly that my child moods on many passing Saturdays evoked the thought which I often spoke aloud to myself: "I am nothing." Aging provides an unmatched experience of self-confrontation.

This essay is an exploration of the meaning of the paradigm of aging as it is conveyed in the symbolic material of religious traditions and in other imaginative material, such as dreams, fairy tales, and art. But the paradigm or archetype in itself is indecipherable unless it relates to a person's experience, revealing the meaning of a basic human intuition in order to communicate something of consequence about the human condition. Carl Jung, who is credited with clarifying the personal connection everyone has with archetypes, once remarked that religions are the schools for the aged.[1] This remains true for many today, but in our times others feel that these schools are not operating for them. For many, the pain of change and growing old is more intensely felt today.

Archetypal psychology advances sets of terms which circumscribe the aging/change problem, two of which for males are *puer* and *senex*. The typical feature of a *puer* personality is the failure to maintain a consistent view of himself in the face of the flux of life while the *senex* personality has too rigid a sense of self, which is often a false view of himself, and indefatigably refuses to look at himself. In women, there is the maiden personality unconsciously bound to the image of her mother; she is counterpart to the devouring mother who refuses to give up what she has produced, the "hag" who cannot look at herself. Both extremes represent an inability to deal with time, and their split portends catastrophe. The same is true of the split between the positive images of the extremes of youth and age — the heroic child and the wise old man; the daughter and the great mother.

Today, youth and age are divided within communities and among streets in communities. There are places where the elderly are never seen, and there are buildings and institutions from which the young stay away. Families are split by age and distance. Many persons of advanced years put on the "youthful look" while others resign themselves to the "mature style." Regions and states are peopled mostly by the retired, and certain cities and towns reflect a young culture. James Hillman, an analyst and editor of a journal of archetypal psychology, comments that the obsession with age and youth today reflects a loss of imagination and a subjugation to historicism. A fatalism has seized many, but others seek to avoid the inevitable crises of aging by mindless preoccupations. Hillman observes:

> *Our polarities — senex and puer — provide the arche-*
> *type for the psychological foundation of the problem*
> *of history.* First, in the conventional sense, puer and
> senex are history as sequence and transition, as process
> through time from beginning to end. And second,
> history as a problem in which I am caught, for which I
> suffer and from which I long to be redeemed, is given
> by the same pair as Father Time and Eternal Youth,
> temporality and eternity, and the puzzling paradoxes
> of their connection.[2]

Temporality and eternity are elements within each of us. The child is father of the man and mother of the woman. Potentially, over the shoulder of every child is a father-mother guide, ideal type, and confidant/e.

When the youth and the aged are associated naturally and symbolically, the elders patiently raise the children; the youth seek the company of their older teachers. Heritage is assured in their connection, and hope is experienced as they face one another. The youthful hero needs the guidance of the wise old man; the daughter is fulfilled through the help of the fabulous mother. The young justify the values of the aged as they provide a future for one another. When the two are split and are inconsiderate toward one another, there is no meaningful future for the aged nor confidence in the youth as they face the crises of living.

One of the common evidences of a split, from the perspective of a youthful mind, is the often heard sentence: "S/he is just too old to change." This represents a projection of one's own fear of change onto the elderly person. The observer is admitting his/her own frozenness before change. Nothing could be more inaccurate and pretentious as a description of the elderly than the inability to change. The human person is expected to make extraordinary adjustments while aging. Strength is no longer consistently trustworthy. Tiresome tasks may be undertaken that require a day or more for recovery. A night of good sleep is often preceded or followed by a night of insomnia. Remembering current facts seems difficult, but memories from decades ago can be recalled in great detail. A great uncle of mine at age 85 was chided when he could not remember the current President of the United States, but at the same time he could relate even the most insignificant details in a day to day summary of a trip which he took forty years previously. Living with the proximity of several sets of opposites is an inescapable adjustment.

Times of solitude are more needed in order to balance times of companionship. The aged seek moments alone, not in idleness or uselessness but in just being alone with oneself, a trait which is cause for criticism when observed in a younger person. Out of sobering reflections a cold honesty about oneself emerges. During a discussion session in a course entitled "The Philosophy of Self Discovery," which I supposedly "taught" to a group of retirees, a woman straightforwardly commented that we were using the euphemism "senior citizens" too much. Why not just say "old people" and be done with it?

The urgency to accomplish certain new tasks or to follow new pursuits is evidence of the importance of the perception of change by the elderly. "To die with one's boots on" may seem wasteful, and exceptions to the laws of aging seem grotesque. The example of Justice Oliver Wendell Holmes is an inappropriate ideal for many. Most people simply do not remain in their prime unto the grave; moreover, many sense that a new and fulfilling role awaits them in the third age of their lives if they can but change to fit it. One author, writing for a C. G. Jung professional society, puts it this way:

> The autumn of a woman's life is far richer than the
> spring if only she becomes aware in time, and harvests

the ripening fruit before it falls and rots and is trampled underfoot.[3]

Jung wrote of the natural aim for youth and the cultural aim for the aged.[4] Young persons are growing and extending themselves out into the world as they develop themselves socially and professionally. Whereas younger persons are motivated by factors outside themselves, the persons of advanced years find an equally intense motivation from interior factors. The bases of this set of internal factors Jung termed "the archetypes of the collective unconscious." They are the primary forms for religious, moral, cognitive, and cultural values, and constitute a universal spiritual heritage reborn in every individual. They are expressed symbolically, for they represent a certain number of shared factors within everyone; hence they are archetypal self-images which give expression to the basic human intuitions that give meaning to the human condition.

The aged begin to understand that the motivation to conquer the world in their youth was really a motivation to conquer the vast world within themselves, but projected externally. We confront ourselves through a variety of self-images throughout our lives, but in old age there may be greater freedom to reflect and to reconsider life values. In old age, the connection between self and life-expressions is more easily made. What may have passed for virtuous conduct in youth may now be seen to be qualified by a degree of vice. Religious images and artistic expressions gain a new power, and so a religious-cultural aim becomes the motivation for living. Immortality no longer means to live as one lived before, but emerges as a more profound dimension of the personality.

Jung called the process of coming to terms with oneself "individuation." It begins to unfold rapidly in the second half of life, but it can be taken up through analytical methods by someone who is mature enough to endure the painful aspects of oneself and sufficiently responsible to deal creatively with self-images. We are talking ideally in both cases. Jung believed that the individuation process is the ideal work or task for the second half of life. Late in life, there may be a stiffening of attitude when the aged must admit the failures along with the achievements. One can become repulsive to oneself and others; regressive and infantile behavior may express these feelings. One finds hypochondria and moodiness in both adolescents and the elderly. The latter are closer to admitting their own unhealthiness and self-regret, but choose the easier course of the youth who externalize their difficulties.

Aging may be experienced as meaningful or pointless. The solution to the dilemma of aging is not found outside but within, and this inner process of growth involves an enormous change of attitude for many. The purpose of advanced years is expressed religiously as the movement toward immortality. The fear of life that can cripple a young adult's career and douse the joy of accomplishment curiously parallels the fear of death that may cause an elderly person to miss the richness of the later years of life. However, as the elderly persons adjust to physical changes, some of which I have mentioned, it should be easier for them to direct attention within. Life is reviewed, in terms of decisions, courses of actions, and omissions, and a stronger, introverted attitude is developed. Such an attitude can help anyone at any stage of life. The accusation that one's parents are too old to change and so one must personally make adjustments to accomodate them is often a disguised admission on the part of the offspring that change is quite difficult for him/herself. Change and rigidity to change are difficulties for everyone. James Hillman concludes his study in this way:

> Thus we conclude that *the senex is there at the beginning as an archetypal root of ego-formation* . . . The senex as *spiritus rector* bestows the certainty of the spirit, so that one is led to state that ego-development is a phenomenon of the senex spirit which works at ordering and hardening within the ego with such compulsion that it must be — as well as the Promethean dynamics of the Hero — an instinctual source of ego energy.[5]

Supporting the ego-centric conscious mind is a vast spiritual resource as well as an underworld of repressed and demonic portraits of self. The potentiality for being an aged personality, with all of the positive and negative implications of age, is there from the beginning when the mind of a child begins to develop. Whereas the physical opposites of life are felt closer together and experienced one after the other in later years, so too are the demons and the saints of the interior spiritual world. The childish person has really failed to appreciate him/herself and consequently neither handles the world confidently nor is aware of the failure to confront the self. S/he is the eternal youth split from the natural aging ideal. If this attitude persists, then the hardworking child (puer) turns into the rigidity of the crotchety old man (senex) too early in life in order to avoid increasingly painful self-knowledge.

Orderliness, rigidity, and boundedness become part of the arche-typal identification process.[6] The typical senex criticism of the puer is for immaturity, failure to grow up and face the world, and the inability to obtain and/or keep a decent job. The puer's criticism of the senex is for enslavement to the past, fear of taking risks, and settled lifelessness. In truth, the senex personality manifests a personal maladaptation to interior change with a consequent inability to know oneself in the varied aspects of the personality. The puer is personally unwilling to develop a sense of identity beyond a particular glamorous role played out socially. Again, the puer suffers from the same inability to take introspection seriously.

Puer and senex attitudes may appear at many stages of development: the former turns away from the responsibilities of a new situation for the security of an inflated and superficial mode of behavior and the latter criticizes the factors contributing to a new situation as bothersome and insignificant.[7] In regard to aging, which is the most personally felt side of change, the puer-senex pair appear especially as images of roles which may serve as evasive modes of behavior. They represent a negative duality in the confrontation with bodily aging.

The puer is balanced by the child hero, the promising and capable youth who stands for hope and fulfillment, and the senex, by the benevolent and guiding sage. The hero-sage pair are a positive duality that enables change and compensates for negative potentialities within the psyche. The man or woman of wisdom assists the young, and together they live through change. In contrast, the senex has lost its child partner and has become cynical, tyrannical and defunct. The real issue of aging is death, and the senex is already an associate of death.

We are back again to a consideration of the duplicity of aging and, in particular, of old age, for it is in the last third of life that the self reascends into one's consideration. The preoccupations of work, family, and social contacts are less intense to some extent. The questions of accomplishment, waste of time, and degrees of satisfaction with work and with oneself come to the fore. In old age many regrets are expressed. It is a this time, too, that one can choose to face oneself, integrate one's personality, and accomplish the religious and cultural task of seeking immortality. On the other hand, one can choose to die to oneself in the face of the changes of old age. The curious and even hopeful truth is that the self does not stop confronting the mind with its self-portraits, consisting of both the positive and negative images of aging.

In traditional societies the religious and cultural values are preserved and taught by the elders. The images of the wise old man and the earth mother or protector-mother occur throughout the mythologies of archaic culture. The grandparents are the transmitters of cultural wisdom, the informing spirits or powers who return to guide and to reassure.[8] They speak with the authority of spiritual insight. They are identified in the accomplished doctor, priest, professor, artist, the grandfather or grandmother, the elder statesman, and in numerous other personalities who combine age, mercy, and understanding. The image is dormant in the background of the mind and reemerges with overriding concerns for self-knowledge. The image comes to the assistance not only of others in need but also to oneself advancing beyond earlier concerns. He or she represents a solution to the dilemmas of aging and the message that there is more to life than the mundane concerns of day-to-day life. He or she may also appear as a deceiver, magician, a fairy-tale godmother who assists in piecemeal answers or with stipulations. The old man on the nearly inaccessible peak will help the young aspirant who makes the rigorous climb, but like the other examples his message or solution was available back from where one started. The elders build up and tear down confidence, care little about the flattery of their students, and are willing to try again and again with each new charge. Whether through trickery, the building up of skills, the imparting of wisdom, or the blunt honesty of age, they offer one general message — the real point to life is what you make of it through what you already possess interiorly.

The great mother or grandmother is understanding, is merciful for all the mistakes of those who beseech her, influences the decisions of her children, but embodies the ideal of harmony. As old wise woman, she teaches that self-interest is not peaceful and leads away from self-knowledge. She represents for women the fruitful and joyful fulfillment of advanced years.

The wise old man intervenes in the busy lives of others by his mere presence, offers an irresistible vision of the future, remains aloof to ordinary concerns, and represents for men the peaceful wisdom of self-knowledge. Together, sagacious father and earth mother are advanced stages on the journey to self-knowledge. The wizard only imparts a greater message than himself — the goodness of home, honesty to oneself, and the power of one greater than himself. The spiritual guide preaches not himself but someone greater. The elder priest can wisely instruct the young man what to do next when God calls in his visions. The great mother supports someone more esteemed, providing the lap for the future king. And she witnesses the lasting character of her creation, continuity through her daughter, and maternal nourishment to life. Many special images come to mind: Eli and Samuel, Merlin and Arthur, guru and initiate, the Pieta, Demeter and Core.

No better set of images imparts the message of aging than the old man and the youth, the great mother and the maiden. They are the poles of self-discovery — the youthful mind and the spiritual heritage of millenia. They share in the resolution of complementary anxieties of the human condition — fear of life and fear of death. Still, the old man and the old woman are only stages in self-discovery.

The changing personality grows to accept him/herself gradually by recognizing that whatever role one plays in society, there is more to oneself than actions and styles. One grows to accept the elements that appear at first as intolerable and even immoral in others, but are to be found within oneself. There are other creative and freeing aspects to oneself which are incorporated into the self-image. Gradually a spiritual core to the personality begins to emerge — especially in advanced years when the question of the meaning of life seems most urgent, but also at earlier times when an interior questioning arises. Whenever an inner spiritual presence is felt, it is heralded or borne by the powerful image of the aged personality. Here there is danger of becoming too comfortable with the sagacious father or mother. Such powers can be destroyers, for they can draw all the energies of personal growth in self-knowledge off course. The goal of the process is not the role of wise teacher or aged nourisher, nor, for that matter, is any role a goal. The elder archetypes are powerful images which can usurp control from the mind and become authorities unto themselves. Personalities that identify with these images are not much different from the senex or the devouring mother. The goal is not identification with the aged personality, which is a powerful but partial view of the self, but rather an integration with the self in its fuller aspects. Ideally, the goal of life is to know oneself, to reach the immortality within, and to integrate oneself spiritually. Hence, Esther Harding observed in her book, *Psychic Energy:*

Thus the image of the Old Wise Man or the Great Mother may be constellated — activated by an access of energy, and come to dominate the individual's psychology. This domination will continue until he can redeem the value represented by the figure and create out of its energy a new attitude or psychic function for integration into his personality. If on the other hand he does not develop such inherent potentialities, he remains the puppet of the archetypal figures.[9]

The goal of aging is not to age properly, for that is an accomodation to change and represents only a step in the direction of the goal. We have been aging since youth, and each new level of growth has its advantages and disadvantages. There are harvests of newly found joy and also resistances to continuity and renewal. Aging and the images of wise old man and earth mother are affirmations of life that lend a profound spiritual quality to life. The self which we come to know is not a mere collection of self-images from youth to old age. We pass beyond the variety of roles and self-images to confrontation with a truth and a reality greater than ourselves. Jung identified the self as the image of God within everyone.[10] It is the center of the personality and finds expression expecially in the images of the sacred in religious traditions. Re-centering on the self is a result of coming to know it through its images, and this can be an important accomplishment of the latter years of life.

Notes

[1]Cf. C. G. Jung, "The Stages of Life," *The Structure and Dynamics of the Psyche,* The Collected Works of C. G. Jung, 8, Bollingen Series, 20 (Princeton: Princeton University Press, 1968), par. 786.

[2]James Hillman, "Senex and Puer: An Aspect of the Historical and Psychological Present," *Puer Papers* (Dallas, Spring Publications, 1979), p. 8.

[3]Irene Claremont de Castillejo, *Knowing Woman: A Feminine Psychology,* (New York, G. P. Putnam's Sons, 1973), p. 150.

[4]Cf. Jung, "On the Psychology of the Unconscious," *Two Essays on Analytical Psychology,* C. W. 7 (Princeton: Princeton University Press, 1966), par. 114.

[5]Hillman, p. 20.

[6]Cf. Jeffrey Satinover, "Puer Aeternus: The Narcissistic Relation to the Self," *Quadrant* (Fall 1980): 78ff. and 90ff.

[7]Cf. Hillman, p. 10.

[8]Cf. Jung, *Psychology and Alchemy,* C. W. 12 (Princeton: Princeton University Press, 1968), par. 159.

[9]M. Esther Harding, *Psychic Energy: Its Source and Its Transformation,* Bollingen Series 10 (Princeton: Princeton University Press, 1963), p. 315.

[10]Cf. Jung, *Aion,* C. W. 9, 2 (Princeton: Princeton University Press, 1968), pars. 59-60.

Aging, Death and the After Life

Robert Fastiggi

I. Reflections on Death's Impact on Life

People are born, grow to maturity, become old and they die. The logic and reality of these facts are so obvious that to state them seems either unnecessary or prosaic. However, we know that volumes have been written wrestling with the implications of these events. Growing old and dying are serious matters. We all acknowledge their existence, but accepting them and discussing them are difficult. This is why there is usually a certain denial of death in the way most of us think and live. We might be able to talk about death intellectually and acknowledge that all those now living will some day die. But when it comes to our own death, the anxiety and dread increase. To look into the mirror and see that face that has been our lifelong companion and to then imagine that face as but a memory captured in a photograph almost seems unimaginable.

We live as if our importance is a given. We take care of our bodies and seek pleasure and entertainment. This acceptance of our own importance can be seen as an instinctual thrust of our will to survive, to persevere and to live. It is only when people feel insignificant or their personal measure of significance has been severely damaged, that this will to live becomes extremely tenuous. Sometimes, the result is listlessness or depression. Other times, the desire for significance becomes frustrated and violence can ensue. This violence can be self-inflicted as in the case of drug-abuse, alcoholism or suicide, or the violence can be lashed out on others. Here, violence takes the form of a perverted assertion of one's own power and significance. It's as if to say: "I'm somebody. I exist because I can do this harm."

The desire to live is certainly natural and healthy. Even very old and very sick people usually still want to live. It is only when suffering or loneliness become oppressive that such people may lose their desire to continue living. However, the natural drive to live must come to terms with the equally natural fact of aging and death. If aging and death are natural, is it unnatural to fear them? These issues weave us into the threads of a most sensitive matter. If the drive to live is so strong while we are living, is it not natural for us to hope to continue living beyond death? Some would say that the desire for immortality is natural and healthy. Others might see it as a wish-fulfillment designed to overcome the fear of death. But does belief in an afterlife make death any less fearful? Hamlet was more impressed by the "dread of something *after* death" (Act III; sc. 1) which makes "us rather bear the ills we have than to fly to others we know not of." Is it the possibility of damnation that we fear about death? Or is it the evaporation of our consciousness and whole self that we've nurtured so carefully into complete nothingness that makes us fearful of death?

Certainly, all of these possibilities can combine to make death more or less fearful. It is the fear of the unknown as well as the fear of our own finitude that can make death so frightening. Death also is a reminder of our own fragility, our own weakness. There is the lurking fear of death as the destroyer, the eliminator of not only our goals, loved ones and accomplishments but most radically of our own personal existence.

Death also stands as a type of judge on the success or failure of our present life. The fear of death is sometimes more really a fear of dying without having lived life to our satisfaction or having achieved what we would like to have achieved. The standard plea of: "I'm too young to die!" carries with it the recognition that what is most fearful about death is that it terminates all our possibilities for the future. Is it possible to ever accept death peacefully and without protest? Is the overcoming of the fear of death a sign of maturity and courage or simply an indication of a more effective armor of psychological defenses? Is a belief in an afterlife the solution to the fear of death or does such a belief only complicate the fear? These and many other questions need to be dealt with if we are to determine the possibility of peacefully accepting death.

What is the relationship of growing old and the process of dying? Dying in an accident, being killed by an act of violence or dying in one's youth of some fatal disease: each of these carries with it a tragic quality all its own. But what about the more deliberate, more inexorable march towards death that old age brings? The fact of aging is a stark reminder of our own finitude. The fear and denial of the aging process are certainly linked to the fear and denial of death.

Many have turned to medical science and improved health formulas for an answer to the aging process. This turn has resulted in a limited and incomplete success. The present population in

North America is enjoying greater longevity as the result of improved health conditions and the advances of medical science, but faces still grow wrinkled and old people still die. Medical science has found ways of alleviating some of the effects of the aging process and in some cases of delaying those effects, but the physically immortal human being has not been created. To a large extent, the turn to medical science for an answer to the problems of aging and death is an indication of our inability to deal with their deeper meanings. This is not to say that medical solutions to suffering and disease should not be sought, but it is to suggest that medical science cannot deal with the psychological, or more significantly, the *ontological* fear of aging and death that exists on a much deeper level.

The psychiatric profession could be looked upon as that branch of medicine which is best equipped to deal with any fears or anxieties that might exist over the topics of aging and death. However, the best work being done in the field of psychiatry in dealing with death and dying is being undertaken by those who recognize the distinctly spiritual dimension of death. Doctors like Elisabeth Kubler-Ross and Dame Cicely Saunders both recognize that the process of dying goes beyond the merely biological. Dr. Kubler-Ross, a Swiss-born psychiatrist, has achieved much deserved praise for such works as *Of Death and Dying* and *Death: The Final Stage of Growth*. In these books, Dr. Kubler-Ross has not only indicated that death can be a beautiful experience (if one is properly prepared and supported) but also that life continues beyond the death of the body. Dr. Cicely Saunders also represents a humanistic and spiritual approach to death with her Hospice for the dying which she runs in Southeast London. Combining the best methods of medical science with the deep compassion of a true humanist, Dr. Saunders offers care for the dying and terminally ill that transcends a mere dulling of pain with drugs and painkillers. She also tries to deal with the families of the dying and offers this observation: "We spend a great deal of time with the families and think there exists a spiritual pain, a sort of unformed feeling which reaches out for truth, forgiveness and certainly meaning."[1]

It is this search for meaning that characterizes the deepest approach to the issues of aging and death. Here medical science in the form of a spiritually sensitive psychiatry joins forces with the great figures of religion, philosophy and literature who have sought to give meaning to the processes of aging and death. Human history and philosophy are full of examples of people growing old peacefully and dying calmly and naturally. There are certainly others who have welcomed death as either the natural end of life or as a way of escaping the pains and sufferings of this life. There have been many (and history seems to indicate the majority) of cultures who have seen death not as the end of life but merely as the transformation into a new mode of existence. Beliefs in reincarnation, resurrection and the survival of the soul after death are widespread. To simply dismiss such beliefs as purely superstitious, illusionary or the products of wish-fulfillment seems somewhat too facile. Even a scientific approach could not honestly state that these beliefs are false. The most that could be argued is that there is not sufficient evidence to prove that humans survive death in some form or other.

It should be obvious that the treatment of the topics of aging, death and the afterlife cannot be viewed in isolation from the cultural context of beliefs, myths and symbols that seek to give structure and meaning to such overwhelming concerns. Part of the present turmoil of our contemporary setting is the lack of any general mythic structure by which people can handle these monumental realities. To be sure, there are still cultures and sub-cultures that provide such religious and mythic support. But if one does not live in a society which is universally Hindu, Islamic, Catholic or whatever, there is the terrible freedom of choosing among a plurality of beliefs and attitudes about aging, death and the survival of death. The curiosity of children growing up in such pluralistic cultures is hardly satisfied by the inability of their elders or educators to give them positive answers of such life and death importance. Some such children might be fortunate enough to seek out an attitude about life and death which can give them structure and meaning. Others, however, might grow to avoid discussion of such topics or simply grow insensitive to their true significance and reality.

We can only speculate as to the effect of films and television on young minds that see death and violence as a matter of course in these media. Do young people watching so many depictions of death grow insensitive to the full import of its meaning? Or do these frequent deaths on the screen only serve to make death more fearful, more incomprehensible and more dreadful? It would seem that the denial of death is impossible when the reality of it is commonly demonstrated in so many shootings and murders on the screen. However, the effect might actually be a more subtle form of denial. Instead of seeing death as a personal and private event that each of us must face with a certain amount of fear and trembling, death can be seen as mechanical and depersonalized. Death then is reduced to the simple removal of one more character out of the plot. As long as it is the other person's death, we can witness so many simulated deaths and never blink an eye.

In spite of these factors which might contribute to the denial or depersonalization of death, the shadow of death still falls on us all. All families are affected by the death of loved ones. What widow who wakes each morning with the weight of loneliness and emptiness in her arms is ignorant of the reality of death? What parent who has lost a child to some fatal illness can build a wall around the pain of death? Death comes for us all. Sometimes as the quiet end to a long and happy life, and other times like a "thief in the night," to quote St. Paul, shocking us into a sudden confrontation with ultimate reality.

If life is a process towards some goal, we need to take a careful look at the process of life whose natural end is to grow old and die. What does it mean to live a life filled with hopes and dreams in youth, compromised to the successes and failures of middle age and finally reduced to a weakened, sickly form in old age awaiting the "end of it all?" What does it all mean? Is it "a consummation devoutly to be wished" to die in a semi-drugged state amid tubes and respirators quietly and painlessly? Is this a fitting end to years of work and struggle, worry and planning? Albert Camus was right to detect a certain absurdity about it all. Where, though, does the honest mind go for possible answers to the meaning of the processes of living, aging and dying?

Reflections need to be made on some of the basic attitudes that philosophers, scientists and religious thinkers have made regarding the meaning of life and death. It is very difficult for me to stand as a judge of other people's attitudes about death and say that this attitude is beneficial and true while this other attitude is unhealthy and false. Nevertheless, impressions and judgments are needed if we are to get at all near the core of such matters. I, therefore, intend to form some reflections on three general and representative attitudes and speculate on the possible impact of these attitudes on people who are growing old and awaiting their own death. These three attitudes can be described as follows: 1) The belief that personal human consciousness ends with physical death; 2) The belief that after death the soul of the person is reincarnated in another body or form; and 3) The belief that life continues after death through the continued existence of the soul and/or the resurrection of the body.

There can be many variations on these three basic attitudes about death. My purpose will be to try to dissect the essence of these three views and show how they could affect the mind of a person who is growing old and facing the reality of death. I will also try to show how these different views of death can affect the whole way one would see life. The realities of life and death interpenetrate. The way one views death will certainly influence one's personal philosophy, morality and sense of priorities. Death is a part of life. It remains to be discovered if life is the other side of death.

II. Death and the Afterlife: Three Attitudes Explored

A) The Denial of Personal Human Consciousness Beyond Death

Those who see death as the end of personal, individual existence do so for a variety of reasons. One reason is the adoption of what is thought to be the rational or scientific attitude on death. As far as science can determine, individual consciousness ends when all vital functions have ceased to function. After that, we know that the body will begin to decompose. For all practical purposes, the deceased is now dead to the world. Perhaps he or she will be remembered by a few generations of descendents. Perhaps if the person was famous or very significant in some field, his or her name will be remembered longer. A footnote might appear in some book, a name might be attached to some painting or poem, a building might be constructed with the individual's name on it: these are the only ways in which a person could be thought to survive death.

In the past century, this "scientific" attitude has won many converts. But there have been others of a scientific bent who have wondered if science could discover evidence for life after death. Martin Ebon, an expert in the history of psychic research, recently wrote a book entitled *The Evidence For Life After Death* (New York, 1977). In this fascinating study, Mr. Ebon shows how many great scientific minds got involved in the study of such phenomena as astral projection, communication with the dead and near-death experiences. Mr. Ebon is careful to note that serious researchers in the field of psychic phenomena maintain the highest standards of scientic method. Although the results have not been absolutely conclusive, almost all of the researchers in this field have experienced enough to make them firmly convinced that there is survival of bodily death.

Raymond A. Moody, M.D., who is both a medical doctor and a Ph.D. in philosophy, has published two books which deal with the phenomena of near-death experiences. In these two books, *Life After Life* (1975) and *Reflections on Life After Life* (1977), Dr. Moody explores many cases of people who have either clinically died or have come very close to death. The remembered experiences of these people show some remarkably similar features among which are the passage through a long, dark tunnel, the experience of being out of one's body, the meeting of dead relatives and friends and an encounter with a "being of light" who helps them view their life in one panoramic, instantaneous insight. In spite of these fascinating and numerous accounts, Dr. Moody has found some doctors who will almost *a priori* dismiss the possibility of survival of death as one explanation for these experiences. Such scientifically-minded individuals will immediately offer pharmacological, neurological or psychological explanations of these phenomena even when the data doesn't support such explanations. Dr. Moody does not believe that he has actually proved that life continues beyond bodily death, but he does believe that these experiences fall into a unique and inexplicable category. He does suggest that life beyond death seems to be the best explanation for the phenomena encountered. The fact that some scientists refuse to accept this possibility only shows how deep their prejudice is on the matter. Perhaps this is the nature of their training.

Some people will deny personal survival of death because they feel the brain must be present for consciousness to be present. Severe brain damage does cause people to lose consciousness. Therefore, it seems safe to say that a permanent loss of consciousness takes place when the brain shows no vital or electrical activity (a flat EEG reading) at the moment of death. This argument for the necessity for the brain is also given support by some philosophers who think that the unity of personal consciousness is impossible without the physical locus of the brain. A disembodied mind has never been encountered, they argue, and there is no reason to believe it ever can be encountered.

The argument for the necessity for the brain makes the ungrounded assumption that because something has not been empirically detected it is therefore impossible and non-existent.

The experiences of astral projection and out of the body phenomena suggest that the unity of consciousness can be maintained apart from the physical brain. But even if such experiences are dismissed, the whole mystery of the relationship of matter, spirit and energy has certainly not been exhausted by contemporary science. As Lewis Thomas, a noted scientist and author, writes: "The greatest single achievement of science in this most scientifically productive of centuries is the discovery that we are profoundly ignorant; we know very little about nature and we understand even less."[2] With this humble and realistic attitude about the progress of science in mind, it seems possible that human soul apart from the brain is a reality that can survive death.

There are others who will rebel at the thought of life after death on what I would call moral or social grounds. These are people who argue that belief in life after death causes a lack of concern for this world and results in a life-fearing, other-worldly attitude. The German philosopher Friedrich Nietzsche is perhaps the most powerful and poetic opponent of the "bad air" created by a guilt-ridden Christian preoccupation with sin, guilt and judgment. He sees the concern for a future life as the establishment of "a nook of disgruntled, arrogant and offensive creatures filled with a profound disgust at themselves, at the earth, at all life . . . ."[3]

Other thinkers, influenced by Nietzsche, include Albert Camus who saw a retreat to the comfort of an afterlife as a form of "philosophical suicide." Jean-Paul Sartre would see such a belief in life after death as a form of "bad faith" and an abrogation of human freedom. The great Father of Psychoanalysis, Sigmund Freud, saw a belief in a future life as a "wish-fulfillment" intended to guard against the fear of death. All of these thinkers see a belief in life after death as a lack of courage and an inability to face reality.

The moral objection to life after death is further nuanced by some philosophers who use the argument of Kant that it is not genuinely moral to do something good with the intention of being rewarded for it. These thinkers point out that a belief in a future life is actually selfish; it is a desire to be rewarded for good things done on earth as well as an egocentric urge to continue one's own existence beyond its natural course of life. Not only is such a belief selfish, they argue, but it also makes people more concerned about their own salvation than with the real problems of society. Marx, to some extent, follows this line of reasoning in his opposition to religion. His statement that "religion is the opiate of the masses" was directed not so much against the masses as it was against those who exploited religion and a belief in a future life as a means of distracting the proleteriat from the misery of their present state.

To be sure, there is a certain measure of truth in these moral objections to life after death. However, a moral objection can be equally raised against the non-existence of life after death. Even Kant himself postulated the necessity for a future life as a means of assuring just punishments for those left unpunished in life and just rewards for those who suffered unjustly in this life. Others have argued that it is only the belief in a judgment after death that will keep the majority of people moral. If evil is left unpunished in a future life, then what is to stop morally weak individuals from giving in to evil and destruction desires in this life?

The moral arguments for and against belief in an afterlife can go back and forth. We should, though, be aware of the deficiencies of both sides. First of all, it can be argued that a belief in a judgment after death is not the only motivation for making people moral. There are many people who will want to do good for the sake of society, their own well-being and a basic human urge to do what is right. On the other hand, it does not follow that belief in an after-life necessarily leads to a lack of concern for this life. The devaluation of the projects for this world might result from an unhealthy religious attitude, but there seems to be no reason to believe that an individual can't love this world and work for its betterment and still believe that life will continue beyond death. In fact, belief in a moral judgment after death should inspire an individual to be socially active and morally concerned about the ills of society and the world. The people interviewed by Dr. Moody in his book *Life After Life* suggest that after their encounters in death, they returned to life with the feeling that life is now more precious and meaningful.

Perhaps philosophers like Nietzsche and Sartre are objecting to some possible dangers of belief in an afterlife. Some of the distortions of Christian teaching and practice could have led to the morbid, fearful and guilt-ridden attitudes that they take to be normative of Christianity. An interesting discovery of Dr. Moody's research is that judgment by the "being of light" is not so much dreadful as therapeutic. His numerous interviews show that in the flashback on life the being of light stresses two things: learning to love other people, and knowledge.

If the reports of Moody's patients can be taken as an accurate portrayal of what judgment by God will be like, much of the dread and terror of "something after death" should fade away. A person who has tried to love other people and has sought wisdom and knowledge should have nothing to fear in what lies beyond physical death. The pattern of loving and learning that begins in this life will continue in the next. Life after death need not be looked upon as a static rapture with the divine but rather as a dynamic and continuous process of learning to love others and gaining knowledge and insights into the mysteries of the universe. The communal aspect of life after death is dogmatically asserted in the "communion of saints" but sometimes too much emphasis is placed on the beatific vision between the individual soul and God. Perhaps more stress should be placed on the possibility of meeting dead relatives and loved ones, of learning to love souls we never met before and of discovering the infinite beauties and wonders of the universe. None of this need conflict with our union with God — for in being united with God we can reach out in a type of "pancosmic vision," as Karl Rahner calls it, embracing the many aspects of the universe.

It can be argued that a belief in life after death need not involve a devaluation of this life. Indeed, did not Jesus Himself say: "I have come in order that you might have life and have it more abundantly?" (John 10:10) A belief in a future life should in no way lead to a hatred of the world but rather to a desire to discover what is of true importance in the world. It is true that some religious people have gone to extremes in the attitude of *contemptus mundi* or hatred of the world. A more balanced view should not be to hate the world but grieve over the suffering and injustice present in the world. It is the malice, corruption and selfishness of our weakened human condition which makes the world often a "valley of tears." The world of nature in itself should never be despised but rather nurtured and protected as a reflection of God Himself. The Bible itself supports this view when it says that: "God looked at all that He had made and saw that it was very good." (Gen. 1:31)

The use of moral arguments, either for or against life after death, ignores a certain philosophical realism. Whether we consider it more courageous and noble to deny a future life or more ethically pleasing to believe in a future life is not really the question. The question is whether or not such beliefs are true. What this realization leads to in certain circles is an attempt to scientifically investigate the evidence for the survival of bodily death. In other circles, it leads to a religious acceptance of life after death on the basis of revelation and faith and not on the basis of scientific evidence. Still others adopt an agnostic anthropological perspective and point out that beliefs in life after death and reincarnation grew out of primitive and superstitious cultures. Unless hard evidence can be given to support the survival of death, these people would say that the probable assumption is that personal consciousness ceases with the death of our bodies.

To search out the truth of this whole matter is difficult indeed. Some thinkers have at least pretended that death should not be as some people make it out to be. The ancient Greek philosopher Epicurus observed that: "Death is nothing to us . . . It does not concern either the living or the dead, since for the former it is not, and the latter are no more." (*Letter to Menoeceus*). Here, death is seen as a painless loss of consciousness to be feared no more than is sleep. Some philosophers have also pointed out that if we are living a purposeful and active life, death will not be a preoccupation with us. This was the view of Bertrand Russell and also of Spinoza who wrote: "A free man thinks of nothing less than of death, and his wisdom is not a meditation upon death but upon life." (*Ethics*, Prop. LXVII)

To view death in this calm, naturalistic manner might be easy for a philosopher, secure in the comfort of his study, but what about ordinary people who are growing old and growing closer to their moment of death? How would the denial of life beyond death affect their outlook on the meaning of their lives? Is it possible to grow old gracefully and peacefully with the conviction that death will mean the end of one's personal consciousness?

I suppose a number of reactions and attitudes are possible. One would be to see life as ever so much more precious and beautiful because it is perishable and impermanent. The recognition of the transitory nature of all things could make us appreciate even more the short and fragile moments of friendship, art and love that make life worth living. An individual life can be looked upon as a flower that grows to maturity, withers and dies. Does the impermanence of the things of nature make them any less beautiful? Likewise, a human life can be seen as the emergence into consciousness of one more person in the cosmic scheme of things. But just as nature is full of brief flowerings of beauty that need to return to the earth, so a human life can be a thing of beauty even though it too must return to earth. There is a kind of naturalistic beauty to this image of life because it places the individual in a cosmic order more mysterious and powerful than any individual life.

It is this sense of communion with the cosmic process that renders this view a type of naturalistic mysticism. In many ways, the Hindu view of the cosmic cycles of birth and rebirth parallels this naturalistic vision. However, the Hindu view of reincarnation does not see the cycle as a purely natural return to the earth. For the Hindus, the soul is immortal and conditioned by the moral laws of *karma*. The person's body might return to the earth, but the person's soul is reincarnated in another body. Nevertheless, the sense of being part of a great cosmic process is similar.

This naturalistic view of death does not always lead to a cosmic spirituality and a peaceful acceptance of the processes of aging and dying. There can be a demonic side to realization that nothing lasts forever. This is seen when the individual becomes immersed in the materialism, greed and self-centeredness that is the supreme danger of a purely selfish and worldly outlook on life. The accumulation of material possessions, the compulsive drive for success, prestige and power, even the craving for affection and love — all of these can so dominate a person's life that death becomes either unthinkable or hidden. The desperate urge for pleasure and success can take the form of a crass materialism and an unprincipled competiveness for the "good things of life." Here, the creative urge to live becomes distorted in a drive for economic power and personal importance. This can lead to a precarious equation of a person's worth with his or her external appearance, financial status and individual possessions. The pace of life might be fast, and the style might be sophisticated and sleek; but one wonders how long such a mode of living can last. The competition for importance, economic gain and individual pleasure can give a person a certain vitality, but how is such living harmonized with the life processes of aging and dying?

For people immersed in the world of crass capitalism and materialism, aging and death can be the most frightening of all realities. The usual response is one of denial. In a culture which glorifies the vigor and beauty of youth, the thought of slowing down or losing one's physical attractiveness can become dreadful. Is it any wonder why the cosmetic industry is so enormous? In the United States, we are impressed by people who might be chronologically old but who still act as though they were artificially young. This is not entirely a bad thing because youthfulness, whether in appearance, activity or attitude, need not disappear entirely with age (although it often has tragi-comic effects). But one wonders if enough attention is paid to the true fruits of advanced years like experience, wisdom and spiritual counsel. Old people are admired to the extent that they still act and think like the young, but why can't they be admired for value of thinking and acting like the archetypal "old ones" should?

Perhaps part of the reason for this state of affairs is that worldly materialism does not recognize the spiritual fruits of aging. An old person is thought to retire gracefully if he or she has earned enough economic power to spend the last years in pleasure and comfort. Elderly people themselves are often made to feel that they have no useful purpose to serve the community. The fortunate ones therefore spend their final years seeking diversions and entertainments while the unfortunate ones are often made to feel a burden to either their families or the state. A purely materialistic view which offers no hope for any future growth beyond death can lead to the pitiful reality of old people being isolated from the general community frittering away their time in various pleasures and amusements. To be sure, old people need entertainment, but the concept of retirement is often empty of any effort to grow in wisdom and prepare for death.

Selfish materialism can often lead to a tragic, frustrated and hopeless view of life. The competitive drive to succeed and prosper can animate and fill a person's life so long as satisfactory results are achieved. The failure to achieve the desired economic power or prestige can plunge such a person into depression or even into suicide. Is it any wonder that teenage suicides are epidemic in the more affluent suburbs where the pressures for success are highest? If a person's values are limited to the material pleasures and achievements of this life, old age can be the gradual demise of the individual's emotional support. As the shadow of death looms closer, the treasures stored up on earth offer little consolation. Sometimes, old people become preoccupied with the future of their estate. Their involvement with capital gains and investments can continue until their final moments of lucid consciousness. Such tragic people can only measure the meaning of their lives by the amount of money and property they leave behind. Often their sad values are absorbed by the awaiting generation. After the funeral, the lawyers and heirs divide the spoils of one solitary person's lonely legacy.

It is perhaps unrealistic to say that all people who become absorbed by materialism die as tragic, desperate souls. Even very worldly people have their loved ones. Values often unconsciously mix in people's lives and their hearts are often torn by conflicting loves. Even church-going people sometimes live and grow old with very materialistic habits and values. Likewise, avowed atheists sometimes mouth silent prayers to some unknown force which they hesitate to call God. Aging and death are not easily digestible commodities for most people whether they believe in a future life or not. Doubt also is a factor in many people's lives. One might verbalize some vague confidence in the world to come, but the slow and sometimes uneasy acceptance of death indicates a gnawing doubt that all that one has believed in might be just an illusion.

There are many possible attitudes old people might take towards the undeniable fact that with each day they are getting nearer to their end. It would be wrong to say that those who deny life after death uniformly approach death with either denial or terror. It is easy to get taken up with the affairs of the living, and many old people are too busy living right up to the end to become intimidated by the thought of death. However, it is the question of the meaning of one's life that is put in such sharp relief by the reality of death. What does it all mean now that it is time to "shuffle off this mortal coil?" An attitude that rules out the possibility of a future life seems to offer only incompleteness as the fruit of all the struggles and labors of life. Some people die more fortunate than others. Some might have lived more nobly, more passionately and more successfully, but when death comes all this doesn't really matter. Hamlet, that great spokesman for matters of mortality, observes: "Imperious Caesar, dead and turned to clay/might stop a hole to keep the wind away." (Act V, sc. 1). In a similar vein, the Frenchman Jean-Paul Sartre made a statement which can be paraphrased as "whether one is a leader of nations or a drunk in a bar, it all comes to the same thing."

Plato saw the task of philosophy as learning to die well. But Plato thought the philosopher could die well because he knew that the soul is eternal. In the *Phaedo*, Socrates remarks: "A man who has really devoted his life to philosophy should be cheerful in the face of death, and confident of finding the greatest blessing in the next world when his life is finished."[4] The question remains, though, as to how one dies well who does not share Plato's confidence in a future life.

Heidegger is one philosopher who emphasizes that death cannot be treated as an external event, but as something which is the innermost structure of human consciousness. David E. Roberts, a well-known philosopher of religion, notes that for Heidegger the authentic view of death sees existence as being "thrown into being towards its own end."[5] The Heideggerian man enters into the certainty of death "not as inevitable external happening, but as something whose inward significance is more certain than anything encountered in the world of objects."[6] The uncertainty of the moment of death prompts the authentic man to live in "a continual confrontation with Nothingness." Death for Heidegger is not something which is clinically accepted as the natural end of living organisms, but rather as an overwhelming tension in our mode of being which heightens our sense of life.

This existential view of death shows a deeper emotional and human involvement in the reality of death than does a merely scientific attitude or a secular materialistic point view. But, to see in the authentic confrontation with Nothingness a resolution to the deeply felt sentiments of people growing old and facing the end of their existence is perhaps expecting too much. The life of an individual might reach its ultimate confrontation with finitude at the moment of death, but does this really help people to die well?

I suppose the existential courage demanded by Heidegger's philosophy is one of the more inspiring attitudes possible for people who are convinced that death is the end of personal existence. The other view which seems somewhat inspirational is the naturalistic mysticism of the body returning to nature and the earth. The human spirit, though, reveals itself as an openness to the infinite horizons of love and being. There seems to be a very profound rebellion at the thought that our spirit will cease to exist at the moment of death. This is much deeper than some egocentric urge to preserve one's being from extinction. It seems to emerge from the very heart of what it means to be human. The idea of the immortality of the soul does not arise as a cowardly fear of being mortal, but rather as a correlate of the infinite and eternal dimensions of being a spirit open to the depths of reality. If we really understand the spiritual side of our humanity, the idea of immortality will be appreciated as the most natural of all ideas. The great Dostoevsky, in his *Diary of a Writer* expresses it well:

There is only a single supreme idea on earth: the concept

of the immortality of the soul: all other profound ideas
by which men live, are only an extention of it.

The concept of the immortality of the soul expresses itself in a
number of beliefs and attitudes. What we need to do is to examine
how a belief in the survival of the human soul after death affects
the process of aging and how this belief can influence a person's
view of the meaning of life as death approaches.

B) The Belief in Reincarnation

We have spent a good deal of time with the issue of belief and
unbelief in regard to a future life. A consideration of the topics of
aging, death and the afterlife would not be complete if the topic of
reincarnation was not considered. Reincarnation is a basic
affirmation that the soul or spirit of an individual does not end
with physical death but rather will be reborn in another form.

This doctrine of reincarnation has its greatest expression in the
religious traditions of India. In Hinduism, reincarnation creates
the endless cycle of birth and rebirth which is called *samsara*. This
cycle of birth-death-rebirth is usually thought of as painful, all-
pervasive and inexorable. The problem of salvation of Hinduism
(and, in a certain sense, Buddhism) is how to escape this painful
cycle of *samsara*.

It should be noted that reincarnation, although most prevalent
in the traditions of India, is a universal concept. The philosopher
and historian, W. Macneile Dixon, notes that: "Of all the doctrines
of a future life, palingenesis or rebirth, which carries with it the
idea of pre-existence, is by far the most ancient and most widely
held."[7] Whether known as metempsychosis, transmigration,
palingenesis or re-embodiment, the basic notion of reincarnation
has fascinated and influenced a great number of people. Two
members of the Theosophical Society of America, Joseph Head
and S. L. Cranston, have compiled two extensive anthologies
containing numerous testimonies and comments on the issue of
reincarnation. These two books, *Reincarnation: An East-West
Anthology* and *Reincarnation: The Phoenix Fire Mystery* are
invaluable and almost inexhaustible sources of insights from
philosophers, mystics, psychologists, scientists and psychics. The
variety of people cited in these volumes shows that reincarnation
strikes a cord of interest in the human heart, for the topic really is
the mystery of life and death.

The impact of a belief in reincarnation will have on one's attitudes
about life and death will vary depending upon the context of one's

beliefs. If one simply feels that one is reincarnated from a previous time period because of certain affinities to that period or experiences of *déjà vu,* but does not integrate this knowledge into a more complete cosmic picture, the notion of reincarnation is only a curiosity. However, if one sees reincarnation as part of a greater cosmic reality as do the Hindus, then it can have very significant spiritual implications.

The Hindu view of reincarnation is linked to the notion of *karma. Karma* is the moral law of cause and effect. It is roughly equivalent to the idea of "as you sow so shall you reap." The notion of karma is used as an explanation for many of the mysteries of life. People who are suffering now are in this state because of the *karma* of their previous lives. Those who are fortunate now are this way because of their inherited *karma.* The Hindu scriptures give some profound insights into the law of *karma.* In the Chandogya Upanishad, it is observed:

> Those whose conduct here has been good will quickly
> attain a good birth (literally womb), the birth (or womb)
> of a Brahman, the birth of a Ksatriya or the birth of a
> Vaisya. But those whose conduct here has been evil will
> quickly attain an evil birth, the birth of a dog, the birth
> of a hog, or the birth of a Candala. (Chandogya 5. 10.7)

While there seems to be a certain fatalism about the law of karma, in reality, it is the supreme expression of personal responsibility for one's own destiny. What might be disturbing is that one could be suffering for some of the bad karma stored up by a previous life that one does not even remember. Nevertheless, a person can always try to perform those good works which will improve his or her situation in the next life. Huston Smith observes that *karma* means that each individual is wholly responsible for his present condition and will have exactly the future he is now creating.

For the Hindus, the soul is eternal. It is only the forms it takes on that change. Although the quality of one's previous lives can be discerned somewhat by attention to one's manifest *karma,* the actual identity of previous lives usually remains hidden. It is only in deep meditation or enlightenment that one might gain knowledge of one's previous modes of existence. The Buddha is said to have gained insight into his past lives at the moment of his enlightenment.

What does all this mean for people living and struggling in their present existence? For one thing, it might enable them to better accept their present condition. As Thomas Berry, a noted cultural historian and thinker, points out:

> The law of Karma enabled the people of India morally and psychologically to accept the human condition in which they found themselves individually. Any affliction was bearable under the conviction that it was merited and that faithful acceptance of the life situation resulting from deeds would assist towards final salvation.[8]

The Hindu view of reincarnation contains a curious paradox. On the one hand, it would seem to be the supreme motivating force for the self-development of the individual. The law of *karma* would imply that the individual should do all in his or her power to cultivate one's virtues in order to rise in the ascending scale of reincarnation. On the other hand, though, the Hindu goal is to precisely transcend the individual self and to escape the endless cycle of birth-death-rebirth known as *samsara*. The ultimate goal of individual self-cultivation is really self-transcendence and the release from the bondage of being reincarnated again. But what exactly happens when the soul has been purified through sufficient reincarnations to now transcend *samsara*?

This is the deepest mystery of Hinduism. Here, we enter the mystic realms of the individual soul, *atman,* merging with the universal soul, *Brahman.* Here we are dealing with the atainment of release from the endless cycle of death and rebirth into the numinous quality of *nirvana.* The descriptions of liberation differ in the Hindu tradition. Some might emphasize the merging of the individual soul with *Brahman* to the point that the individual soul becomes totally merged with ultimate and its individual identity is lost. Other descriptions might emphasize not so much the absorption into the ultimate as the discovery of the ultimate from within. In this view, there still is the identity of the individual soul intact, although now it has been transformed into realm of *nirvana.*

How does all of this affect an elderly person? For one thing, the Hindu notion of reincarnation emphasizes the spiritual or contemplative dimension of the human person. Spiritual growth means more than just doing good works. It also entails a deepening of one's contemplative nature. The escape from the endless cycle of birth and rebirth is above all else a contemplative experience. The various yogas practiced by Hindus all reach their most profound levels in the act of contemplation. Growing old should therefore include a deepening of one's contemplative nature.

The Hindu religion is very sensitive to the need for spiritual enrichment during old age. In the *Laws of Manu,* it is suggested that when a man begins to see his skin wrinkled and his hair turn grey and when his children are all on their own, it is time for him to go to the forest with or without his wife. Thus, a man abandons the life of a householder, and retires to the forest to seek contemplation. If he really progresses in the spiritual life, he may eventually become a wandering ascetic, totally renouncing all earthly possessions.

This built-in structure of the Hindu religion allows for people to be active and productive during their middle years but increasingly detached and contemplative during their later years. It is a way of encouraging old people to prepare for death and penetrate the meaning of life before their body expires. The result should be a willing acceptance of death and a confidence in the cosmic law to continue one's soul in another life after death.

Gandhi believed that a true understanding of reincarnation should make a contemplative person neither fearful of his own death nor mournful over the death of loved ones. The genius of the Hindu scheme of *karma* and reincarnation is that an individual life is not an isolated being facing death. Instead, the individual soul is caught up in the great cosmic laws of *karma* and rebirth, and salvation is also according to the cosmic design of eventually realizing that the universal and eternal are in union with the individual and the transient. *Atman* is *Brahman,* and *samsara* is *nirvana.* A person who practices contemplation during his old age will lose his attachments to the world. The transition from death to rebirth will be easy and natural.

Perhaps the actual goal of the Hindu cycle of birth-death and rebirth is hard for us to grasp. This is partly because the goal is a mystical one and therefore difficult to describe. Moreover, the ontological state of having transcended the cycle of birth, death and rebirth is often described in vague and elusive terms. Perhaps it is best to say that the notion of *nirvana* or freedom or release from the world of endless change, whether Hindu or Buddhist, is a mystical state of consciousness. Even if descriptions are difficult, the consequences are clear. The individual is now liberated and insight into the mystery of life and death is achieved. In the *Dhammapada,* the Buddha offers this discourse on old age:

. . . Him I call a Brahamana who knows the mystery

of death and rebirth of all beings, who is free from attachment, who is happy within himself and enlightened . . . Him I call a Brahamana who knows his former lives, who knows heaven and hell, who has reached the end of births, who is a sage of perfect knowledge and has accomplished all that has to be accomplished.

The belief in reincarnation and the subsequent transcendence of the cycle of birth and rebirth has given structure and meaning to the processes of aging and death to countless millions of people in the world. This mythic structure and attitude allows an individual to deal with his own old age and death with both meaning and acceptance. It offers an explanation for suffering and injustice as well as a motivation to perform good works. An anthropologist of religion might marvel at the social and political functions of these mythic beliefs but see them as merely devices of a culture to deal with some rather painful realities. Indeed, the caste system and the slow progress towards alleviating poverty in India have both been attributed to the negative aspects of their religious beliefs. Even if the mythic structures of *karma,* reincarnation and liberation have allowed millions of people to find meaning in their suffering, it does not justify an unconcern for that suffering. This is the worldly humanist response to benefits of belief in reincarnation. However, it should be noted that both Hinduism and Buddhism advocate compassion for all who suffer, in addition to a cosmological scheme for finding meaning in their suffering. One wonders also if the attitude of atheistic materialism has produced results which are any more solicitous.

C) The Belief that Life Continues After Death Through The Survival of the Soul and/or The Resurrection of the Body
    Many of the implications of a belief in life after death were dealt with in the section dealing with the denial of such a belief. There, we tried to deal with some of the objections to the notion that life continues beyond physical death. Our conclusions were that a belief in life after death has not been disproven by modern science or shown to be destructive by modern philosophy. If we see the *human person* as more than just a material body, it is quite plausible that *the soul* survives death. Moreover, the belief that life continues beyond physical death does not necessarily suggest a devaluation of this life or a selfish concern for one's own ego. Rather, the belief in life after death arises from a profound

understanding that a human person contains a spiritual dimension that seeks love and knowledge in this life but yearns for a completion of the urge to love and to know in a life beyond this one. Thus, the human spirit is always reaching out towards the future.

Secular expressions on this urge are found in a concern for the future of one's tribe, race, nation or, on a grander scale, in a concern for the future of the human family. Yet there is a deep urge for future completion of our individual yearnings and aspiration that seems to transcend the mere concern for the historical and the secular future. True apocalypticism leaps out of the boundaries of space and time. The apocalyptic future is colored with the images and symbols of the spiritual and the transcendent. Even though much of Old Testament apocalyptic thought centers on the transformation of the earth into a new age, there is no doubt that the new earth will be more than a peaceful and satiated completion of the yearnings of this life. It will be an age of spiritual communion with God. It will be not only the transformation of this earth alone, but it will also be the harmonious union of the earth with heaven. Thus, the future is seen as the spiritual and material completion of all reality.

The question of our survival of death is inexorably linked with our vision of the future. Some people might argue that the future of the human race should take precedence over our concern for our own individual destiny. But the value of the human community as a whole is also conditioned by the infinite value placed upon each individual as well. Many individual lives have been offered up as bloody sacrifices to the god of a new future society. The "unfinished revolution" has been used as an excuse for the devaluation of individual lives. Our most profound yearnings for the future go beyond the revolutionary mentality. The spiritually sensitive person realizes that our openness to love and knowledge is so deep that it can only be satisfied in a transformation of our material and historical mode of being into a mystical dimension of communion with the real (which does not obliterate the material but rather unites it with the spiritual).

The issues involved here are delicate, elusive and difficult. The exact relation of the material world with the future apocalyptic transformation has been fertile matter for theological speculation. The more archaic apocalyptic images depict future life as the mere resuscitation of the bodies of the dead. The more sophisticated images depict a spiritualization of the body which allows for a fuller and freer expression of the "whole man" in the union of body and soul. The spiritualized body is capable of reaching out in love and knowledge towards God and towards all of humanity in a way that was impossible during earthly, historical existence. Here is where the image of the "pancosmic vision" seems helpful. The individual soul is able to realize in his or her most profound depths the image of all of humanity and the image of God. This spiritual community unites the internal and external dimensions of communion and love. In loving his humanity, the individual loves all of humanity. In loving God, the individual loves all of God's creatures. The depths of the human soul reveal the unimaginable depth and beauty of God. This is so because God is present in the very depths of the soul that open out to the infinite horizons of reality. Yet the individual soul reaches outward as well as inward. The spiritualized body has an expansive potential which transcends the limits of our earthly body. In the expansive embrace of love towards God and God's creatures, the individual soul is able to see the unity and diversity of reality coincide in remarkable splendor. God becomes all in all, and the future has now joined with the eternal.

The language and imagery of the future life always fall short of the anticipated glory. Likewise, our image of what mode or form the human person will take also remains a mystery. One thing is certain, though, and that is that a belief in a future life demands an affirmation of the spiritual side of our humanity. St. Paul speaks of our "spiritual body" (1 Cor. 15), and "just as we resemble the man from earth (Adam), so shall we bear the likeness of the man from heaven." (v. 49) Jesus makes it very clear that our future destiny involves a more than bodily existence: "When people rise from the dead, they neither marry nor are given in marriage but live like angels in heaven." (Mat. 22 v. 30) It is clear, at least from the Christian perspective, that our future entails a spiritual transformation of our person after death.

How should such a belief influence the elderly? Here, we move once again into the arena of speculation, for it is very difficult to know the inner feelings stirring in the heart of any fellow human coming face to face with God. Very often there is the pull of many different emotions. Certainly sadness and sorrow are not inappropriate emotions when thinking about death. To leave a place, a home, to venture forth into the unknown — all of these involve both sadness and fear. It seems that all profound transformations in life strike a very deep cord of emotions in our heart, and it is not uncommon to feel overwhelmed, saddened or enthralled by such events as birth, marriage, retirement and death. These key moments of joy and sorrow hit us where we are most vulnerable. They bring us into the heart of the mysteries of life and death and make us realize that all our science and sophistication is powerless before them. We become as children, yearning for instruction and guidance in a world that overwhelms our ability to grasp it. The gush of tears, the dull throb of grief, the eyes raised to a religious symbol seeking solace — all these give solemn homage to the One who is author of life and death.

The old person who has lived a life in solemn homage to the author of life and death will gracefully and peacefully walk the final steps of his or her journey in life. When trust in the mysterious powers that control life, growth and change have been constant companions through life, this trust will be the final blessing of old age. Just as the mystery of life demands an attitude of reverential trust, so also does the mystery of death. The elderly person who trusts in God will live with hope for the future. The dynamism of love and knowledge will continue even in the midst of physical diminishment and sickness. A person who loves God will trust in the eternal quality of the love of God. Love never ends, and neither will the relationship of love that exists between the human soul and God.

The attitude of trust should also help an old person overcome the fear of death and the fear of judgment. The arrival of old age has often been thought of as a time to spiritually prepare for one's final reckoning with God. Many terrible sinners have been given the solace of God's forgiveness through the grace of the sacraments of either reconciliation or anointing of the sick. The Catholic Church is very wise to have these ritualized expressions of God's love and forgiveness for the human person. As a creature of the sense world, we need the visible expression of the spiritual in order to be psychologically convinced of the reality of God's compassion.

In facing death, the three theological virtues of faith, hope and charity all come into play. The old person awaiting death has faith in the promise of a future life. This faith gives rise to hope for a world which is the completion of the inadequacies of this one. This is a hope that our deepest aspirations and yearnings are not frustrated dreams but realizable realities. Finally, charity should emerge in the heart of an old person facing death. The love for one's children should broaden into a deep love and compassion for all humans struggling through life. Nothing is more sad and tragic than an old person who is full of anger, bitterness, criticism and reproach towards the people of the present generation. An old person might be saddened by the evils and failures of the world, but a peaceful heart will look with compassion and forgiveness on the foolish and the wicked. Charity's greatest test is often faced in old age. This is so especially when the elderly are made to feel like they are a burden, or they are made to feel useless. Without the theological virtue of charity (which is a gift from God), an old person can easily grow into a very lonely, bitter and tragic figure.

The passage from this life to the next is made much easier when an old person has been recognized as a creative resource up to the moment of death. In a healthy family environment, the elderly should be seen as the "links to the past." They should be the storytellers to the young generation. When an old person has led a full, happy and resourceful life up to the very end, death should come as the final ripening of his or her humanity. Karl Rahner, among others, has made a point of seeing death as the end of a life-long process of dying. Childhood dies with adolescence; adolescence dies with adulthood, and so forth. Yet in each one of these "deaths" the memories and events of the previous stage are not lost but rather brought to completion. If this is the pattern of life, then death should be the "final stage of growth" to use the phrase of Dr. Kubler-Ross. An elderly person, therefore, who has flowed with the process of dying (which is part of life) should be able to flow gracefully into the final and ultimate stage.

The key to the belief in a future life is an abiding trust in God and an abiding recognition of the spiritual dimension of our humanity. The two of these go hand in hand. An old person who has lived life with a concern for God and with a recognition of the spiritual will have the faith and trust needed to face death peacefully and courageously. Death is not made less painful by faith, but it is made more meaningful. The old person opens his or her soul to God at the moment of death. This opening of the soul should have been a lifelong process and habit. The old person of faith will place the same trust in God on the deathbed as he or she placed in God throughout life. The soul submits itself to the mysterious darkness of death and awaits the emergence of the light.

Final Thoughts and Conclusion
It should be obvious to the reader that the author of this chapter

believes in a future life and feels that such a belief should help in the process of growing old and preparing for death. It is difficult to remain totally objective when dealing with a topic as personal as death. Nevertheless, whether or not one believes in a future life or reincarnation, death places us all in the same boat. When all is said and done, no one can really be an expert on death for it is a subject that transcends our ability to write or talk about it.

Scientists, philosophers, psychologists, theologians — all may treat death in their own special ways, but after all the studies have been made and all the theories have been proferred, death still stands there like a lurking shadow: unmoveable, omnipresent and mysterious. Perhaps it is this sense of mystery that needs to be developed. Death brings us into the kingdom of the mysterious, and we are all subjects to its majestic elusiveness. But death is more than a subject that involves the unknown. It is a deeper mystery, a mystery that grips and shocks in sudden moments of lucid simplicity. We see that we are growing old and can do nothing about it. We see that our lives are on a quiet course towards death, and we cannot escape. We look at ourselves, and we wonder what it's all about. Then, we approach the dark road towards death with nothing to guide us — except some hopes, fears and a vague but profound trust in the loving powers that be.

Notes

1. International Herald Tribune May 12, 1981
2. Thomas, Lewis Editorial "How Should Humans Pay Their Way?" *New York Times* August 24, 1981 p. A15
3. Nietzsche, Freidrich *On the Genealogy of Morals* (trans. W. Kaufmann) (New York, 1967) p. 117
4. Plato, *Phaedo* in *The Last Days of Socrates* (Trans. H. Tredennick) (Middlesex, England, 1954) p. 107
5. Roberts, David E. *Existentialism and Religious Belief* p. 155
6. Ibid
7. Dixon, Maceille in *The Phoenix Fire Mystery* p.3
8. Berry, Thomas *The Religions of India* (New York, 1971) p. 14

The Mystical Dimension of Aging

Wayne Teasdale

Perhaps the most basic, enduring and vivid experience for us all is the reality of constant change. For no matter the direction in which we look, everything is in a state of perpetual growth and decay, an endless cycle of beginning, development, decline and transformation, of birth, maturation, death and the Beyond. We perceive the operation of this principle on all levels of existence, and there is no being that is not subject to its law in the realm of temporality. Even a child knows that yesterday is not quite the same as today, that there is a difference between this day and tomorrow. Indeed, the perception of time through the process of change is a universal phenomenon, attested to in all ages and cultures.

On the human scale, we designate this experience of constant change as the process of aging, for aging, in its structural aspect, is simply the reality of flux, of movement and becoming applied to human life, and is the measurement of such life. Moreover, we divide human existence into stages: childhood, adolescence, adulthood, or maturity, and old age. This division, however, does not comprehend what aging as such is; it merely acknowledges this process as a fact of life.

Aging, furthermore, is not confined only to "living" organisms. Everything ages in the sense of development. For stars and galaxies are born, live and die, changing form in the process. Similarly, planets and moons also have such cycles. In a real sense, the entire cosmos is going through this aging process that we call change or evolution. This fact and the *organic* nature of the universe's growth have led some astronomers and cosmologists to conclude the the cosmos is itself a living organism, the galaxies being its members and the stars its cells.

What is the cause of this state of continuous flux that Heraclitus took note of some twenty-five centuries ago? What is the essential meaning of aging? Why does everything change or become? What purpose does growth or development serve? Is there a purpose to the process of change? Is there a goal or terminus to which aging itself is oriented?

In this chapter, an attempt will be made to present the insight into the actuality of aging as a process of *spiritual* growth (as the environment of the mystical quest) that mysticism *is* the meaning of aging, and that the nature of wisdom — the end towards which the various stages of life are moving — is *mystical*. The elucidation of this issue will necessitate a discussion of what mysticism is — what its nature is — and what the stages of mystical consciousness are. Consideration will also be given to the transmission of mystical wisdom in the master-disciple relationship, the model of how the generations should interact with each other. This will then set the stage for identifying contemplation or mystical life as the supreme *value*, the depth wisdom that can transform the world when it becomes the focus and motivating center of man's activity in himself and in the world. In this way, we will understand the proper function of aging, restore the "old ones" to their important role in society as venerable sages and teachers of the mystical dimension of life (revaluing on a higher plane) the honor due the aged and permit them to contribute their wisdom and experience to the renewal of mankind.

Change, Becoming and Aging

In the spatio-temporal domain, everything is constantly changing and becoming, because, in a real sense, nothing is actually fully what it ought to be. The seed is not yet the tree, though it will become so in time. The point is that, in an ultimate sense, the reality of change is the fact of becoming, which has its *raison d'être* in a lack of reality or actuality at the core of temporal being. Everything is *striving to be* because nothing has yet achieved the fullness of existence within the limits of the time-space continuum. Beings change because they are trying to hold on to, or comprehend in themselves, the plenitude of existence, to become completely actual. All things are racing towards that absolute "place" that will actualize them and bring about their consummation. Change, becoming and aging are the processes of realizing the potentiality for being for reality, of the actualization of that which each thing must be in order to fulfill its nature.

Consequently, a being assumes many different moments in the progressive actualization of what it intrinsically is. A person goes through innumerable changes and traverses certain stages — on the level of physical structure — in the course of his or her life, but as we will see, the meaning of this process is not found on the physical plane. We must look elsewhere to understand it.

Even when we examine a supposedly substantial physical body, when we subject it to the analysis of subatomic physics, we discover, to our astonishment, the insubstantial character it has, its essential lack. We find rather, that matter is really not "solid" — not completely independent in its being — but is composed of *dynamic patterns* of energy constantly changing into one another and following a certain theme of order which interconnects them with the totality. This means that a merely materialistic or mechanistic conception of reality is false. The cosmos, in both its *macro* and *micro* phases, is *dynamic* or living. It also has a definite government, which we do not grasp because of the vast extent of its order and the numerous processes involved.

What is real is the totality of the process, the integrated whole, the overarching principle that unites all the elements into one system of reality. Now, the really telling note in this picture of physical reality is that of a patterned or ordered dynamism as the basis of the universe's flux. What this suggests is that Spirit is the ultimate foundation of the cosmos, for order, pattern, indeed dynamism itself are essentially spiritual in nature. The implication is that this theme of subatomic order, structure or pattern is itself serving a symbolic function, which points not only to the reality of *meaning* and purpose in the cosmic/evolutionary process, but also to the *within* and the *beyond* of the process itself.

Reality is the product of a totality of processes. This does not mean that reality is, itself, process or a mere result of it, but that reality requires duration or time to unfold; it requires a certain sequence of temporal becoming to make explicit what it is or will be. This is true of everything in the cosmos. We can see this truth graphically illustrated in the case of the seed that will eventually become the tree. The actuality of the tree is not the seed, but without the seed, it would not become the tree. The being of the tree stretches from its seedling form all the way to its complete maturity. Hence, reality is the totality of the existential moments that constitute a being, and Reality as such. This means that there is a complete notion behind the process of the unfolding of the whole, a plan. The immediate moment is only one element in the process — real, but incomplete. For only when the immediate is seen within the context of the totality is it rightly understood.

Aging is a process that encompasses long periods of time and is only evident through the course of duration. On the structural level, aging involves consciousness possessing a time-sense which is partially subjective. In the actual flow of time, the conscious knower is observing certain relations among objects, and these relations change as new details are introduced while others are superseded. It is consciousness that is experiencing the reality of aging. Aging takes place in the perception of the knowing subject as well as in the body of the knower. It is thus a spiritual state as well as a physical fact. It is part of man's self-understanding and one of the greatest challenges in life.

Aging, in its ideal condition, is a progressive *clarification* of what life is. It is characterized by the enhancing of one's perspective on existence. For the process of aging — when the person is awake to its significance — is a *spiritual* phenomenon. It is growth in one's awareness of what is. Aging is also the environment of our search for the Absolute, the unfolding of the Mystery of life in our lives. It is also the revelation of the meaning of death, since all life — and aging as such — is a movement in relation to death and beyond. The Mystery of life, death and eternity is not something the mind constructs, but is something objectively *meant* for consciousness. It is not subjective in origin, nor is it merely objective, since it engages consciousness. It is somehow tailor-made for us.

Aging, as a process of striving to know and to live the Mystery of existence, takes its impulse primarily from the great puzzle of death. It is in this orientation that mystical wisdom is born. Wisdom is the insight into this question and its answer. Aging is the drama of living this answer. Socrates maintained that the whole point of life is to learn to die well, that life is a preparation for death, but that only he can die well who knows what life is all about. This knowledge is what constitutes wisdom. And this wisdom, 'the pearl of great price,' is essentially *mystical*. Thus, when life is lived in its depth, it is a process of spiritual growth, and aging is the medium through which this growth occurs. Aging is fulfilled in mystical awareness. This is wisdom in its profoundest sense for true wisdom is the search for the Absolute which is constitutional to human nature, and aging is the process of unfolding this search.

In the modern world, the elderly live in a state of spiritual deprivation. They are made to feel ashamed of their age. This is because the contemporary world does not live from a deep contact with the mystery of aging. Old people are alienated, because society values a productive function in its citizens rather than simply being a person. Function determines worth. The elderly who are not aware of their spiritual dimension, tend to be lonely, bored and lacking a sense of direction and self-worth. They consider themselves useless, as does society, because they cannot *do* something in the way of work. Since the modern world values *doing* rather than being, our elderly feel that their existence is devoid of purpose. Our world has lost its focus. It is out of touch with the meaning of being human. And it is because civilization has lost its spiritual focus that so many elderly lack such an awareness in their lives. They have become victims of a spiritually dull world, a world torn by violence, injustice, hatred, selfishness and a monstrous indifference to the sufferings of others. Is it not possible to measure the moral and spiritual health of a society by the way it treats its older citizens? The world must regain its contact with the transcendent, with mystical wisdom, and rediscover the "old ones" as teachers of this wisdom.

Mystical Wisdom

Mysticism, or contemplative spirituality, refers to that heightened consciousness arising from an *experiential* penetration into the realm of the Divine. In itself, it is not philosophical or theological speculation about the Absolute or God. Rather, mysticism is an intense, intimate *awareness,* or *experience,* of the Absolute. Mystical wisdom is grounded in, and aims at an existential, concrete *oneness* with, Ulitmate Reality. In this sense, it is a practical wisdom. Mystical knowledge comprises all the insights into the Divine that have been culled from the human experience of union with the transcendent. The entire purpose of life is found in the mystical quest. For it is in the mystical quest that aging achieves its goal, which is to allow each person sufficient time to discover the spiritual dimension of life and to bloom in its garden beyond space and time.

Just as the reality of aging is universal, so also is mysticism. It is present in every culture, from the most primitive animistic tribes to the most sophisticated and technically advanced societies. It was the thirst for the Divine Life and for immortality that inspired the great *rishis* to retire to the forests of India and dwell in caves, keeping silence and practicing meditation. These Hindu saints discovered the Source of Being living within the depths of the Self. Likewise, it was the search for God and perfection that led the early Christian monks into the deserts of Egypt, Palestine and Syria. Their hunger for God bore fruit in an experiential knowledge of His inner being, much like the Hebrew Prophets before them, who became absorbed in the Divine *Pathos.* This same passion for the Absolute was later institutionalized in the form of the great Catholic monastic Orders and in the freer monastic style of the mendicant Orders (friars). In the Eastern Orthodox Church, we see the same spiritual motive at work in her monastic structures, which have given birth to countless contemplatives.

In Buddhism as well there is a rich mystical tradition which emphasizes the realization of liberation (*nirvana*) through the practice of meditation and compassion, nurtured within a diverse and thriving monastic culture. In Islam, the *Sufis* are the great masters of mystical life who have represented for centuries the depth dimension of Islam and the profoundest aspiration of the soul. The *Sufis* also have many affinites with the mystics of Christianity. The quest for the Absolute has its most archaic roots among the primitive cultures, which are guided by their *shamans,* the seers of the other world. Among the North American Indians, the mystical journey takes the form (among others) of the vision quest, in the context of a culture that has always experienced an intense identification with nature and a solidarity with all living beings.

It is the universality of the mystical dimension that offers hope for the future transformation of the world. The nations of the earth are divided along so many lines of economic and political interest, but in the spiritual dimension we all come together. It is this realization that has led one contemplative master of our time, Abbot Thomas Keating, to say: "The contemplative (mystical) dimension of life, present in all the great religions, is the common heart of the world. There the human family is already one."[1]

This desire for the Absolute, for unity with it, and the desire for immortality, are what established us as fully human, and they are conducive to perfection. Man cannot, in truth, dispense with this level of existence and be happy, for it is only in this way that his life will be fulfilled. He has been created for the mystical quest, which is a *permanent* dimension of human experience. It is what defines his life, and it takes form as man strives for the Infinite. Furthermore, any state that fails to make room for the mystical quest eventually runs the risk of collapse, since it is not rooted in the essential and is superimposing its own program. And that is to distort life. Moreover, there are already signs of decay and collapse in a number of states. For all we have to do is take a good look around at the condition of civilization globally, and we will see that it is afflicted with a terrible spiritual *malaise* that does not bode well for the future, unless corrected in time. Mankind's dangerous situation — the nuclear arms trap and mass starvation in the Third World — is the result of a spiritual illness and a moral myopia that has been gaining ground since the 18th century "enlightenment." An irony of history, perhaps? Is it any wonder that the elderly of our planet feel so estranged and, in a sense, stateless?

The old ones are compelled by a prevailing cultural mood, which is informed by consumerism (the lust to have more and more things, especially things that are unnecessary to one's well-being) and the youth cult, to seek useless ends in which they do not themselves believe nor really want. Society psychologically compels its older citizens to live estranged lives in the time remaining to them, since it is ill-equipped to guide them along the path of spirituality. This distressing situation exists for a number of historical reasons: exclusive emphasis on reason and science, leaving no room for the play of intuition; the pursuit of material goals to the detriment of mystical wisdom; the 'easy' life of affluent secularity, propped up by technological advances; and the preoccupation with acquiring money. As a consequence, there is probably not one modern industrial state that really understands the needs of the elderly, needs which are primarily *spiritual* in nature. And the mystical inclination is simply the ultimate manifestation of such needs, for God has implanted the mystical desire, the essential need like food itself, in the depths of the soul, and He has given us the means to attain the end. Indeed, aging is itself the chief of these!

Another example of a means or a method is given in the Psalms when Yahweh or God says: "Be *still,* and you will know that I am God." (Ps. 46:11) Be still, and you will *experience* His Presence. Now this method is similar to the various forms of meditation in the religions of Asia which stress the importance of inner *quiet* or the cessation of though processes. This is also close to the meaning of the *hesychia* of the Desert Fathers, the practice of *interior silence* and waiting upon the initiative of God. The point is that the mystical life, once awakened, has to be cultivated with extraordinary care and assiduous practice, which usually involves some sort of method, since certain methods are beneficial in assisting us to reach the goal.

In Hinduism, which sets aside the last stage of life, beginning at sixty (and this is marked by a special celebration) for the purpose of pursuing the mystical quest, and cultivating this dimension, the significance of age and wisdom was discovered very early, for before Europe was even civilized, the *rishis* and *sadhus* had stumbled upon the truth. These holy men and women had encountered the Divine Presence dwelling within the 'cave of the heart.' They found God at the center of their being. The *Chandogya Upanishad* waxes lyrical when it proclaims: "In the city of Brahman (the 'cave of the heart') there is an abode, within it a small lotus flower; inside, a little space; what there is within, it is that (which) one must seek, that one must desire to know!"[2]

Today in India, the spiritual descendants of the rishis — the Hindu (and now also Christian) monks or *samnyasis* lead that same intense practice of meditation and ascetical discipline that culminates in mystical experience. They seek the immortal Self or the Divine Spark within the deep subjectivity of the soul. This Divine Spark or Atman *is* God *immanent* in the heart. The *Katha Upanishad*, in a celebrated passage, expresses it this way: "What is hard to see, hidden in the depth, set in the cave (of the heart), primeval . . . smaller than the small, greater than the great, is the *self*, the life interior to all beings, the only Master!"[3] Dwelling there with God in the 'cave of the heart' one develops the contemplative capacity, which is the mystical perception of the Presence in all things, and a sense of one's own immortality.

One important difference — at least on the surface — existing between the religions of the Orient and the Occident, in the mystical life, is the emphasis on the Divine Presence as either *immanent* or *transcendent*. Actually, both are found in most traditions, but a certain emphasis is characteristic of each. In the East, the emphasis is on the immanence of the Divine in the 'cave of the heart,' in the deepest center of one's being, where the world and creatures have no direct influence. That is the untouched core of a person's being. It was the spiritual genius of India that had made this crucial discovery. In the West, the stress has been on the transcendent, totally other character of the Absolute, the Divine Presence, symbolized in the spiritual journey to the summit of the mountain, as in the theophany that Moses encountered on Mount Sinai, where God revealed His Name as YAHWEH or "I AM WHO I AM," I am the fullness of Being, Existence and Presence (Exodus 3:14). This is the transcendent life of God, the Inaccessible One, Who manifested Himself in the *Shekinah*, the sacred Presence hovering above His friends.

When we take a deeper plunge into this mystery, however, we find that both immanence and transcendence converge in the

Divine Unity when the soul is *one* with God in the consciousness of mystical union. Going within the mystical 'cave of the heart,' we discover a door that opens into the great splendor of Divine transcendence, the Light of eternal glory, where the finite is perpetually coming forth from the Infinite One. Immanence and transcendence, as modes of Divine Presence, are *one* in the Mystery of God's eternal Now, which is beyond time and space.

The final consummation of the process of mystical life, the process of aging and its very meaning, is *unity*. Unity is the whole point of the mystical quest, to rest in the Divine One. In that height of contemplative experience, on the summit of life near the horizon of eternity, in the mystical oneness with the Source, duality is overcome, and the subject-object polarity, so characteristic of everyday consciousness, is superseded in the experience of unity. Plotinus describes this experience of unity and the paradox it involves. He says: "Soul must see in its own way; this is by coalescence, unification; but in seeking thus to know the Unity, it is prevented by that very unification from recognizing that it has found it; for it cannot distinguish itself from the object of this intuition."[4]

The paradox is this: one experiences unity but cannot see or feel the distinction between oneself and God, that being in the Unity means that is what one is conscious of, since if one were aware of a difference, then one would not be in a state of unification with the Absolute. If there is total unity in an unqualified sense, how can there be difference? But if there is no difference, how can the soul experience the Divine Unity and retain the vivid memory of it? What happens in mystical union is that God draws the soul into a *unity of consciousness* with Himself, not a unity of being, and the soul is overpowered by the sheer intensity of God's infinite *act* of existence, His unlimited power *to be* expressed in His oneness, in which all His knowledge and the totality are united with Him in that eternal Now which He *is*. The soul experiences this unity of consciousness. Furthermore, what the mystics are aware of in the experience is not a pantheistic identification with the Ground of existence, but a unity with God that entails *panentheism,* that is, that all things subsist *in* God. And it is only God Who can initiate this expansion of our consciousness into an explosion of awareness, as we are embraced and surrounded by the Divine Unity. If we were this Unity itself, then we could bring it about at will, but we cannot. And so we are completely dependent on the mercy of God, as in all things.

It is this experience of unity with the Absolute that is one of the essential elements of mystical life. Indeed, if unity were absent, then an experience could not be claimed to be mystical in nature. When the soul enters into the Unity in its ultimate degree, then she experiences it as pure bliss and the gushing forth of Love. Jan Van Ruysbroeck, the Flemish mystic of the 14th century, comments on this aspect when he says: "And in this (Unity) there is a delectable passing over and a flowing-away and a sinking-down into the essential nakedness, . . . for there is nothing but an eternal resting in a delectable embrace of the flowing-out of love."⁵

Thus Unity is also the Presence of the Divine Life, which often arises in one's consciousness in a sudden flash, in a moment of extraordinary clarity. The Divine Presence "invades" the soul without warning, and brings her into its Unity. It happens when one least expects it. The power of God's Presence is so great that it begins to transform the soul in His Unity. Before this Presence one is dumb and passive, like a gentle feather floating in the immensity of a whirlwind, and the soul desires only to have this mystical inpouring of God's ineffable love.

Sometimes she may be carried away into the Presence, through Unity into the Trinity, where she perceives the eternal event of the Divine One knowing Himself in the dynamic Mystery of the trinitarian interaction. The Trinity is the Source of God's Identity, His knowledge and His love. To be on this high plane of mystical consciousness is to witness how Unity contemplates and knows itself in Trinity, and how Trinity is the eternal actualization of God's supreme *act* of inner Identity. Unity and Trinity are the endless ebb and flow of the Divine Life, which is captured primordially in the *tao*, in the symbol of *yin* and *yang,* a representation of the hidden being of the nameless One. And the inner, dynamic nature of Unity resolving itself into a threefold *unmoving-movement,* which knows itself in the intimacy of the personal, is also reflected in the Hindu mystical intuition of *Saccidananda,* the absolute conscious moments of Being (*sat*), Knowledge (*cit*) and Bliss (*ananda*), which correspond to the three Divine Persons of the Trinity. *Sat* would be the Father (Source of Being); *cit* is the Son (Logos or Knowledge), and *ananda* is the Holy Spirit (Bliss, Love and the Divine Energy).

The Christian intuition and experience of the Trinity is that it is the perfect metaphysical identity of the Divine nature. The soul is caught up into the dynamic life of the Trinity, and sees it from *within* the actuality of the Trinity's eternal activity. The Father as Source of Being (fullness of Reality) proceeds from the Divine Unity, the Godhead. As the implicit actuality of all things, He flows into the Son, the Logos as a 'movement' of self-knowledge. In this eternal act, He knows Himself in His Son, and both know each other in the Spirit. The Spirit is the eternal fruit of the Father's contemplation of the Son and the Son's perfect imaging and explicitation of the Father's infinite being. The act itself of this relationship generates eternally the unifying bond of Love which is the Spirit, the inner Self of God and the Ground, or inward Life, of the Godhead. It is the Trinity, as the dynamic Center of the Divine Unity, that is also the creative Origin of the cosmos and of all things, for the act by which the Trinity *is* the Identity of God is also the act by which the generation of everything occurs. And this creative act occurs through the Son, for Christ *is* the link between heaven and earth and *is* the *way* to the God-head.

In the progressive growth into mystical life, which is the process of spiritual aging or unfolding, the direct path to this high estate is the way of *love*. Love is the purity of one's deepest desire for God ever knocking at the gate of His domain. It is only by way of love that we can ever arrive at mystical union, that we can touch God or rather, be touched by Him. Speculation will not reach God's being or yield any positive knowledge of His nature, and certainly not grasp His essence. To achieve oneness with Him, we must persist in our loving desire for Him; we must become single-minded in this intention. This is the way or method of love.

Although it is true to say that thought cannot grasp or produce mystical consciousness, it is also true that the ultimate level of the experience includes both knowledge and love, that mystical union gives us a metaphysical knowledge of God's being, the Divine Unity, the Trinity, Christ, the Son of God, the various mysteries and a glimpse of the principles that govern the creation of all beings as they arise out of the fecundity of the trinitarian interaction at the heart of the Real.

The relationship between knowledge and love in the act of mystical union is a very intimate one indeed. It is somehow understood in the biblical notion of *da'ath,* the Hebrew word for knowledge based on intimacy, on love, as in "Adam *knew (da'ath)* Eve," and this is the model of a relationship with God. It is a knowledge, a knowing of a concrete personal nature in which love

produces a profound understanding, although it remains in-
expressible. This is what happens in the depths of the soul as she
enters deeper into the Mystery of God's being and hidden life.
Knowledge and love converge and mutually expand each other's
range in a greater and greater penetration of the Divine Mystery.
Love enlivens knowledge and knowledge magnifies love, and both
become *one* in a mystical enlightenment of affectivity, for both
are enlarged into a new form of knowing and loving — a single act
— in which there is an enhanced experience of God's inner life. It is
a state of blissful omniscience, as in the Buddhist understanding of
nirvana in which there is a simultaneous awareness of emptiness
and fullness; emptiness implying that the mind is not aware of any
particular object, and fullness because it is conscious of the totality
at once. The latter is similar to the Divine act of knowing, since
God comprehends everything in knowing Himself.

Aging — to apply the above — allows the forces of nature and
grace to unite body and spirit in the expanded experience of living.
As one lives and grows old, one actually experiences growth in the
profoundest kind of knowledge, which is knowing *how to love,*
and this is something only the Spirit can teach us. In the following
section, we will deal with the three stages of the mystical life or the
levels of spiritual growth in the process of contemplative aging.

The Stages: Purgation, Illumination and Union

In the steady course of development in mystical awareness, from
the faint flashes in the beginning to its zenith in the Unitive Life,
there are three significant stages that often overlap and which
eventually become simultaneous. These stages or degrees can be
found, in one form or another, in the mystical literature of all the
great world religions. It was Plotinus in the Western world,
however, who first took note of them, and the Pseudo-Dionysius
who later developed the stages more systematically. Furthermore,
it was St. John of the Cross who developed these stages into a
comprehensive psychology of spiritual growth that is applicable to
the experience of growing in love and knowledge.

In the first stage, that of the Purgative Way, there is, to begin
with, an *awakening* to the reality of the spiritual life. Once this
knowledge is grasped, the soul has to *will* to traverse the difficult
path of the mystical quest that will eventually lead to the Unitive
Life. This act of the will, which is a continuous commitment, is
what is usually referred to as *conversion.* The initial stage of
purgation assumes that the person is already aware of the mystical

goal of life and is totally committed to its pursuit. The task of the purgative period is to grow progressively in interior freedom by a steadfast *renunciation* of all the lesser goods of life, and the rooting out of all vices. One must let go of sense pleasures, and the very desire for them. And one has also to be liberated from the chains of the ego, from its dangerous illusions and self-deceptions. The Purgative Way, moreover, has the purpose of freeing us from the psychic scars of our unconscious life and the wounds that previous experiences have left. Further, purgation increases the perceptive powers of the person, thus permitting the Divine Light to shine in the soul without obstacles in the way of its deifying activity. In this manner, the Divine Life takes its birth in the soul's freedom, and ultimately bears fruit in mystical union as well as in the growth of the virtues.

The most essential attitude to learn in this period is that of *detachment,* freedom from self-will and ego-centricity. The hardest thing in life is to let go of the ego. For it hounds us day and night, and we barely find peace from its insidious influence even in times of prayer. The ego is the source of all mankind's troubles. Since the root of all evil (of all sin) and the chief obstacle in the way of mystical life is an inordinate self-love (ego or pride) the process of *undoing* its hold can be long and very painful. The suffering arises from a profound dose of self-knowledge that is characteristic of the entire spiritual journey, but which is especially acute during the time of purgation.

How is the ego overcome? The ego is tamed or overcome primarily through continuous acts of the will and fervent prayer. It is very difficult though, and requires the wisdom of a spiritual master who can guide one through the many traps and pitfalls of the inner life. Of course, this whole idea runs counter to the values of the world, which gloats in an attitude of sheer self-indulgence. It takes enormous discipline to stir a clear path through the rocks and shoals of the spiritual life.

In addition to other factors, detachment is aided by a practice of prayer in which the person surrenders his or her thoughts, for in a real sense, to give up your thoughts *is* to give up yourself. Thomas Keating maintains that in order to arrive at vision or the Unitive Life, it is even necessary to abandon one's ideas on how to get there. This practice of the prayer of interior quiet (giving up thoughts and attending to God) cultivates in the soul the ability of calm detachment and a disposition of just 'letting be,' not trying to control events, others or even the unfolding of one's own life. This attitude of renunciation of self-will, or detachment, is absolutely indispensable for spiritual growth to happen.

The gradual growth in the disposition of humble renunciation and detachment, the purification of desire before the soul enters the Illuminative Way, is also part of what is called the first"dark night of the soul," because one experiences great trials during this period of being weaned away from self-will and the many allurements of the world. There are two dark nights, one before entrance into the stage of mystical Illumination, called the "dark night of the senses," and the other occurs in the crucial transition period between the Illuminative and Unitive Ways, and is called the "night of the spirit." More will be said on this, later.

Purgation is furthered by the trials of the nights. Now, the sufferings of the first night are fairly tangible in human terms. They consist of rejections, humiliations, failures, the death of a loved one, illness, misfortunes, misunderstandings, all the experiences common to life, ways in which we are freed from our illusions. Their purpose is to assist us in letting go, in learning *detachment* or spiritual poverty by acceptance, quiet acceptance of difficulties. It *is* suffering that is the great teacher of love and mystical wisdom. Perhaps aging is the most common experience of the first" dark night,"for is not aging itself a continual purgation, a process of being liberated from the ego-illusion, in order that the person may be one with God? In each moment we are dying, being purged, and so aging is a positive struggle from which something beautiful and precious is striving to be born. When the soul has been purged of self-will to a certain degree, and her character has been remade so that the image of God shines through her thoughts and actions, and when she fixes her attention on God and the goal of union with Him (Reality itself), then she is ready for the stage of Illumination.

The Illuminative Way is characterized by the perception of God's Presence in all things, and by a mystical understanding of the cosmic and angelic orders. Everywhere one looks, one sees the Presence of the Divine bursting forth. Flowers, trees, rocks, mountains, birds, the fish, the stars, the sun, the moon, events, people and situations all become theophanies or manifestations of the Presence. Everything assumes a sacral nature, and becomes virtually a sacramental sign. Illumination is a state of sensitivity to and reverence for God's Presence, for God Himself, for even in the midst of the trials, the aches and pains of old age — the purgation of life — there can be a perception of God's Presence.

Illumination is also a keen awareness of the Divine indwelling within one's own being, in the solitude of the "cave of the heart." The mystical life, the blissful life in the Spirit, is going on all the time, but our preoccupations and imperfections are stumbling blocks to a realization of this *experiential* truth. Our minds and hearts are too cluttered with ambitions, strong emotions and desires. When the soul, however, achieves inner *simplification* through a process of purification of the will and interior quiet, then she is able to perceive the radiant Presence of the Divine within the heart and in all things, even in one's own sufferings, especially those associated with growing old. We see it all as actually coming from God.

This profound experience of God's indwelling stimulates the growth of the virtues, especially those of humility, affective charity, zeal, simplicity and patience. One is able to forgive injuries quite spontaneously without effort. Everyone and everything become signs of God's Presence and Love for you, which causes a deep interior peace and an abiding mystical joy. This experience of Illumination only magnifies the yearning of the soul for God, for a total union with Him. It makes the mystical quest a single-minded passion, the passion of the infinite.

To the mystic in this stage, the world is transfigured in the Light of eternal glory, and the process of aging assumes a new value, a positive one. All things are seen as arising from a hidden unity, the Divine oneness. All of nature, every creature (including trees, plants, the grass and life itself) has a certain luminous integrity, for one is seeing them in their purity. There is an almost idyllic and mythic quality to everything. The extraordinary beauty and subtlety of nature, its order and harmony, its olympian grandeur and vastness, its musical and heavenly charm enflame the imagination of poets, artists and mystics, awakening profound archetypes and esoteric associations, which often find expression in their poety and art, monuments to human genius inspired by the Divine.

The Illuminative Way oftentimes grants an intellectual vision of the Absolute, and the relation of all being and reality to it. This is the metaphysical component of mystical experience which allows the mystic a glimpse of *totality*: to see the whole process of existence flow forth from the Source, showing also how all things arise from their Divine Ground in the Unity of the One, the One-in-Three.

Such an experience gives to the soul a flash of ineffable insight into the general structure of reality, and this accounts for the origin of many philosophical systems and intuitions, East and West. At times, however, in this stage of the spiritual life, the soul is touched by the Divine *clarity* which illumines her in the mysteries, but it is different from mere intellectual vision. This Divine clarity is the awareness the soul has of God's inner being and truth, in the Godhead or pure Unity and in the Trinity, its Identity; and it is completely ungraspable.

As a person nears the end of the Illuminative period proper, he or she becomes more and more recollected interiorly, and achieves a profound peace, joy and equanimity. This recollection is what, in the Christian Tradition, is called the, "Prayer of Quiet," but in the traditions of the Asian religions is designated as stillness and the suspension of thoughts, which is the end of all meditative techniques.

Before the soul can enter the Unitive state, she must endure the extreme trials of the second night, the "night of the spirit." This is a period in which the soul feels abandoned by God, which of course is not the case. It is the final test before the fullness of mystical life dawns. The purpose of the second night is to purify the soul of any residue of self-will; it is in fact a purification of the will, every inch of it! For prior to the soul's entrance into the plenitude and enjoyment of mystical union — and henceforth — she must belong wholly to God. Thomas Keating gives some valuable and wise advice concerning this time and other periods of dryness and spiritual suffering, when he remarks: "One has only a single support — the mercy of God — but that support is not felt. It is the time of trust, of hoping and continuing to hope against hope."[6] By this trust, hope and silent endurance, the soul eventually is given the grace to experience her unity with God again, but to a much greater degree than before. The fruit of this union is the transformation of the soul *in* God or "deification," the actuality of becoming Godlike, so that she is then always aware of His Presence, and reflects Him in her own being. At this stage, even the ravages of age seem less annoying, since the person has achieved detachment, for one is so united to God that one's sufferings become insignificant in comparison to the glory of mystical union.

In the Unitive Life, the consummation of contemplation, of mystical experience, the unity which the person enjoyed in the earlier phases only in sudden moments or brief flashes of transcendent exxperience is expanded into a *permanent* perception that pervades all of the person's life. The union has thus become the "mystical marriage" between God and the chosen soul. It is this element of *stability* in the Unitive Way that Thomas Keating emphasizes when he comments:

> The growth of the contemplative dimension leads to the stable perception of the transcendent in the midst of the secular. By the contemplative dimension, I mean the growth of faith to the point that one's actions are motivated by an abiding awareness and sensitivity to the Presence of God and to His will in all that happens inwardly and outwardly.[7]

This description seems to suggest the essential characteristic of Illumination, which is the consciousness in us of God's Presence, but in the Unitive stage, the mystic's awareness of the Presence is the result of an intimate *contact* and perduring *oneness* with the Absolute, the Divine Life. It is not a detached intellectual experience or knowledge of God's indwelling in the soul and all reality that characterizes this final period of spiritual development, but a continuous perception of the soul's unity with Him, even in the daily situations of life. It is to live in the Spirit, and to come to the conscious realization, existentially, that "in Him we live and move and have our being." (Acts 17:28)

This enlarged identity that the soul finds in God — for we are beings whose ultimate identity is in *relation*, in relationship to the One Who knows who we are — is the *reality* of a vivifying and constant love. That is why the Unitive Way leads to and *is* the mystical marriage, the state of permanent intimacy between God and the soul, a state of loving awareness of His activity in the depths of the heart where we are *one* with Him. St. John of the Cross describes this state that began as a tiny spark of faith in the period of conversion and Purgation, being expanded in the Illuminative stage, and growing into the vital and awesome awareness of God, as the 'Living Flame of Love,' for as this "Living Flame of Love," God, the "tidal wave" of intimate Presence wounds the soul in her deepest center by His power as this purifying and consuming affection, dwelling secretly in the soul, in the "cave of the heart." The Divine spark, awakened in conversion, becomes an all-encompassing Presence, permanently residing in the interior domain of the soul. This experience of Divnine intimacy, in its permanence, *is* 'a taste' and a promise of eternal life. The price of eternal life, however, is the *cross,* which is a dying in God, a letting go of self-will. By losing one's life in God, one finds true life in Him, and this is to share in His inner being and to abide in His love. This flame of Divine love totally absorbs the soul's desire, and she is transformed in His Presence. He becomes the absolute Center, the gravitational focus of her longing, filling her with the inestimable glory of His love. And this occurs even in the midst of the struggles, the joys and sorrows of life, as one ages and is being purged of the "little self." The soul is united to God in the obscurity of this love.

The Unitive Life is the goal of the mystical quest; it is the end towards which the relentless process of aging is directed. It is the crown of life, and the promise of its ultimate fulfillment in eternal happiness, in the beatitude of the endless vision of God. It is the great indication of immortality, which is the triumph of the Spirit in the consummation of life, an eternal process of living in Divine love, the inner perfection of the trinitarian Mystery at the Center of "He Who Is." Here, in the height of the Unitive Way, aging achieves its true significance, which is realized in spiritual growth or mystical enlightenment. This is the completion of aging, its ever inviting terminus, the meaning of that restless call of the heart to be *one,* and this desire can only be fulfilled in the enhanced identity found in the Divine Life.

It is a hazardous activity indeed to speculate about the relationship of the stages of spiritual growth to the particular age level at which awakened souls enter these degrees of spiritual development. Such a correspondence can only be relative to the concrete situation of a particular person who must traverse these mystical steps. This situation will depend on his or her nature, grace and the time involved in the hard work of purgation, the plucking out of ego at its roots. This work can be accomplished fairly quickly in a few, as in the case of St. Therese of Lisieux, who had passed through all the stages and dwelt in the Unitive Way in her early twenties. In others, purgation takes considerably longer. Some never reach this point in life, and others never even awaken to the reality of the spiritual quest. Generally, contemplation reaches its zenith in the Unitive Way late in life. The intent of monastic *ascesis* is to work away at the cultivation of contemplation on a fulltime basis, and thus accelerate the *interior* process of spiritual maturity.

It is the elders who have been traveling the mystical path for a long period, who are best qualified to teach these matters to the younger generations. If they are completely formed contemplatives or mystics, and have the required skill, experience and perspective in the direction of souls, then they may take on the task of transmitting mystical values, insights and methods from one generation to another. The aim of the next section will be to examine this perennial relationship of the master and disciple, with an eye to two objectives: (1) the elucidation of the relationship in transmission, and (2) the presentation of the guru-disciple relation as an archetype or model of how the young relate to the old, how youth interacts with the wise. This is the crucial area of the value and role of the elders in society.

The Master-Disciple Relation

The master-disciple relationship is one of the most *natural* of human bonds. It is *primordial* and *universal*. Its image can be seen in a child sitting in the lap of a grandparent. This is the pristine state of it in tribal society, the picture of the wise elder sharing the secrets of life with children and youths around a camp fire, in some remote jungle. In the relationship of a grandparent to his or her grandchildren, we can discern the actual prefigurement of the more spiritually refined relation of the guru and his disciple. Grandparents are the original teachers of human wisdom. Consequently, the notion of such a relationship has its inception at the heart of human community. It is thus a very *human* bond.

The role of guru or master is an extension, a natural evolution, of the function of grandparents. Those known for their knowledge in these early communities, as time passed, became elders. Slowly, the very significant office of *shaman* arose. These men were seers who had made contact with the mystical realm. They had special powers, and possessed certain occult knowledge. Thus in shamanism, there is a quaint mixture of magic and mystical intuition.

In the forests of India and the deserts of Egypt, the relationship reached its perfection as it developed spontaneously out of a life devoted exclusively to contemplation, the mystical quest. In these environments, and later in the monastic milieu of Europe and Asia, the master-disciple bond took definitive form. Certain individuals, usually advanced in years, having discovered the mystical dimension of life and cultivated its fruits, became celebrated for their spiritual wisdom. In time, disciples gravitated naturally to them in search of instruction about life, death, self-knowledge, immortality and how to grow in mystical consciousness.

The master became a *guide* and teacher of spiritual wisdom. He was also a kind of mirror in which the disciple saw himself and the state of his inner life. Henri Le Saux or, Abhishiktananda, maintains that in the encounter with the guru, one comes face-to-face with oneself, or one's own depths. The master is one who, having touched the heightss of the mystical Reality, and knowing what is possible, has the gift of discernment, for he can read hearts. The definitive meeting with the guru, however, happens beyond time and space in the Infinite, but by entering deep into the "cave of the heart." It occurs on the plane of *unity,* not in the usual condition of knowing, i.e. the subject-object duality. Guru and disciples are bound together on the contemplative level of depth.

It is a bond characterized by spiritual love, supported by the natural ambience of the quest. Its motivation is the mystical journey and a profound sense of responsibility for each other: the teacher for his beloved disciple, a concern for his interior growth, and the disciple, a feeling of veneration for the master in whom he discerns the embodiment of mystical wisdom and of life's pupose. This attitude of homage and veneration often takes the form of service to the guru, like a loving child looking after the needs of his parents. The bond is even deeper than marriage, because it is grounded in the Spirit. In this depth, there is no place to hide, nor does one desire to do so. Abhishiktananda elaborates on the relationship when he declares: "The guru and the disciple form a couple, a pair of which the two elements attract each other and adhere to each other. As with the two poles they exist only in relation to one another . . . a pair on the road to unity . . . a non-dual reciprocity . . . ."[8] It is too profound for words.

Hence, the relationship is one of trust, absolute *openness* and honesty. The master is a guide in the ways of the Spirit; he is a teacher of contemplation. Instruction is thus an essential part of the relation, but it is not primarily philosophical; it is more in the realm of the *experiential,* since it is a concrete, living instruction — by word and example — in the rudiments of mystical wisdom, which aims at *praxis* or the practical task of getting to the summit of contemplative experience. The master is one who leads the disciple, and shows him how to transcend the ego, thoughts and imagination, in the process of the ascent to the Absolute. This function is clearly revealed in Dante's *Paradiso,* where at a certain point, St. Bernard takes the place of Beatrice in guiding Dante to the ultimate vision of the Divine nature. This is also the reason why Jung believes that St. Bernard is the archetype of the old wise man, representing contemplative wisdom. He is the symbol of the master who takes his student to the heights of mystic science. He is the experienced guide who knows the terrain firsthand.

What is transmitted in the master-disciple connection is a certain *attitude* of confidence and openness to life, of humility, and ultimately, the knowledge of God. The master communicates a quiet zeal for the mystical quest, a disposition of total dedication, and a responsibility for his students. He is after all their spiritual father! He is the perfection of *compassion* and *charity,* but most of all, he is a "deified" being, one who has become like unto God, for the guru, the sage, the master is a teacher of that holiness he exemplifies, and this holiness is the substance of "deification." The master is a reflection in the living flesh of God's Presence in the world. Finally, the guru teaches his disciples certain techniques of prayer, methods of meditation which are designed to cultivate a total *receptivity* to the activity of the Spirit in the "cave of the heart." These techniques are ways to learn to *just be;* they are exercises in an effortless journey to the Source. Their function is to teach us a non-discursive attention to the Presence within the "cave." This instruction in spiritual methodology is the *practical,* indeed esential, aspect of the relationship. It goes far beyond this, however, since the guru is pointing the way to *perfection* in his words, his silence and his example. In sum, the master is the immediate source of the disciple's inspiration, a visible manifestation of the invisible Mystery.

In this relationship of love and respect mutually existing between the two, evident in the attitude of openness, trust and honesty, we see the *model* of how the generations must learn to interact. In the image of the disciples sitting around the master in veneration and communion, in awe of his holiness and wisdom, and in the master's loving, selfless concern for them, do we not actually have the very *archetype* of association between the elders, the "old ones" and the young? For in this relationship, we can glean a sense of how we are meant to relate and how we are supposed to encounter each other in a creative, positive realization of each other's gifts. To achieve this ideal association in human community requires that society *regain* a feeling for the *mystical,* and that the elderly be restored as the teachers of this wisdom, which necessitates that they first learn it themselves. If we create the environment, there can be no doubt that they will. Once the old ones assume again the spiritual leadership of our societies as teachers of mystical truth and method, then it will become possible to solve the serious global problems, and this can only occur as we apply *contemplation* to the process of *renewing* the earth, making it the foundation of all value. This is the issue we will explore in what follows.

The Aged, Contemplation and the Transformation of the Earth
   The "old ones," in the positive connotation of this term, are those who have confronted, understood and accepted the fact of their aging. They are not running away from it. Why should they, since they realize that aging has an indisputable value? They perceive this value in a concrete sense of integration with the unfolding of their lives in the mystery of life's mystical or spiritual purpose. Those who have discovered this truth, and have allowed themselves to grow spiritually, age with extraordinary dignity and grace. Pope John XXIII, Mother Teresa and Bede Griffiths are good examples of this attitude. The old ones are at peace within and with others. For they have found the source of happiness and genuine fulfilment in the mystical quest. And so they are joyful and full of hope. These men and women embody crucial values that are needed in the process of renewing the planet on all levels. These include: love, justice, peace, faith, unity, humanity and *solidarity* with all living beings, to mention a few.
   The aged contemplative is one who has the quality of "agedness," which F. Franck, quoting R. H. Blyth, defines as the possession of " . . . all of youth with none of its stupidity, insensitiveness, egoism and cruelty. Agedness is oldness without cynicism, obstinacy and pride of power . . . (and is) the wisdom that is life aware of its livingness. It affirms the sacredness of life and of the human."[9] It is this attribute and the reason for it that we must incorporate into our future, for it is preeminently a contemplative attitude. The elders *are* our teachers in this wisdom, which has a practical benefit: it can *save* our planet from destruction. It can also be the basis for a new order of valuation in society. This quality of agedness is a fruit of wisdom, and it emphasizes *being* rather than having or doing. If we are going to change the world, then we will have to alter the world's exclusive emphasis on *doing* and *having*. Thomas Keating makes the same point within the context of the spiritual quest, when he says: " . . . we need to cultivate a practical awareness of the primacy of being over doing."[10] This is true for two reasons: one as the way to discover the mystical, our ultimate vocation as human beings, and the second as the practical, necessary

disposition for all to learn, in the process of reordering the earth's resources for the good of every member of mankind, and for the preservation of the planetary cycles and processes. Until we absorb and live the attitude and capacity of *just being,* rather than simply having and doing, we cannot make any progress in the spiritual life, nor can we stop the mad rush towards nuclear war, the exploitation of the poor, world hunger, or curtail the willful devastation of the natural world and its numerous species who contribute to our physical *and* psychic well-being. Learning to *just be,* we will also discover who we are in relation to the Divine, to others and to nature, and will be at peace with all three. It is that aggressive attitude that wants to *control* everyone and everything that *must* go, for alas, it will destroy us in the end if it is not rooted out, and soon! And is not that destructive, manipulative attitude nothing other than the bloated ego dressed in the disguise of respectabiity, and employing noble rhetoric? And yet, when we unmask this evil tendency, we will find that it is nothing less than that demonic lust for power!

The primary contribution that the elderly can make to every society and in every age is *wisdom,* mystical wisdom, which refocuses the value of life on what is ultimately essential for our happiness. As the aged recover the mystical sense, it will give them the necessary perspective and the vision to guide the rest of mankind in the historical re-ordering of the focus of value and motivation in society, away from an exclusive preoccupation with material ends — doing and having — to a new appreciation of our mystical vocation, which is the call to live in a state of permanent *intimacy* with God in the "cave of the heart" — the realm of *being.* It is the elderly, because of their wisdom, experience and leisure, who can most of all cultivate the contemplative dimension. They can then share this precious wisdom with the younger generations, and get them started on the mystical quest.

This quest or contemplation has to be awakened in the hearts of all people. It must become the *primary value* in the process of transforming the world from a place of nuclear nightmare and the shadow of death, of exploitation, persecution, repression, terrible hunger, neglect, poverty, disease, economic and spiritual injustice, indifference, ignorance, homelessness, and the continuing plunder of the natural world, to a planet at *peace,* free of the weapons of war, which are the instruments of ignorance and hatred under the pretext of security — a place of *sharing,* love, mystical life, community, enlightenment and understanding, where people are not hungry and everyone feels a deep sense of *empathy* for everyone else. Such a world could be the beginning of our entrance into Paradise, the Kingdom of God among us.

It is because we are so attached to having, doing and dominating that we fail to hear the subtle but persistent call of the heart to enter into contemplation, and to have spiritual *joy,* treasures that do not pass away. In these spiritual treasures, all can share to their capacity, and that is limited only by their desire. Indeed, the *key* to mankind's *survival* is found in the degree to which we can rebuild the social motivation of the world on the firm foundation of contemplation or the mystical quest, for we are not fully human unless we are living from the depths, the wellspring of our authenticity. And if you doubt this truth, just ponder the meaning of all the savage acts that daily occur around the world. They happen because something essential is missing, and that is a *contact* with the mystical spring of our inner lives. That is why the world is out of focus, off balance, and why there is so much barbarity in man and contemporary civilization.

There can only be lasting peace when each person — after the basic necessities are met — is in touch with the contemplative dimension in his or her own being, the spiritual level of human existence. Only when nations comprehend the mystical wealth hidden in the heart of us all will they be ready to give peace a real chance. As long as the world is based on illusory values, such as power, status, money and domination, there will never be peace. And yet we cannot afford not to have it. The time has arrived for us all to *renew* our planet by rejecting the ignorance that separates us, lulls us to an uneasy slumber, and compels us to hide behind the false security of nuclear arms. Let us recall that poignant question that Pope John Paul II presented to the United Nations General Assembly, when he asked soberly: " . . . will there continue to accumulate over the heads of this new generation of children the threat of common extermination . . . ? *Are the children to receive the arms race from us* as a necessary inheritance?"[11]

There has to be a worldwide awakening of the masses against nuclear arms and all armaments, and a decision by humanity's leaders that the *survival* of our planet is far more important than the selfish, myopic interests of competing states. Political ideology and imperialism, especially in its *hegemonistic* form must go, if we are to survive. The world will not tolerate a one-system view of political, economic and social life. We are a pluralistic planet, and nothing can change that fact, not guns, tanks, missiles, secret police, terror or torture. We have to find a new way, through contemplation, for it creates the psychological climate by fostering the necessary *trust*. And so, there must be *total global disarmament* by all the states, and this can only be possible when we banish fear and insecurity, which have held us captive for too long. The future life of the planet will not accept domination by any nation or group of nations. The only path that will lead us out of the web of ignorance and danger that has so enwrapped the world — and entrapped it — is the penetrating spiritual activity of the mystical quest or contemplation. Contemplation is the answer to the crisis of humanity that so haunts this anguished epoch of history.

Contemplatives are natural peacemakers, and contemplation is the ongoing process of realizing that "peace which passes understanding" within the depths of the soul, and which spreads a healing peace wherever contemplatives go. Is it not peacefulness that is the hallmark of an enlightened elder? Does not wisdom wear the gentle smile of this peace, so elusive to contemporary man? The contemplative *value* is the only way to implement peace on a global scale. All of us have the sacred trust of being peacemakers, and peace is born spontaneously in contemplation, which is always life-affirming.

The narrow, selfish politics and economics of the present world, which are daily proven to be morally destitute, must be replaced with the hope-filled politics and economics of the heart embodied in living contemplative values. When mystical values are chosen and become the center of our lives, then we will be able to find solutions to all of our problems that now tear apart the fragile tissue of international relations, for when we are all living from our "common heart" in contemplation, then no problem is insoluble and no challenge is too great. The application of the contemplative vision to a solution of mankind's problems is *love-in-action*. And that is the practical nature of contemplation, since it always begets fruitful results.

We really have no choice: either we choose life in embracing the contemplative value, and in this choice find the eventual resolution of our troubles, or else continue our present no-where course which will end in global suicide. Let all of us keep in mind — whether the powerful or the powerless of this world — that the leaders of this planet are only the *stewards* of this brief period of history, and *do not* have the prerogative to play with the destiny of our world. The future belongs to the other generations to come, and we have to serve their welfare. Let us reject the geopolitics of the past, the dangerous divisions of ideological and economic ambition. Let us give our earth its heart back by rediscovering the contemplative heritage present in us all, and affirmed in all the world's great religions.

The way to this contemplative *transformation* of the world is first to take the step of acknowledging it as the *essential value* of life and the primary factor in our future interactions. Each nation has to recover its mystical heritage from its own tradition, and then together we can *share* the fruits of this wisdom that the toil of centuries has produced. The mystical treasures of the various religions belong to the whole of humanity as part of our collective experience.

Once the contemplative value is made the basis of culture and the focus of our lives, then we will discover a new, expanded identity, for then we will have found our "common heart," which makes us *one*. As this interior revolution takes place in the souls of mankind, a fresh breeze of understanding will dispel ignorance, the hatreds and feuds that have been the cause of so much suffering in this century of sheer brutality and injustice. When we live from our common heart in the mystical dimension, we will perceive our ultimate unity not as a theory, but as the *reality* it is. This will be the final revolution, for the *definitive* revolution *is* the spiritual awakening of mankind. Then we can begin to banish hunger from our globe by *sharing* our food and other resources with one another. As the weapons of mass destruction are set aside, we will then be free to feed all of mankind.

As man finds that inner harmony that comes from living with God in the "cave of the heart," and as he reaches out in trust and makes peace with all others, sharing resources, then a new life will dawn on our planet, and peace *will* be a reality, rather than an elusive dream. When we are living from our contemplative depth, we will then feel our *oneness* with the natural world as well, and all of its wonderful creatures, whose rights we have so shamelessly violated. The natural environment and its many creatures have rights just as nations and peoples do. The planet is as much their home as ours. The United Nations has formally acknowledged this fact in a special charter devoted to the rights of these creatures. We must allow the natural world to restore its balance and revitalize its cycles and processes. We have to respect the earth and its sovereign right to exist in its own way, unmolested by our technology, for the earth sustains us all. Man has dominion over the earth, but he does *not* have the right to destroy it or interfere with its vital operations.

Let us lock hands together across the barriers of the centuries, overcoming our ignorance, and build a civilization based on *love,* which is contemplation in action. A civilization founded on love was first envisioned in our time by Pope Paul VI. Somehow he saw the faint glimmerings on the horizon of a new dawn of civilization, a great spiritual renaissance. We have the unique capacity to make his dream a reality. The question before this hour of history is: do we have the will to change the world into a place of *love* before it is too late? Contemplation, the mystical value, "the pearl of great price" buried deep in our hearts is the blueprint for such a new civilization. For does not civilization, in its higher cultural expressions, aim at such a state of genuine humanity and refinement of character? Does it not long for a heart, a soul? Contemplation *is* this heart or soul, and courage is the only way we can achieve it. We must *seize the initiative of history* and implant this seed of the spiritual transformation of the world.

My uncle, John Cosgrove, now in his early eighties and a beautiful example of that quality of *agedness,* a man of great spiritual wisdom, is fond of a saying that epitomizes what the elderly have to offer society, when he says: "Mysticism or contemplation is a treasure so difficult to find, and so easily lost if not worked at." Clearly, it is our collective and individual vocation to discover and cultivate the mystical garden within the "cave" of our own hearts. This is the entire significance of aging, as we are granted sufficient time to pursue it. In this regard, Thomas Keating has an important insight. Speaking to our contemplative depths, he says:

> The greatest accomplishment in life is to be what we are, which is God's idea of what He wanted us to be when He brought us into being; and no idea of ours will ever change it. Accepting that gift is accepting God's will for us, and in its acceptance is found the path to growth and ultimate fulfillment.[12]

To be what we are, in the profoundest sense of Abbot Thomas' meaning, is achieved in its plentitude only in contemplative experience, in mystical life, in an enhanced identity found in that union with the Divine at the center of our own being. And so, aging is a spiritual process which finds completion in mystical consciousness the progressive clarification of our being in God's.

Notes

[1]Thomas Keating, O.C.S.O., *The Heart of the World: A Spiritual Catechism* (New York: Crossroad, 1981), p. 1.
[2]*Chandogya Upanishad* 8, 1.
[3]*Katha Upanishad* 2, 12 and 20; 5, 12.
[4]Plotinus, *Enneads* VI. 9. 3.
[5]Jan Van Ruysbroeck, *The Spiritual Espousals,* trans. Eric Colledge (New York: Harper & Harper, 1957), III, ix, p. 190.
[6]Thomas Keating, O.C.S.O., "A View of the Spiritual Journey in the '80s," *Origins,* vol. 11, No. 7, July 2, 1981, p. 109.
[7]*Ibid.*
[8]Abhishiktananda, *Guru and Disciple,* trans. Heather Sandeman (London: SPCK, 1974), p. 29.
[9]Frederick Franck, "Living Ancestors," *Parabola,* vol. V, number 1, 1980, p. 27, 31.
[10]*Op. cit.,* "Spiritual Journey," p. 110.
[11]Address of His Holiness, Pope John Paul II To The XXXIV General Assembly of the United Nations Organization, 2 October, 1979, par. 22.
[12]*Op. cit., Heart of the World,* p. 69.

Epilogue: Wise Elders and Old Fools

Francis V. Tiso

Imagine that you are an ancient alga, languishing by the shore of a pre-cambrian sea. How foolish you are as you find yourself growing old, drying out, perhaps drained of energy after a thousand cell divisions, complaining of your age and your wrinkles when all of life is still so young. Disconnected from an evolutionary consciousness, the alga's aging is total disaster. For us humans, that same absence of the broad perspective has raised up a harvest of fearful selfishness. What is so terrible if I age, if I die? Even if I feel that death is fearful, whom do I benefit with that feeling? What does that feeling change? Added to the vast flux of things, does that feeling make any statement of value?

Why is it so hard for people to grasp that our center of value is in the *others:* those who have shared my love, those who have known fellowship at table, those who grew up at my feet, those who carry on that reality which is more important and larger than any of us? Surely this deeply known reality is a power in the face of the great Emptiness. The larger reality of things is absolutely dependent on us; we are the indispensible embodiments of all that is, of the Tao, the Word, the Dharmakaya, but only when we live in some sense outside ourselves and not for ourselves. This, it is no surprise, constitutes the perennial spiritual wisdom of the ages.

Humanity begins with the tribe, the clan, the family. The Fourth Hill of the Ojibway represents the experience of collective moment, the flow of life as known in archaic societies. At its most gracious peak, the tribe can be a nurturer of human order and human diversity, mediated by visionary encounter with transcendant guardians of the past and future. At its most stringent, the tribe defines all human action by means of normative behavior and excludes the deviant. The individual lives on in the tribe and is held by the collective mind of the tribe. Except for the shaman and visionary, solitude is unthinkable and unendurable.

In many ancient traditions, among them the cultures of the Semitic peoples, the young are invited to consider contrasting portraits of the wise and the foolish. The wise one is prudent, circumspect, a man of few words, loyal to family, friends, king, and "the system." He is aware of the liabilities of evil doing, and so avoids sin. A deep inner relationship to the gods is secondary to the focal point of this "wisdom literature." There is instead a rational presentation, in proverbial form, of the way to live by a defined norm. One belongs to a tribe with complex structures, somewhat distinct from the archaic tribe with its internally validated myths and tradition of visions. In the wisdom literature, there is adherence to community values and standards, perhaps with more than a touch of — shall we say — a certain bourgeois idealism. Indeed, much of this is "how-to" literature for the young man on his way up the royal bureaucratic ladder. The wise man of Proverbs is a kindly bureaucrat.

The fool is characterized as a scoffer, laughing at the stabilizing values of the group, denying the gods, living in lust and greed, practicing adultery, and speaking his mind without considering the consequences. A touch of envy mars the portrait; sometimes the wicked fool prospers.

In the New Testament, and among the prophets of the Old Testament, we find a strange sort of fool. This fool is a clown in a holy parade, one who has made himself foolish for the benefit of many: Paul on the way to Rome, Jesus on the way to Golgotha, Hosea with his harlot wife, Jeremiah in the high-priest's stocks.

Both fools and wise ones may be of any age. As civilizations grow old, and layer falls upon layer, leaving only the outcroppings accesible to memory, new understandings of the elderly person circulate in the folklore. The archetypes change. In an archaic society, few survive to old age. In a bureaucratic kingdom, somewhat more live on to see "children's children," and shape their society to accomodate the urban clans in peace and security.

The Industrial Age devalues the aging person as an individual, and experiences the mass of the elderly (created by advances in medical technology) as an ambiguous burden. In purely economic terms, the elderly are a problem. They are less productive, they have high medical bills, and they have little to say to a world that has changed too rapidly for any one person or generation to grasp. The ancient role of the wise elder has been outstripped, it would seem, by a society that creates itself anew every decade with a burst of mind-boggling technology. "Wisdom" can now be handed on by computers, into which scores of scientists, technicians, statisticians, and accountants have poured raw data. The very young technician is at the peak of his productivity; what need do we have of old age, much less experience, in a world that designs obsolescence into the machinery upon which it most depends?

The social impact of this rapid change is to produce old fools. The elderly of the West hardly know what's going on. The general bewilderment produced by the consumer culture is intensified among the old; the rate of social change is too great for any one to absorb. Life is experienced in great haste; things are not savored — they are devoured and discarded. Repeated activities lose their impact. Sex, food, and clothing have to be diverse to be exciting. Always a new fashion, a new mania, a new name, a new need to fulfill.

In the end, this consumer (consuming?) culture attacks the diversity of human adaptations. Marketing strategies obliterate the small pockets of special interest and seek to bring everyone into conformity with the mass mind, mass needs, the mass patterns of behavior. This makes selling easy and predictable so as to maximize profits. Profit-making tends to supplant ethics and obscure the actual needs of people. The elderly are statistically on the periphery of this process, so their particular needs are of lesser interest.

Oddly enough, developing countries seem to be astonishingly vulnerable to the marketing ideology of human existence. During his recent trip to Africa, an astute friend observed the great preoccupation with "prestige" in a continent that is everywhere slipping into chaos: "Prestige Motors;" "Prestige Laundry;" "Prestige Drug Store." Government statements criticizing this mentality seem to have little real effect.

How are we to find a path to wisdom for our times? I would suggest that we at least try to come back to reality. We are all aging towards death. The fact of death is an anchor point which, when all else fails, holds us inescapably to the otherwise thwarted fact of our humanity.

We have already seen how, in the teachings of the Zen Abbot Hakuin, we may all be counted among the aging and that our lives hang precariously in the balance. The proximity of death to our fragile bodies is the great equalizer that unites all persons in a common fear, a common mystery and a common realism. At the same time, our decline into death carrying the burdens and the wisdom of living is suggestive of our journey toward the Absolute. Aging and death have both the fascination and awesomeness that we associate with the Holy itself.

This paradox of the ordinary and the transcendent may be found among the shopping bag ladies of New York's West Side, with whom I spend evenings from time to time in a Franciscan house of hospitality. They are the elderly of the streets; often they are recognizably the prematurely old. These women are not to be romanticized. They are not saints. Some strive in that direction, but even the best show the crumbling side of their personalities in lurking madness, broiling, selfish tantrums, or in the hunger of the streets that catches one by surprise. They are truly stripped down to the nakedness of humanity. Thanks to my Franciscan friends, the fragrances of their unwashed humanity are now and then moderated. And yet the paradox of their lives lingers to haunt one.

They hold our imagination, these street creatures, with their ability to expose our own darker side. Let's admit it, much of their madness is chosen. But the bureaucrats along the way have played their part in putting them on the streets, too. It is not poverty, in some abstract economic sense, that puts them on the streets. It is human indifference and the whole cold system of forms, security deposits, insurance, politics, advertising, and drugs. There they are: the cast-off whore, the mad stockbroker, the fashion designer appareled like a second-hand queen, the leathery lesbian, the would-be nun, the discarded wife, the sweet and sour black momma, the "exotic dancer," the old Slavic woman who mutely weaves her peasant robes from denim fragments, and so on. Some move sweetly in a daze; some sit and chatter blindly of their ailments, of forgotten rapes, of one another, of nothing at all. They preach sermons, or brag about their welfare children. They bum cigarettes, eager, as if for cocaine. They sit sullenly in a dusty corner, sipping tea. They frolic when I open the clothing room and the second hand wares are shared out. "Green's just not for you, my dear," I protest. "Here, try this; it'll be warm and it's *almost* the right length." "That purse is You!" "Please, Gertie, don't throw the blouses on the floor when you don't like them." "No, Madge, we haven't any furs."

The ladies could hardly be called the "wise." Yet they are too mad to be considered deliberate fools. I suspect that they were all foolish at one time or another. That time of folly led them into the impossible situations that ejected them into the streets. They can't cope with life as it is in our expensive, on-time, high-speed cities. So they live in the cracks, in the subway tunnels, in the bus terminals, beside hydrants, often surrounded by ramparts of stuffed shopping bags. Yet, ironically, these women are the truest urbanites, the ones most wise in the ways of these "mean streets." They teach us that same disillusionment that was liberation to the Buddha; they detach us from our daily cravings and our egoistic mirror-gazing. As all true fools do, they heal us with folly. The foolish, unconcerned, even jaded liberty of the old and worn-out is a kind of teaching, a kind of crazy wisdom.

These ladies are dangerous. They are truly undefinable. There is no way to explain them statistically; they blur at the edges of our categories. Their wild tales defy the fact-finder who dares to draw a bell-curve among them.

They shadow us and parody us, formulating for us a certain image — not a trite "there but for the grace of God go I" — rather, they mock the young, the employed, the clean with existential disdain. They are living placards, holding up our hidden selves unashamedly to view. They are our secret selves, blatant on the streets. Like the portrait of Dorian Gray, they soak up horrors while we rub on the Estee Lauder skin cream.

The spiritual traditions of the world have their holy fools. There are the "crazy wisdom" gurus of the Tantric schools, the Holy Fools of Russian Orthodoxy, the comics among the Taoist sages, the clown guilds of the Amerindians, the prophetic parodists of ancient Israel, and unpredictable lightning-bolts from the Zen masters. Sacred fools have always been the guides from the too-secure ways of the tribe and bureaucrat into new visions of wholeness for a community in transition. Fools are a relief and liberation from the drudgery of daily conformity, from values gone run-down in ordinariness. They liberate the person from the straits of the collective. The ways of the wise go down to defeat before the antics of holy fools. New choices are born in the ecstasy of madness. Embarrassing debates are held: An old hag confronts and confounds the learned Abbot Naropa; the hag turns out to be a magical transformation of Naropa's destined guru, Tilopa. The scholar becomes a master after twelve "trials" that prove him to be nothing but a pompous fool. For only a fool can scale the heights; the fool alone dances even to the edge of the precipice, and so redeems the whole plateau.

In our world today, we desperately need more fools and fewer lawyers and accountants. We need to raise up some crazy hags, some mad street creatures to tell us beguiling tales and thus break the evil spells of books and laws and dollar bills. We are a bound and gagged people, too rich in the wisdom of bureaucrats and technicians. Even our "liberation movements" lack humor. Our fear of death, of annhilation, of being out of fashion and out of favor has made fools of all of us. When the fools have made fools of the foolish, we will at last know one another's true names and have fear no longer. We need the folly of an old age that cares no longer for power or wrinkles, but which can face death as friend faces friend. So I hope to age in foolishness, and so find healing. Healing, and not therapy. I'll seek out clowns for my innoculations, and let time give me a face-lift of leathery wrinkles.

Author Biographies

1. Muhammad Abdul-Rauf. (Islam)
   Director of the Islamic Center, Washington, D.C. Born in Egypt; a renowed Islamic scholar, and Professor of Islamic studies at the University of United Arab Emirates, Abu Dhabi.

2. Kofi Appiah-Kubi (African tradition)
   A lay theologian of the Ghana Presbyterian Church; an advocate of African theology and African traditional healing practices. Former theology secretary of the All-Africa Conference of Churches.

3. Thomas Berry, C.P. (Preface)
   Founder of the Riverdale Center for Religious Research and Professor, Department of Theology, Fordham University, N.Y. An elder and mentor to many scholars addressing research to interreligious dialogue and the wisdom of the planet.

4. John Borelli, Ph. D. (Paradigm of Aging)
   Assistant Professor and Chairman of the Department of Religious Studies, College of Mount St. Vincent, Riverdale, N.Y. Specialist in interreligious studies and Jungian psychology.

5. Rev. John B. Chethimattam, C.M.I. (Hinduism)
   Professor in the Department of Philosophy, Fordham University Born in Thottakad, India, in 1922. Noted for interdisciplinary studies in Indian philosophy and culture.

6. Professor Albert Chi-Lu Chung (Chinese tradition)
   Former Professor of Philosophy and Logic, Chengchi University, China, and Columbia University, N.Y. An expert in *I Ching* studies; born in China 64 years ago.

7. Msgr. Ettore DiFilippo (Director)
   Founder of Opera Pia International in 1978. Was born in Civitella del Tronto, Teramo, Italy, 59 years ago. Ordained a priest in 1945, he studied at the School of Journalism, Università Pro Deo in Rome. He is Counselor to the Permanent Observer Mission of the Holy See to the United Nations and a doctoral candidate in the History of Religions at Fordham University.

8. Robert L. Fastiggi (Death)
   Religious educator and doctoral candidate, Fordham University, Department of Theology. Currently teaching Doctrine, Ethics, and Scripture at St. Joseph's-by-the-Sea High School, Staten Island, N.Y.

9. Rabbi Asher Finkel (Judaism)
   Born in Jerusalem, holds rabbinical degree from Yeshiva University and the Ph.D. from Tübingen University. Professor

in the graduate department of Judeo-Christian Studies, Seton Hall University, and visiting professor of Scripture at Maryknoll School of Theology. Author of *The Pharisees and the Teacher of Nazareth* (E.J. Brill, 1974).

10. John Grim, Ph.D. (Native American religion)
    Holds doctorate in the History of Religions from Fordham University. Assistant Professor, Department of Religious Studies, Elizabeth Seton College, Yonkers, N.Y. His specialization is shamanism among the Native Peoples of North America.

11. Dr. Buddhadasa P. Kirthisinghe (Buddhism)
    Representative of the World Fellowship of Buddhists to the United Nations. Expert on Buddhism and the modern world, especially Buddhism and science.

12. Jose Pereira, Ph.D. (Christianity)
    Associate Professor of Theology at Fordham University. A specialist in the theology of world religions, Indian cultural history, and ethnomusicology. Author of *Hindu Theology: A Reader* (Doubleday, 1976).

13. Dom Jean Leclercq, O.S.B. (Monasticism)
    A monk of the Abbaye Clervaux in Luxembourg. He is a professor at the Gregorian University in Rome and is one of the great living church historians and authorities on monastic spirituality. He is the author of *The Love of Learning and the Desire for God*, and numerous other studies.

14. Wayne Teasdale (Mysticism)
    Doctoral candidate in the Department of Theology, Fordham University. Author of *Essays in Mysticism: Explorations into Contemplative Experience* (Sunday Publications, 1982) and active in peace work and interreligious dialogue.

15. Francis V. Tiso, M. Div. (Editor, Buddhism)
    Assistant to the Publisher and Editor, the Seabury Press, New York. Participant in interreligious dialogue. Adjunct faculty, Department of Religious Studies, Mercy College, Dobbs Ferry, N.Y. Author of *A Young Person's Book of Catholic Signs and Symbols* (Doubleday, 1982).